BEYOND THE PALE

Beyond the Pale

Folklore, Family, *and the* Mystery *of* Our Hidden Genes

EMILY URQUHART

HARPER**AVENUE**

In memory of Rodsella Morse Spencer,
who lived not in your time, not in my time, but in the old time,
and for Andrew and Sadie, my happily ever after.

———————

Published by Harper Avenue, an inprint of HarperCollins Publishers Ltd

First edition

HarperCollins Publishers Ltd
2 Bloor Street East, 20th Floor
Toronto, Ontario, Canada
M4W 1A8

www.harpercollins.ca

Library and Archives Canada Cataloguing in Publication
information is available upon request

ISBN 978-1-44342-356-4

Printed and bound in the United States

RRD 9 8 7 6 5 4 3 2 1

Contents

Prologue

MY DAUGHTER WAS BORN WITH A GENETIC CONDITION I KNEW NOTHING about. It was so foreign to me that I wasn't able to recognize or see it. It is a deceptively obvious medical mystery, one that crops up in both holy and medical texts and in supernatural beliefs across time. In some cultures, people like my child are revered; in others, they are seen as harbingers of evil. In my own society, they have been fodder for legends, believed to live in backwoods colonies, cloistered together, insular and removed. In the recent past, they've been exploited and exhibited like animals in a zoo. The most extreme stories are from East Africa, where people are being murdered and mutilated for bearing this disorder's recessive traits.

I study folklore, the intimate truths we reveal through the stories we tell. Legends, fairy tales, and beliefs are the screens onto which we project our fears, hopes, secrets, and desires. After my daughter was born, I felt that knowing the cultural tales about people with her condition, whether they were frightening or beautiful, would help me understand the shape of her life. Because she will encounter these stories too: on the silver screen, via the Internet, in the news, and from the lips of unpredictable strangers.

I've never met or known about anyone—family or acquaintance—who shares my daughter's difference. It can pass silently on from parent to child for hundreds of years, so I also didn't know where it came from. Then, a few weeks ago, there was a clue. A series of family photographs from the early 1900s show two women who bear a striking resemblance to my daughter.

I mined archives and census records to learn more about these people, but none of those fraying documents could identify them, or provide the human details I craved about their lives. Specifically, I want to know if these long-ago women were happy, despite living with a disability and standing apart from their peers because of their unusual, if beautiful, appearance. It's a risk-laden query because the answer will shape how I see my little girl's future.

Now I am meeting a distant relative I discovered while trying to understand my daughter's inheritance. At age ninety, she's the only connection I have to several women who lived a century ago, tangential ancestors whose lives might illuminate my child's present. My dad is driving me to this meeting; he has never met this relative either. He is calm; I am nervous. Neither one of us knows what to expect.

I tell my dad that we've passed the building. We drive around the block, then pull into the parking lot of a modest retirement residence where our cousin many times removed is expecting our arrival. My dad sits patiently by my side while I shuffle and reorder the family photos I brought with me. I think back to when I'd sat in a different car, in a colder season, years and miles from here, parked outside our doctor's office in Newfoundland. I wept in the passenger seat while my husband stared wearily out from behind the wheel. Our infant daughter was in the back, wearing thumb-less mittens and a tiny woolen hat. She was two weeks old. During our first visit, the physician quelled my husband's fears, but on that day, our second trip to her office in a week, she acquiesced and referred us to a specialist with a long wait-list.

I'd looked out the car window and spotted a speck of steel in the gray sky. A plane rising. I wished I were on it. Turning back to see my sleeping infant, I crashed to earth. I resolved to stay there. Although we didn't know it then, inside that car, sitting in the frozen, snow-crusted parking lot, some of the answers were within us, in our cells, soon to be extracted from our blood.

Over the next three years, we consulted a slew of experts—medical, cultural, regular, and extraordinary—but the person who would teach us the most—tiny, mute, sleeping in the back seat—was our daughter. The rest we uncovered over a series of journeys. These voyages took us across North America and as far away as Africa. Each one was more harrowing than the last, and each time there was a moment when I contemplated retreat before heading forward.

Today, in autumn's pale light, my hesitation evaporates. I turn to my dad, who has been waiting quietly for my lead.

"I'm ready now," I tell him, then open the door and step outside to meet my daughter's past and her future.

ONE

DISCOVERY

CHAPTER 1

Some White

THE VISITORS COME FROM ALL WARDS OF THE HOSPITAL. THERE IS AN audiologist, a social worker, a lactation consultant, a rotating cast of doctors, and an endless stream of nurses. We have a private room, but our newly formed family of three is rarely alone. This is not unusual in the maternity ward. What is curious, however, are the nurses who visit with no service to offer. They arrive at my side, somewhat apologetically, to catch a glimpse of our newborn daughter. "Some white," they whistle and coo into her plastic bassinet, using the vernacular emphasis that has become so familiar during my five years in Newfoundland. They say it to me, and they repeat it to one another: "That hair is some white."

Sadie Jane is born in the usual excruciating manner on Boxing Day 2010. Overdue, she is unwrinkled and chubby, with perfectly formed features and a shock of white hair on her head. Her mouth a tiny *O* and her arms flailing, she reaches constantly for my arms, my milk, my warmth. Her eyes flutter open occasionally, but mostly they're shut. In one of our baby's fleeting moments of wakefulness, the ward pediatrician probes her pupils with a tiny flashlight. Afterward, she looks past me and my husband, Andrew, past my parents, fixing her gaze on the spruce-clad hills behind the hospital. "You have a very fair, very healthy baby girl," she says. We never see that doctor again.

My child is the fairest of them all. The weight of my pride is unbearable, too big for our tiny room on the maternity ward. I stage a photo shoot on my bed, and Andrew takes the picture that will become Sadie's birth announcement. I beam the image across the globe.

The next day, Andrew takes Sadie in his arms and goes for a walk down the hall. The nurses crowd around, making a fuss over her white hair and scolding him in the same breath. "No walking with babies in the hall! That hair! The liability!" He is heading back to our room when he overhears one of the nurses ask, "Is that baby an albino?"

They return trailed by a heavy-set nurse with dark hair and few teeth. "Is she an albino?" the nurse asks, lisping slightly, a note of alarm in her voice. "No," I tell her firmly. The woman stares back at me, bug-eyed, bewildered. Then she lets herself into our bathroom, where she cleans the toilet, empties the trash bin, and wipes down the sink. She is wearing nurse's scrubs, but it is clear now that she is a janitor.

As Andrew recounts this strange tale to his mother over the telephone her heart sinks. She doesn't know what to say, because both she and Andrew's father, Don, asked the same question when they saw the first photographs of their granddaughter. Don, a family physician in Georgetown, Ontario, grows increasingly tense as the days pass. *Why didn't the pediatrician say something?* he wonders. He is 99.9 percent certain, as convinced as he can be without examining her, that Sadie has a genetic condition called albinism. It is stable, and there is no treatment (you can't substitute good genes for bad ones—at least not yet). He believes that the doctor opted to spare us, for now.

In a week's time, Don will be on a plane to Newfoundland. His role as a grandfather is not to deliver grim medical news. He is the support staff, not ground control, and he feels certain that our family doctor will say something at the one-week checkup. After that, he can offer guidance.

Albinism, a genetic disorder, is both obvious and mysteriously complex. (As with the pejorative "retard," those in the know don't use the word "albino" anymore.) People with oculocutaneous albinism have little to no pigment in their skin, hair, and eyes. They have relatively little protection against the sun; burns are quick and dangerous and may cause skin cancer.

The current understanding of the way pigment affects vision is more complicated. Normally, when the irises are faced with glare, they activate the pupils, a pair of gatekeepers that control how much light reaches the back of the eye. Without this regulation system, stray light enters through the pupil and iris, impairing the development of the retina and interfering with the optic nerve (the wiring system that connects the eyes to the brain). Albinism also affects the development of the fovea, a cluster of cones in the middle of the retina that are responsible for visual acuity. At around six weeks, almost every baby with albinism will develop nystagmus, in which the eyes dart back and forth involuntarily. We don't know why this condition is present in albinism, but it is unrelated to pigment.

What we also know is that low pigmentation results in photophobia, meaning that daylight, particularly the searing rays of high noon, can be intolerable. It resembles those initial moments of squinty-eyed discomfort the rest of us feel when exiting a dark theater into the light of day. Together, this complicated cocktail of eyesight issues is called low vision, and it is like seeing the world through an Instagram filter. The pixels are bigger, the world is a little brighter, and while it is not blurry, the finer details are lost.

There are few experts in the field of albinism. The condition falls across a spectrum of medical specialties—genetics, ophthalmology, dermatology—and most general practitioners will never see a patient with albinism during their careers. When we visit our family doctor a week after Sadie and I are discharged from the hospital, she dismisses my husband's concern about the janitor's comments. "I've seen babies this fair before," she tells us. Her file notes from our visit on January 5 list that Sadie has very fair skin, that her eyes are normal, and that she is thriving. Thriving! My maternal pride swells. My baby is flourishing. My husband, however, is not doing well at all.

Hours after the doctor's appointment, we take the dog for a walk and stop at a nearby schoolyard, where he runs in circles, chasing his doggy shadow across the floodlit snow. Sadie is tucked into her dad's coat, strung up in a contraption that keeps her close to his chest and out of the cold. We silently shuffle back and forth to keep warm. A heavy darkness fills the air between us. It followed us here, stalked us down the stairs from our apartment and along the night streets. It has been with us since we left the hospital. Something is wrong with Andrew. Later I will find him sitting quietly in the dimness of early evening. I switch the lights on, and he turns them off again. Even his camera, a constant flashing light from Sadie's first cry, has gone dark. But when I ask him what is wrong, he cannot find the words to tell me.

My husband is the kind of person who leads the pack in a crisis. This strength, along with his height, his dark hair and green eyes, and his ridiculousness, are what had me pining to be his sidekick. But since the birth of our first child, he has come loose. He is distant, and unreachable. Parenthood exposes his Achilles' heel, shocking both of us. What I don't know is that, like his parents, Andrew is convinced our newborn baby girl has a rare genetic condition.

My in-laws arrive the next day. Don carefully examines Sadie, using the contents of his doctor's tool kit, a ritual I wrongly assume follows the birth of every grandchild. He takes on the responsibility that, as a grandfather, he had hoped to avoid. He waits until morning, when his son, so clearly tormented, comes to him. Andrew is saddened but receptive to the possibility of a problem. Later, when we are alone, Sadie sleeps in my arms while he relays his father's concerns, releasing his own bottled fear in the process. To me, the suggestion is infuriating and impossible.

When noon comes and I still have not contacted my parents, it is gently suggested that I make the call. Sitting in a rocking chair by the nursery window, phone in hand, I stare out at the familiar scene and find it distorted. The row houses, stacked one above the other up Prescott Street, the two towers of the basilica, the gray winter sky—it is all askew. I dial and wait for my mother to answer.

"There might be something wrong with Sadie," I tell her. I have a catch in my throat, and can't continue.

My mother, listening on the other end, does not hesitate.

"No one will love her any less."

I DO NOT FAIL TO NOTICE THE PECULIARITIES OF MY DAUGHTER'S ARRIVAL, but I interpret them in a completely different way. My husband is a biologist, attuned to the natural order of the world. I am a folklorist, and walking the line between fantasy and reality is my work. I believe in science, but I understand fairy tales. My new baby's astonishing white hair and unusual beauty, her immediate legion of admirers, even the timing of her arrival—a labor that stretched across some of the holiest days of the liturgical calendar—have the markings of a supernatural tale.

We mythologize even our routine birth stories. The most extraordinary reside in the world's grand narratives, from ancient Greece to the foundations of Christianity. Like the detailed version of Noah's birth, brought to public attention in the 1940s with the discovery of the Dead Sea Scrolls. In it, the boy is born with flesh as "white as snow," hair as "white as wool," and unusual eyes that illuminate the room. His father, Lamech, is disturbed by his newborn son's appearance, so different from his own. He is suspicious too. Recently, there were rumors that angels had been cavorting about with mortal women, and this child has definite angelic qualities. He consults his father, Methuselah, who in turn seeks the counsel of his father, Enoch. What Lamech ultimately discovers is that the pale flesh, white hair, and luminous eyes are attributes of the child's divine calling. "Call his name Noah," Enoch advises. "When all mankind who are on earth shall die, he shall be safe."

Texts from some of the scrolls are published in the mid-1950s, and this birth story catches the attention of a British ophthalmologist named Arnold Sorsby. In 1958, he publishes an article titled "Noah—An Albino" in the *British Medical Journal.* He writes that the narrative is "clearly not that of a miraculous child but of an albino." To help prove his point, he includes a genetic breakdown and an adjoining diagram explaining the possible inheritance pattern of Noah's albinism. Only in the final paragraph does he suggest that the article is a parody, when he earnestly considers the recessive genetics of angels.

I read this paper shortly after the birth of my own ethereal child ("Your baby looks like an angel!" exclaims another new mom at the hospital). I search for Sorsby online but find an obituary rather than a white pages listing. What I glean from his life story is that he edited the *Journal of Medical Genetics* for seven years in the 1960s, he was an ophthalmologist employed at London's Royal Eye Hospital, and he specialized in genetic conditions of the eyes. All of this posits him as a person whose theories you would be inclined to take seriously. Case in point: when the first American albinism advocacy group forms in the 1980s, it takes the acronym NOAH (National Organization for Albinism and Hypopigmentation) as its official name.

I show Sorsby's article to Dr. Daniel Machiela, a professor in the Religious Studies Department at McMaster University in Hamilton, Ontario, with special expertise in the interpretation of the Dead Sea Scrolls. He is interested but unconvinced.

"There is a metaphorical and symbolic attachment to the way he looks," Machiela says. "And that clearly seems to be what is going on here."

I want to connect Noah's story to my own, so I suggest that his ancient Near Eastern parents theoretically would have had dark hair, skin, and eyes, and therefore a child born with white hair would be very unusual.

"The point in these stories is that he was not just like anyone else who was born then—the way you would expect them to be born," says Machiela. "He stood out."

WHEN SADIE IS FIVE WEEKS OLD, WE MEET WITH A GENETICIST, Dr. Lesley Turner. She is exquisitely gentle examining our infant daughter, and I trust her immediately. We have seen an ophthalmologist, and we understand that Sadie has characteristics of albinism, but the doctor refers us to the Provincial Medical Genetics Program for conclusive tests. Andrew and I sit at a round table in an office at the Health Sciences Centre in St. John's, and I nurse Sadie while Dr. Turner and a genetic counselor draw our family tree—a narrative of various disasters that includes an uncle who died too young of multiple sclerosis, a brother who died even younger of alcoholism, and on both sides the shattering experience of Alzheimer's.

Sadie has five milliliters of blood taken, half the regular amount because she weighs just eleven pounds. She is silent when the needle pierces her skin, but she pees from the shock of it. The tiny vial of blood is flown to the University of Minnesota Physicians Outreach

Laboratories, where I imagine a flurry of strangers in white lab coats carrying beakers and punching codes into complicated machines. The results arrive four weeks later: Sadie has oculocutaneous albinism type 1 (OCA1) variants A and B.

In OCA1A, the enzyme tyrosinase, which converts the amino acid tyrosine into melanin, fails to carry out its assigned task. In OCA1B cases, it makes a partial effort, and there is some pigment formation: yellower hair and eyelashes, darker eyes. OCA1 occurs with one in every forty thousand births. The recessive gene can be passed on silently for centuries because both parents must be carriers for the condition to manifest. It is so rare, so improbable. Of all the gin joints in all the towns in all the world, Andrew walks into the Ship Pub in St. John's on a blustery June night. I spot him across the bar and think he looks familiar, so I introduce myself. The rest is genetic history.

It is a strange relief to succumb to your DNA. Earlier that week, I had fought back tears when a worried nurse at a lactation support session looked into Sadie's eyes and asked, "Does she smile at you? Does she make eye contact? Can she focus on an object?" No. No. And no. But with the albinism diagnosis, I throw out all of my "baby's first year" books and ignore the monthly milestones attributed to normal development. The first time Sadie reaches for an object (a garish purple dragon hanging from the handle of her bucket seat), the first time she holds my gaze, the first time she smiles back at me, these will happen on a different timeline, and they will be some of the most exciting, profound moments of my life.

When I meet with Dr. Turner a year later, I ask her how it feels to be a genetic code messenger. She considers this for a moment. In our case, she has noticed a shift toward accepting Sadie's condition since our first visit, particularly in me. In the beginning, I denied the possibility of a problem, or at least I saw it in a different way. Andrew, his earlier depression having lifted, seemed open to the diagnosis during the initial meeting.

The hardest cases are when a child's prognosis is terminal. She tells me about walking into the small room where we met the previous year and facing an entire family (child, parents, and both sets of grandparents) to deliver the news of the fatal genetic flaw. The mood was heavy. The father was weeping. Dr. Turner excused herself for a moment on the pretense of finding a few more chairs. She went to her office, put her head down, took a few deep breaths, and said, "Okay, pull yourself together."

"Then what?" I ask.

"And then I was fine to go back in."

"It's not supposed to look like this," says a fierce, sad-eyed mother in the outpatient waiting room at the children's hospital in St. John's. "You get pregnant, and you have a baby, right?" She shakes her head. "I had a big bleed at thirty weeks, and it's been hell ever since." I have seen this mother before; I take Sadie to a slew of specialists with offices here, and our appointments often coincide. The woman points out her daughter, a small eighteen-month-old with a wiry build and corkscrew curls, seated at a miniature yellow table, coloring with conviction. I don't see the problem, but it turns out that no one does. She suffers from "a failure to thrive." This is the term allotted to an infant or a young child who stops developing at the same rate as his or her peers. The child's development begins in the regular way, and then there is a change.

In European fairy lore, a newborn whose nature turns foul, who screams with colic or falls suspiciously quiet, whose chubby cheeks turn gaunt and whose bright eyes hollow, is called a changeling. It is sometimes believed that the human child is switched by the fairies for one of their own offspring. The fairies persisted in North America, stealing infants from cribs throughout Newfoundland and leaving cross, wizened, unfamiliar babies in their places.

Some scholars attribute changeling narratives to cases of failure to thrive. A supernatural explanation absolves the parents of guilt; rather than a genetic hand-me-down, it is a case of switched identity. It allows them to grieve for the stolen child, the one they had conjured over nine long months—because that child is gone, away with the fairies, and with it any preconceived ideas of parenthood.

There are no changeling stories connected to albinism because, with the exception of nystagmus—the darting of the irises, which appears at around six weeks—the condition does not develop after birth. However, the ethereal whiteness does inspire albinism lore across the globe, particularly where people typically have darker skin, hair, and eyes. In the early twentieth century, New Zealand ethnographer Makereti Papakura found that Maori people with albinism are believed to be the offspring of mortal women and supernatural men who belong to a tribe of fair-haired mist dwellers.

Around the same time, Western scholars sought to verify rumors of an "albinotic race" residing among the Cuna people of the San Blas Islands, off the coast of Panama. The theory has been debunked, but the place still appears to have a high incidence of the genetic condition. D.B. Stout, an intrepid anthropologist, takes up residence among the Cuna and discovers that, in some communities, individuals with albinism are associated with higher intelligence, godliness, and magic powers that enable them to ward off a demon that periodically eclipses the sun and moon. Stout's successors find that Cuna people with albinism are called moon children, alluding to their mothers or fathers staring too long at the night sky during gestation.

I print the albinism-lore articles I've found through my university library's database and keep them in a folder on my desk. They sit side by side with Sadie's five-section medical binder. In some ways, what I learn about the moon children of the San Blas Islands is just as important to my understanding of the condition as the literature from our genetic counselor.

In spring we drive from St. John's to Northumberland County, Ontario, where we plan to spend the summer at my family cottage by the lake. The ferry ride is dark and bleary. The province of Nova Scotia is a continuous scream. New Brunswick, a long, low wail. Quebec is Stan Rogers, roadside nursing, and cheese curds. Ontario, endless highway, more tears, then relief when we pull down the treed lane and see the little blue cottage that will be our home for the next three months.

My parents' home is a short drive from the lake, and Sadie and I spend afternoons there with my mom and dad. I sit in my mom's office, transcribing interviews I'd conducted for my dissertation, listening to the stories from a Newfoundland outport. Normally, this is where my mom writes, but lately she is more babysitter than novelist. Often I'll wander out and find my mother reclined on the couch reading, while Sadie lolls around on the floor beside her, thumping her heels on the ground, sucking on the lid of a yogurt container, or removing her socks. It astounds me that they can achieve this kind of parallel amusement. As the mother, and the main food source, I'm never afforded the same kind of reprieve.

My father is usually there too, working in his studio, which is a room off the back of the house. He'd recently rediscovered a series of his early tondos, circular oil paintings he did in the 1960s, along the back wall of the barn on their property. The building originally belonged to my maternal grandparents, and he must have stashed them there in the late 1970s or early '80s, having run out of storage space in our home. If my parents hadn't bought the house after my grandmother died in 2007, the paintings would have vanished—auctioned off or carelessly discarded. He's reinspired by the almost-lost work, reviving and adding to the brilliant orbs of abstract landscapes. On the afternoons we spend there, I take Sadie out to see her grandfather working on his art, dipping her head close to the colors and whisking her away before she's able to mash her fingers into the gobs of wet oil paint.

Down at the lake, we keep Sadie inside, afraid the sun will scorch her pale skin but equally frightened by the warnings against applying sunblock to a baby less than six months old. I try a few different natural brands, but they are gritty, or oily, or so zinc-filled that the lotion looks like war paint. As the sun sets one evening Andrew carries Sadie down to the edge of the water so that she can hear the waves raking the beach stones. She is awake, but her eyes are closed. She rarely opens her eyes outside unless she's peering out from beneath a floppy wide-brimmed hat. I don't know if she will grow less photophobic with time or if she will always close her eyes against the day's light.

IN JUNE, WE TAKE SADIE TO SEE DR. ELISE HÉON, THE CHIEF OPHTHALmologist at the Hospital for Sick Children in Toronto. She is a tall, handsome woman, wearing a sleeveless Anthropologie dress stamped with a bucolic landscape print. She graciously acknowledges the distance we have traveled and makes us feel like visiting royalty. She is a commanding presence, and her underlings are practically tripping on her white coattails. Even Sadie, traumatized by an earlier test involving electrodes plastered to her head and a strobe light, succumbs immediately to the doctor's charm and reaches for her arms. In faintly accented but excellent English, Dr. Héon informs us that our daughter will never drive a car.

I can no more picture six-month-old Sadie driving a car than I can imagine her using a fork. The future is slippery and hard to grasp. Sometimes I imagine approaching her teacher to discuss how to avoid flash photography on picture day. "Perhaps you would consider taking the pictures outside this year?" my future self will ask Sadie's future teacher, explaining how the flash makes her blue eyes appear red. But when I visualize this, I am standing in the foyer of my own elementary school and speaking with Mrs. Vijendren, my grade-two teacher. I have no frame of reference for Sadie's future—nor, for that matter, for my own.

After our morning at SickKids, we walk over to the Art Gallery of Ontario to see the abstract expressionist show. In the hushed world of the exhibition space, my mind wanders. Sadie is asleep in her stroller, buried beneath the hulking gray UV shield. Several of Mark Rothko's giant color field paintings dominate a corner of the gallery, floating landscapes of shimmering hues, detail-less and yet so emotive. This is how Sadie will see, I think, in giant fields of color, as an abstract expressionist does.

A few days later, I am cornered at an afternoon gathering by an acquaintance, a tireless raconteur of questionable narratives.

"My aunt is an albino," she says. "She had to wear a blanket over her head during the day if she ever went outside, but mostly they had her working in the fields at night during rainstorms. Everyone thought she was a witch."

"Really?" I ask, unconvinced.

"You got the short end of the genetic stick," she says, shaking her head.

It enrages me that this woman is calling my beautiful baby a manifestation of poor genes. But it is the interactions during the most mundane aspects of life that wear me down. A flash mob of shoppers comes alive at the grocery store when I push my daughter along the aisles in the cart—craned necks, pointed fingers, wide-eyed astonishment. "Does she get her hair color from you or your husband?" they ask. The answer is both, of course, because it's a recessive trait.

WE RETURN TO ST. JOHN'S IN EARLY FALL, AND AFTER A CONSULT WITH our ophthalmologist, Sadie gets fitted for glasses to help control her nystagmus and improve her distance vision. Something about the pink plastic frames digging into her chubby cheeks upsets me deeply. I erupt in great, galloping sobs at the optometrist's office. Even after I pull myself together, a snivel will escape at random, like a hiccup.

Around the same time, I am roused from sleep one night by a drunk abusing the cars parked on our downtown street. His fists repeatedly rain down on hoods and trunks and windshields. The bashing of flesh on metal and glass sounds like an offbeat drum, punctuated by his raging diatribe. The next morning, I see two cars with smashed windshields on our block. Later that week, a neighbor tells me that the offender returned, leaving an envelope with $250 on the windshield of one of the damaged vehicles. Inside was a note that read, *I'm sorry I smashed your windows. I don't know what got into me.*

This outburst and the man's apology resonate with me. Some days I want to scream out my front door like a banshee and smash my world apart, then leave an apology note and get on with life.

Instead, I rub two shiny worry spots into either side of my scalp. While organizing photos from a spring vacation, I am shocked to see the round bald spots peering out of my hairline, like a second set of eyes. Motherhood, with its saggy-bodied sleeplessness and the baby's constant cry, is a foreign country. Not Tibet exactly, but certainly Denmark, or Croatia.

AT EIGHT MONTHS, SADIE BEGINS TO SPEND TIME AT OUR LOCAL CNIB (founded as the Canadian National Institute for the Blind), a center where we can use a playroom designed for children with limited sight. It is called the Snoezelen Room (an awkward neologism that pairs the Dutch words for "sniff" and "doze"), and it conjures hazy memories of

European discotheques from the year I spent in the south of France. A darkened lair, it is a wild array of flashing lights, mirrors, padded floors, lit-up toys, and beanbag chairs, under a convincing projection of stars. Another projection on the wall is of an underwater scene in the shape of a circle, as if we were peering out a submarine porthole. Sadie's vision progresses in tandem with these visits, until one day she notices the stars on the ceiling.

Along with the music lessons, playgroups, and kids' gym, the Snoezelen Room becomes just another new-mom-and-baby excursion. Months back, however, pushing my stroller through CNIB's doors for the first time, I agreed with the woman I met in the hospital waiting room in St. John's: "It's not supposed to look like this."

But it does. And it will. I see lots of other kids wearing sunglasses, and we live in an age of UV-proof clothing and SPF awareness. Visually impaired or sighted, we all carry technological devices that facilitate our everyday tasks. Sadie is beautiful, smart, and funny, and most important, she is loved. Her network starts with her two smitten parents and expands across family and friends, a team of doctors, and a beloved dog that waits with tail-thumping enthusiasm at the nursery door every morning. Her fans include the PhD-wielding mamas in our baby group, her sitters, the besotted employee at our local grocery store, and our postal worker, who for a year delivers weekly gift packages to the little blond girl at number 62.

Before Sadie came along, smug parents would tell me that you can only really know love when you have a child. I interpreted this to mean the love you feel for your child, which I now know is vast and indefinable. But I wonder if they meant it in a greater sense. It is the love we receive that astounds me. You never know how much people care about you until you fall apart a little and everyone picks you up, piece by piece, and puts you back together again.

I AM THE ANTHOLOGIST, AND THESE ARE THE STORIES IN MY REPER-toire. Occasionally, snippets of darker narratives sidle their way into my collection. I read about folk beliefs in Zimbabwe and Tanzania, where some see albinism as a curse, a contagion, or punishment for a mother's infidelity with a malevolent spirit. In these nations deci-mated by disease, there are rumors that sleeping with a woman with albinism can cure HIV/AIDS.

"The same culture that can elevate me to a god can turn me into a demon," says Peter Ash, a BC resident with albinism who founded Under the Same Sun, a Vancouver nonprofit that strives to better the lives of people with albinism in Tanzania.

Ash is a fast talker, and he rhymes off the atrocities visited on Tanzania's albinism population in rapid-fire succession: rape, vio-lence, dismemberment, social stigma, abandonment, orphanhood, and infanticide. He tells me about visiting a little boy who had lost a hand to poachers—a transaction set up by his parents. The poach-ers sell "albino" body parts to witch doctors, who believe they hold magical properties and use them for curative potions.

Ash remains remarkably objective when discussing these issues. I am less so. Whispers of colonial judgment shroud my objectivity. "How do I interpret this?" I ask my former teacher Diane Goldstein, a folklore professor at Indiana University, and a renowned belief scholar who describes herself as a cultural relativist. She reminds me to look at the context, and says that in her own work (on AIDS legends and beliefs and, more recently, infanticide), she finds that "at the heart of these beliefs are important cultural issues that are very humane."

And how different are these beliefs from our own? Hollywood is North America's witch doctor, and he can also be barbaric. Such popu-lar films as *The Da Vinci Code*, *The Matrix Reloaded*, and *The Princess Bride* all feature albino villains. Despite our perceived modernity, much of our faith and knowledge is wrapped up in make-believe.

AFTER MONTHS OF READING PARENTING MEMOIRS AND MEDICAL JOUR-
nals, I return to novels. I pick up Michael Crummey's *Galore*, and in
the first few pages a "bleached white" man is cut from the belly of a
beached whale, to the horror and fascination of the outport villagers
who witness the event. The man is christened Judah, and there is a
hint of the supernatural in his muteness and whiteness. He is often
referred to as "the albino."

I have crossed paths with Crummey a few times over my years in
Newfoundland. He is kind and affable, and I like how he peppers his
soft-spoken sentences with emphatic curses. He agrees to speak with
me about Judah's character.

We meet in a soulless boardroom in the library at Memorial
University—Crummey's alma mater, where I am working on my
PhD—and he tells me that Judah's whiteness is not related to a genetic condition. (In the book, a doctor's examination reveals that Judah
is "not a true albino," and Crummey jokes, "I guess given your own
experience he could have just got it wrong.") The decision was practical: Judah was bleached by the whale's stomach acid. However, the
whiteness opened up a variety of literary possibilities.

"White is the empty page," says Crummey. "It's the blank canvas,
and so what I saw happening in the book was that Judah was the blank
canvas people could project whatever they desired most—or whatever
they feared most—onto. The community created Judah over and over
and over again because he was blank."

White is the noncolor, both enigmatic and profound. I think of
Noah's whiteness, symbolic of a divine path. I think of the fair-haired
people who live in the New Zealand mist, the moon children on a
string of islands off Panama, and the infants who went away with the
fairies of Newfoundland. I think of the tiny white-haired baby who
slept in her plastic bassinet while half of the hospital came to her side
in awe.

23

I can't go back to those few days in the maternity ward, before the janitor's Cassandra-like prediction, before science threatened my version of the story—when I spun my own tale and accepted my daughter's beauty as otherworldly and magical. I am not certain that we are better off for knowing the molecular story rather than the folktale, or whether there is room for both. Science can tell you how genetic anomalies and birth defects happen, but not why they happened to you rather than to your neighbor. Medical facts can rarely offer the level of comfort that stories can. At least in our personal narratives we have control. Here is the value of folklore: it gives shape to the unknowable. This can be uplifting or dangerous, but ultimately it explains human difference in a way that science never will. Some days, I yearn for my short-lived dark age, but it is a curious nostalgia because I can't imagine life—and more specifically my daughter—to be any different, and in the end I don't want to.

When Sadie is a year old, Dr. Turner invites us to share our tale of genetic discovery with her first-year medical students. We nervously over-prepare with a twenty-one-slide PowerPoint presentation and seven pages of notes.

The talk goes smoothly until we broach the topic of having a second child. There is a one-in-four chance of albinism, and one in two that the baby will be a carrier regardless. There is also a one-in-four chance that the gene will not be present at all. These numbers tell me as much as tea leaves or tarot cards. A second child will have this condition, or she will not.

For now, it is just a line in our printed notes: "Talk about DNA/ in vitro testing." The rest of the sheet is blank because we have come to the end of the story so far. We have to look out at the fifty or so faces in the room and shrug our shoulders, helpless to fate, helpless to a wiring system I barely understand, the invisible ruler we must obey that hovers, depending on what you believe, somewhere between God, fairy tales, and science. The talk stops here. The students clap, and Sadie looks up from the third row, where she has wedged her walker between a desk and a knapsack. The clapping ends, and the students ask us questions we can confidently answer, about events that have already happened. Sadie dislodges her walker, turns, and races off in the other direction, happy to receive the students' attention, content to hear her parents' voices in the background, knowing that we are there watching her and making sure (for now) that her world is padded and safe.

Telling our story to the medical students is not as frightening as I had thought it would be. The reality is that I tell versions of this story every day. I tell inquisitive grocery shoppers, and moms at playgroups; I tell my seatmates on airplanes, and strangers at the park. I perform the narrative like a folktale, many times, and it changes depending on the context and the audience. One day, I will pass it on to the person who matters most, because it is her story, after all. I wonder how she will tell it.

CHAPTER 2

Imaginings

I AM AT A WEEKEND PLAYDATE WITH SADIE WHEN MY FRIEND JENNY tells me she is pregnant with her second child. I smile, and I say the right things, but inside a viscous dread envelops my chest, drips through my ribs, then pools in my stomach. I can't name the feeling—something between fear and regret—but I am shocked by it.

Sadie and I spend a lot of Saturday afternoons in Jenny's light-filled home, a tiny timber-frame rental on a panhandle lot with a view of the St. John's narrows. We gather there with other new moms, a group of women I knew through the university but had grown closer with after the arrival of our children. It is an international assembly of first-time mothers from Italy, Australia, the United States, and several Canadian provinces. Many of them have recently defended their PhD dissertations, most in science, using their second language. They could be an intimidating group if the talk when we met wasn't all about the babies. We discussed how they slept and ate; what they drank and how often they peed and pooped; we shared info on playgroups; we talked about how much the babies grew. We also talked about the accessories: playpens, strollers, bibs, blankets, cribs, soothers, and those amber teething necklaces all the toddlers seem to be wearing these days.

Occasionally, we discussed our various career options—post-doctoral positions, academic jobs, papers accepted to journals—but generally we focused on the kids. What was surprising about this group was that there wasn't any competition. Not professionally (we weren't vying for the same jobs) and not when it came to our children. I've met moms with sharp elbows at community playgroups and music classes. When I sense a competitive edge, I point out that I don't follow milestone guidelines. I tell the mom how I relegated my baby books to storage when my daughter was diagnosed with a genetic condition that caused low vision. I say that she might develop slower, or she might not, but that for now I'm happy with our pace, and this generally gives me a pass from the occasional parenting rivalries I encounter.

I didn't need to explain Sadie's white hair or visual impairment to the moms who met at Jenny's house because they already knew; they'd watched the story unfold. I am grateful for that sanctuary, and in particular to Jenny, who set the tone. She's a polyglot whose English sentences are peppered with her native Italian, and she has a casual, accepting manner. As a friend, she is a constant advocate. This made my reaction to her pregnancy news all the more surprising, and unsettling. Pushing Sadie in her stroller on the way home, removed from the jubilance and chaos of the babies and their moms, I mull over my strange emotional response. It was sudden and unexpected, like a rogue wave on a peaceful sea. But like the water phenomenon, I know there is an undercurrent at its center.

Andrew and I aren't talking about it yet, but I think about having a second child a lot. I imagine having amniocentesis done despite the risk to the fetus, and how I'd feel if the invasive test resulted in a miscarriage, as one in every two hundred to four hundred procedures will. The risk would be closer to one in a hundred if I opted for chorionic villus sampling, where a probe extracts tissue from the developing placenta, and which can be done earlier in the pregnancy. I envision refusing these tests and how at the first pangs of labor I'd begin to wonder, not about the child's gender, but about her eyesight and about the color, or lack of color, in her hair. I never stop there. I conjure our friends and family looking at the first photos of our second baby on their computer screens: "Well, she obviously has the white hair," they might say. Or possibly worse: "I bet they're relieved."

Can't we just stay here a little longer while I figure this out? I'd thought as my peers had their second children. From the outside, it looked easy for them. This is foolish, I know, because every new life is a chance taken, made clear by the many tests offered to women in early pregnancy. High risk or low, we are all given the option to prescreen our offspring. From the earliest prenatal blood work, or even before, we begin seeking messages from our unborn encoded in their cells. These can be difficult to decipher, like the 2 to 4 percent of integrated prenatal screening that turn up false positive results for Down syndrome, or they can be very precise, particularly when using amniocentesis to detect specific conditions, such as spina bifida or cystic fibrosis. Once the discovery is made, there is no turning back. You can't erase the information. You must decide to soldier on with the pregnancy or to terminate. It puts parents in the bewildering and emotional position of placing value on a potential human life, puzzling out what is worth bearing, for the eventual child, and for themselves. In the bigger picture, these quandaries are relegated to ethicists and lawmakers, but mostly this task and the ultimate decision unfolds over pillow talk in the bedrooms of regular folks in their ordinary homes.

The crux of the problem with selection is that parents can feel vilified for procreating despite knowledge of an existing genetic trait, but they can also feel condemned for choosing to terminate based on the same information. In either case, the psychological effects on them can range from troubling to torturous.

It's a hard topic to wrestle with on my own, so I contact my friend Georgina Blanchard, who practices midwifery in Toronto, and ask her opinion.

"People think you are foolish now if you don't have genetic testing, but it's a myth that you have to do it," Georgina tells me over Skype while nursing her small son, her older boy occasionally whizzing between her and the computer screen.

"It does seem like just another part of the pregnancy experience," I say. "We wouldn't have known to screen for albinism, but I'm grateful that was never an option."

"A lot of people don't want genetic screening," she says. "What if they want a baby and they don't have a position about whether the baby is normal or perfect or healthy? What if the baby is perfect for them because it's their baby?"

She's right. Parents love their children because they are their own. Decisions, whether to screen or to select, are personal and shouldn't involve the tongue-wagging masses. So why do we, the mothers and fathers, care about the societal pressure to have perfect children? Why do I worry about the reactions of relatives and strangers to this phantom second child and feel a lingering sense of guilt? This is particularly perplexing in light of the overwhelming, enveloping love we and others feel for our daughter.

A 1998 study on mothers of children with some form of genetic or birth defect noted that each woman interviewed—about twenty-five from varying backgrounds in New York State—felt some level of responsibility for their child's disability, "both through her obligations to undergo prenatal screening and selective abortion of defective fetuses, and through her control of the uterine environment."

As a feminist and academic I know it's absurd to blame myself for passing on a genetic condition to my child, or to any future children. As a human being I struggle under centuries of maternal blame. Most of what happens within the sanctuary of the womb is beyond the woman's control, but historically, and in contemporary folk beliefs, a pregnant woman is seen to exert supernatural power over her unborn child. In the Age of Enlightenment, some French philosophers believed that the mother's imagination could produce a child with birth defects. Others dismissed the notion that a woman could wield such power.

The science of embryology developed over the nineteenth and twentieth centuries. In reality, it was what a pregnant woman consumed, not her thoughts, that could affect the development of the fetus. In the 1940s, a pediatric researcher named Josef Warkany, who worked out of the University of Cincinnati's College of Medicine, made a discovery that would forever alter prenatal guidelines. Warkany's findings, published in the journal *Science*, were that environmental factors could affect the fetus and cause birth defects. In his research with laboratory animals, he found that a mother's diet could have an impact on her unborn child. It was a pregnant woman's consumption, not her imagination, that could have a bearing on her offspring.

It would take researchers another thirty years to coin the term "fetal alcohol syndrome," though the negative effects of drink on the unborn had been suspected for centuries. The condition was diagnosed when a group of children from different backgrounds and ethnicities presented with similar medical problems. Several studies between 1968 and the early seventies noted one commonality: the children's pregnant mothers were chronic alcohol abusers. The researchers who wrote the 1973 article in *Lancet*, Drs. David Smith and Kenneth Jones at the University of Washington, named the constellation of abnormalities for the cause. This is because naming a condition for the teratogen—the substance causing the developmental irregularities—makes it clear that there is a correlation between the act and the outcome.

Today, the posters in doctors' offices and on public transit delivering messages to pregnant women about eating well and the risks of alcohol consumption and smoking, which have been linked to low birth weight for more than fifty years, seem almost outdated. I clearly remember the face of the pregnant woman I met outside my OB's office one day. "You pregnant too?" she asked casually, taking a long haul on her cigarette. Had she missed the public service ads in the waiting room? Was it a deliberate act of defiance? I'd never seen a full-term pregnant woman smoking. It was as unlikely as standing next to a Sasquatch.

Common folk beliefs are closer to seventeenth- and eighteenth-century French imaginationist views. A pregnant mother's behavior, where she rests her gaze, her yearnings and unfulfilled desires, have been attributed to birth defects, marks, and genetic conditions. I came across this often in my folklore research on albinism. Like the myth in Malawi that a pregnant woman must refrain from looking directly at a person with albinism or her child will be born with the condition. If she does look, it's not too late, she can protect her fetus from turning slowly white in her belly by hawking on the ground. The pale grow accustomed to the sound of spit hitting dust.

Many folk beliefs center on prenatal behavior because a pregnant woman is a particular kind of taboo: she embodies life, sex, and mystery. In a 1964 study, folklorist Lucile F. Newman discovered a series of social controls embedded in folk beliefs about pregnancy in Contra Costa County, California. Women in her study, which was conducted among white and African-American patients of prenatal care clinics, told her that laughing at a person with a disability can cause your child to be born with a similar condition, and pitying them will have the same result. Cravings were also taboo. Several women said that wanting something too badly and exhibiting strong desires would mark the fetus. This is a common belief across ethnicities; in France and Italy, the notion is so enmeshed in the culture that the words for "longing" and "birthmark" are interchangeable.

Is there any truth to the possibility of a psychic connection between a mother and her unborn child? Medical researchers at the Johns Hopkins School of Hygiene and Public Health's Department of Population and Family Health Sciences were baffled when they set out to debunk pregnancy folklore about gender prediction and instead discovered an even more mystical connection. Of the women questioned, 71 percent correctly guessed their baby's gender and most based their prediction on a feeling or a dream. When the women used traditional folk beliefs to determine the sex, their results dropped dramatically. In a strange twist, there was a correlation between the mother's level of education and correct gender prediction. Those with a high school diploma or higher were more likely to be correct. The scientists threw up their hands in defeat, unable to interpret the results. "As researchers we must confess to being troubled by the better validity of these methods when compared with those having some biological plausibility, and it is always possible that this was a spurious finding," the authors write. "It is equally likely that there is simply much about the maternal–fetal connection that we do not know."

AFTER I HAVE A STORY ON ALBINISM PUBLISHED IN A NATIONAL MAGAZINE, the host of a local afternoon radio show calls to interview me. I'd prepared by brushing up on genetics and the inner workings of the eye, so his more personal questions catch me off guard. Near the end he steers the conversation toward the possibility of having a second child.

"How worried are you about going through this again?" he asks.

"I've had a lot of opinions floated about by family and friends, and some people think it is irresponsible or tell me that I should adopt," I say. "But knowing Sadie as she is now, and the joy that she is and that she's brought to so many people, I just think it's not a good enough reason not to have a second child. If we're able to down the road, then that's definitely a possibility."

My answer isn't untrue, just indirect. When I imagine a second pregnancy and envision the scenario where I get the screening results, the baby always has albinism. I never consider termination. This condition doesn't warrant that heart-and-mind-bending conversation for me, or for Andrew. So I was surprised when I came across an article on embryo screening in January 2012, shortly after Sadie's first birthday, in which the reporter listed albinism as an example of a condition people might weed out. These were cases where the gene has already been isolated, as with the genetic testing we did to determine exactly what type of albinism Sadie has. It rattled me to see this view in print, this suggestion that other parents like us, people who knew they carried the OCA gene, were doing the test to avoid having a second child with albinism.

Medically, these tests are referred to as preimplantation genetic diagnosis (PGD), which is an option for couples with known genetic mutations, and the more common preimplantation genetic screening (PGS), a chromosome number evaluation. In both cases, embryos are harvested via in vitro fertilization (IVF), and those that carry the gene mutation or have an abnormal chromosomal count are not implanted. The cost for both procedures is prohibitive, starting at $10,000, including the IVF cycle (where mature eggs are collected from a woman's ovaries and fertilized with sperm, and the embryos then implanted in the uterus) and embryo screening. The genetic testing is done in the United States, as currently no lab in Canada has the technology to facilitate that part of the procedure. About one hundred PGD and three hundred PGS tests are performed in Canada per year.

In a *New York Times* article on embryo screening, the founder and director of the Institute for Human Reproduction in Chicago, Dr. Ilan Tur-Kaspa, refers to regular conception as "reproductive roulette." Later in the same piece, a bioethicist named Janet Malek, from the Brody School of Medicine at East Carolina University, says she sees embryo screening as a moral duty when parents are aware of a bad gene mutation and can afford the procedure. Reading this, I can't help but apply these strangers' ethical standards to my own life and wonder if their feelings would hold for my child's genetic condition, and where we might fall on their scale of what is considered worthy of screening.

It isn't simply an issue of ethics or a quibble over the quality of a human life. I am primarily concerned with the emotional impact on my daughter. The choice to abort a fetus that tests positive for albinism, or to discard any embryos that carry this genetic mutation, carries an inherent message. What these decisions would say to Sadie is that, when faced with the option, her parents decided against having another child like her. Maybe as she grows older she might understand the difficult position we are in, acknowledging the challenges of one's low vision, sun sensitivity, and the social difficulties of looking different from your peers. When I try to imagine explaining this choice to her, I don't get very far. Even the most logical human being would see this as a form of rejection.

The new moms in my orbit aren't grappling with the same constellation of issues as I am. They are facing other concerns, unique to their own lives, which are also confusing and emotional, but sometimes I can't find a way to connect. I am grateful for my support network, but I long for someone who can say two words: "I know." This is what happens when I meet Carrie Lentz.

Carrie lives in Alberta and her second son, Jonah, was born with albinism about two months after Sadie. NOAH's executive director Mike McGowan put us in touch over email in February 2012, feeling we had a lot in common. Carrie is in the process of forming a Canadian chapter of the albinism organization while working full time and parenting two young boys. She's a type-A personality in all aspects of her life. She gets things done. I email her my phone number, and she calls me three minutes later. We talk for an hour, for as long as our husbands and kids can spare us. We swap birth and diagnosis stories and our babies' medical histories and say, "I know, I know, I know." We discuss the upcoming NOAH conference in St. Louis, which Carrie and her family plan to attend, but on which we remain undecided. Then we talk about having another child.

"I only want another baby if I can guarantee that it will be a girl, and that she will have albinism," Carrie says.

"Really?" I ask.

"Yes," she says. "I've always wanted a daughter, and Jonah could have a sibling he can relate to."

Carrie's take on having another child is unexpected and refreshing. She would choose albinism. She meant this hypothetically, but her comment spurred my thoughts in a direction I had never considered.

In certain communities, parents do choose to have children who share their genetic difference. My understanding of embryo screening had been one-sided. Moms and dads want to have children who resemble them and who they can relate with. Why wouldn't parents choose a child who was like them or, as Carrie suggested, like one of their other children? A parent who is deaf, or has dwarfism, or has albinism might want a child who looks phenotypically theirs. I wonder if we could choose an embryo to ensure our next child would have albinism, should we conceive via IVF and go through the PGD screening process. Statistically, one in four of our embryos would express the genetic mutation, and considering my age, we'd probably manage to harvest about six. Chances are good that at least one of them would test positive for albinism.

If I were in the United Kingdom, it would be illegal for me to select an embryo with a known genetic condition. The Human Fertilisation Embryology Authority has disallowed the use of PGD to select for disability or for gender and also sanctions which conditions are deemed serious enough to screen for. More than one hundred items are on the list (including oculocutaneous albinism 1 types A and B), with another sixty currently under consideration. In Canada, it is illegal to select an embryo based on gender unless there is a medical reason for doing so, but the decision to select for or against disability is left to the patient and doctor to tussle with. This means that Canadian and American fertility specialists can accommodate this request—but would they? I contact Dr. Carl Laskin, a specialist in reproductive immunology and autoimmune diseases in pregnancy, who works for the LifeQuest Centre for Reproductive Medicine in Toronto, to ask for his opinion on selecting for rather than against disability. LifeQuest was the first clinic in the country to offer PGD, beginning in the late 1990s, and today they accommodate about twenty cases per year. (PGS is more common, and this number is closer to one hundred.)

In a 2008 survey of 137 fertility clinics in the United States, researchers at the Genetics and Public Policy Center at the Johns Hopkins Berman Institute of Bioethics in Washington found that 3 percent of clients were using PGD to choose for a disability. There have been no similar studies done in Canada, but Dr. Laskin, whose clinic performs the largest number of PGD screenings in the country, says he has not been faced with this scenario. However, he sits on several ethics committees and says it's something they discuss often during workshops. They tend to cite the case of Sharon Duchesneau and Candy McCullough, a lesbian couple in Washington, DC, who are both deaf, and chose a sperm donor who carried the genetic trait for deafness to ensure their child would be born without hearing. Their case garnered immense publicity back in 2002, and, based on

Dr. Laskin's account, is still used as an example among fertility specialists when discussing ethical taboos.

"We've had many discussions using the deaf scenario as the kick-off point, and the stance depends on the physician and their personal feelings on this," Dr. Laskin says.

"When you're dealing with these kinds of questions, you have to remember that the physician brings their own baggage to the discussion. Now, that baggage may be that they have two children who have never had a problem. Can the physician look at [the patients' situation] dispassionately and say, 'Okay, I have no problem and I can go forward with this?' Or, 'I simply can't get around this, but let me find someone that would.' That basically is the end of the discussion, and the final conclusion that we came to is that not all of us would take it on."

"Would you take it on?" I ask.

"I would be one of the ones who had difficulties," Dr. Laskin says.

"Why?"

"The issue is—certainly when we talked about the deaf scenario—that I am going to assist in bringing a child into this world that is going to have a lifelong challenge with hearing, and in your case, a lifelong challenge with vision. I understand where you're coming from, I really do, but I can't walk a mile in your shoes. I don't make a value judgment on you, but I look to myself and say, 'I'm having trouble with this.' I would simply recuse myself and find someone that would do it."

"I hadn't really considered it from your side," I say. "How as a physician you have to be comfortable with it because it's your ethical quandary as well."

"Sometimes you'll have couples say, 'Don't you think this is my choice?'" says Dr. Laskin. "My answer is, 'Yes, it is, but it's also my choice as to whether or not I participate.'"

I wonder about the medical researchers, the people who work to isolate and identify the genes that we are now selecting for, but mostly against. Does it present a similar ethical debate for them? I contact Dr. Murray Brilliant, an aptly named American geneticist with special expertise in albinism, to ask for his opinion on prenatal screening. Dr. Brilliant was responsible for discovering the location of two genes associated with oculocutaneous albinism: OCA2, which is most prevalent in Africans and people of African descent, and OCA4, which is most commonly found in Japan. His laboratory also identified the gene associated with Hermansky–Pudlak syndrome type 1, a rare bleeding disorder with varying levels of severity that also features oculocutaneous albinism. His worldwide work on albinism, as well as his pigment-augmentation studies, are ongoing.

Gene isolation is significant work and I'm grateful to scientists like Dr. Brilliant, whose research is minimally funded and mostly fueled by small-scale donors, interest, and passion because studying a rare genetic condition is not lucrative. Still, I'm curious to know his feelings on genetic screening. When I try to ask him, I begin with a long preamble about having a second child, but trail off.

"You can ask," Dr. Brilliant says, knowing where my question is leading.

"As a geneticist you're able to isolate the gene, and this is important for people like us when looking for a child's diagnosis and subsequently managing or treating them," I say. "But could identifying the gene help to eradicate the condition altogether in the places in the world where we have the means to do that?"

"You can't eradicate a condition," Dr. Brilliant answers. "On average we all have about seven really bad mutations. It's just the draw of the genetic cards. Albinism is a condition that we can see, but you can't see other mutations that lead to coronary artery disease or diabetes or something else. We all have something."

"But what about selective abortion?" I ask.

"I have no real opinion on what a parent chooses to do when they have children, how they want to select. I do know this: I've seen a number of parents who have recently had a child with albinism, and they're desperate for some kind of test so they don't have another child with albinism, and then after a year or two, after they get to know their child, that's not on their radar anymore."

Which bad mutations will manifest in your child depends on whom you mate with.

"Are you two related?" our first ophthalmologist asked during our initial consult when Sadie was just a few weeks old.

"No," we told her, stifling incredulous giggles. Later, furious and embarrassed, I asked Andrew why it would matter to her. "What's done is done," I said.

"Not necessarily," he countered, always the scientist. "If we were second cousins, they might look for a number of other issues." It's not that inbreeding spontaneously causes genetic disorders, he explained. Instead, sharing a common ancestor makes you more likely to carry some of those same very bad seven mutations that Dr. Brilliant mentioned. As we learned, when both parents carry the same gene mutation, the chances of their child expressing a condition increases, in some cases from nearly zero to 25, 50, or even 100 percent.

Testing revealed that Sadie has two types of albinism, which means the gene didn't come from shared branches on our family trees, but in the time between the ophthalmologist's comment and our results, I briefly wondered if somewhere in our shared Irish ancestry our forebears had crossed paths.

Early in our relationship, Andrew and I visited Ireland, tracing his roots the long way back to County Tipperary, where we found both a mansion and a castle bearing his surname. Remembering my failed attempt to commune with my own Irish ancestors in my twenties, when I mostly cleaned youth hostels and drank beer with Australians, I didn't expect much. But when we arrived at his family's ancestral manor—now the headquarters for a bovine insemination business— he was treated like the prodigal son.

The manor's grandeur had faded over the years. The halls were cobwebbed, the walls were mottled and worn, and the tiled floors had lost their sheen. The elaborate foyer had been transformed into a reception. The family crest painted across a skylight was dimmed by debris. The desperate grunting of heated bulls followed us as we walked the grounds, and the beasts roared when we passed their gated pens. The true gem, far from the penned animals, was the family castle, which sat in an adjacent field—a sixteenth-century stone fortress that had been partially burned by the Black and Tans for being a purported IRA meeting spot. My husband's paternal family were Norman landlords, though my father-in-law once told me that his great-grandfather "ran off with the maid, so I guess we do have some Irish in us."

Some of my family lore remains obscured in the twists and folds of our DNA, like how my maternal grandfather fervently denied his mother's possible Jewish roots. "Weiss is a Scottish surname," he told his children, despite occasionally donning a yarmulke and attending synagogue. "It's for business," he explained. *What business?* his children always wondered. Long dead now, his descendants will never know if he was attending synagogue to impress contacts in the mining industry or to appease a sense of spirituality, looking to connect to a missing piece of his identity. We can't ask him these questions, but there are new means of unearthing buried ethnicities.

After our initial genetic mapping, I wanted a bigger picture. I wrangled Andrew into having his cheek swabbed and sent the sample off, along with a swab of my own cheek, to a genetic genealogy company that will test your DNA against the hundreds of thousands of other people's genetic results stored in its database and give you a rough outline of where your ancestors came from. It isn't the kind of test that predicts the various ways you are likely to die (I'd rather not know). Instead, the results show where your DNA falls over the map of the world. When my test has been processed and I log on to the company's website to find my results, a small box appears, prompting me to choose an ethnicity that relates to my background in order to best interpret my results. There are four choices: Iranian, Arab, Jewish, and "None of the above." My finger hovers over the box beside "Jewish" for some time. Nothing but family lore links me to Judaism. In the end I choose "None of the above." Still, my results do indicate that at least 6.86 percent of my overall makeup is Middle Eastern, and possibly Jewish. It could explain my maternal grandfather's trips to the synagogue. The surname Weiss—which, interestingly, means white—is popular among Germanic people and Ashkenazi Jews. (No one ever believed it was Scottish.) The results could also be a mistake, as the margin of error is fairly wide. My DNA mapping pointed in a direction, but I'm left to invent the rest. So in some ways, the test told me nothing at all.

DNA is the code by which our cells carry out their assigned tasks to eventually form a human being with all its working parts. It is science, but it also encapsulates the life histories of our ancestors, a long and twisted love story. It's about emotion and chance, decisions made with wild abandon or practicality, a ship that sailed, a fallen soldier, a blind date, a missed appointment, a late spring night in a half-filled pub in an island city off the North Atlantic coast. An introduction, and what followed. Life's intricacies, some mundane, some profound, are housed in our cells.

IN THE FIRST BLUSH OF OUR RELATIONSHIP, ANDREW WAS PLUCKED BY helicopter and dropped into a mountain range in central Labrador for two months. It was spring 2008. He was collecting biological samples, living in a tent, and eating oatmeal for breakfast every day.

"We will not be able to speak on the phone," he had told me. It seemed impossibly old-fashioned. So I wrote letters that arrived in the folds of fieldworkers' backpacks. Responses came in fat envelopes filled with handwritten pages and sprinkled with maddening insects. They were delivered from the mountains by burly northern pilots after their food drops to the campsite, and mailed from Goose Bay. When the phone rang in July and a crackling satellite call broke through, failed, then broke through again, I thought someone was phoning from the research camp to tell me that Andrew had died.

"Hello? Can you hear me now?"

"Are you okay? I thought you couldn't call?"

He could call. It was expensive and risky to block the lines, but he could call, and he did.

We were married two years later on a rocky outcrop in Bonavista Bay by the community of Upper Amherst Cove, where we lived that summer. I was researching the changes second-home ownership was having on former fishing communities and how this was reshaping the stories inhabitants tell. Andrew was often away doing fieldwork in Labrador. I was pregnant with Sadie. We'd been engaged for several months, but one day, as Andrew was about to leave for the north, we decided not to wait. I planned the wedding in a matter of days. Wesley Shirran, the elderly justice of the peace in Bonavista, handed me a form on which I signed my name, while his wife cooked him a cod's-head supper in the next room.

IT SEEMS BOTH PREPOSTEROUS AND INEVITABLE THAT WE WOULD HAVE to leave the island of Newfoundland. In the early spring of Sadie's second year, Andrew is offered a postdoctoral position at the University of Victoria. Vancouver Island is twelve thousand miles and two ferry rides away from Newfoundland. We sell our purple row house in May. Andrew leaves for British Columbia the same day that the new owner takes possession and moves into the apartment downstairs. We now rent the space we once owned. Over the five weeks that Andrew is away, I dismantle our support system: pediatrician, geneticist, ophthalmologist, dermatologist, low-vision specialist, friends, colleagues, neighbors, the postwoman, and the grocery store stockwoman who has been so kind.

I'd been here six years, Andrew five, and although it isn't my ancestral home, St. John's—indeed, the whole island of Newfoundland—will be the mausoleum in my graveyard of abandoned geographies. I will mourn its passing from my life in a large and monumental way. Moving here was the least practical and best decision I ever made. But we had to go. My scholarship funding was running out, and Andrew's had dried up the previous year. We needed an income; we needed to secure a future that we hoped included at least one academic job, medical benefits, and a decent income.

"We'll come back," we tell each other occasionally that summer. It is a temporary salve, a way to avoid the finality of departure. *But we have to come back*, I think. *We were married here. It's where our daughter was born.*

When Sadie is old enough to care, but not old enough to find it boring, we'll take her to St. John's and watch a live music show at the Ship Pub, where her parents met. We will stand in front of what had been our purple row house and ask a stranger to take an embarrassing photo of us on the front stoop. We can show her the hospital where she was born and, behind it, the hump of spruce-covered hills that I stared at in the days after she arrived. We'll go to Upper Amherst Cove to visit the friends we made over the three summers we spent there, and take Sadie on a hike to the rock where we got married. We will drive into Bonavista, where I can show her the baby-blue trailer where eighty-nine-year-old Wesley Shirran, the justice of the peace, helped me to secure a wedding certificate. I'll tell her how he nodded kindly at my swollen belly. *That was you*, I'll tell her. *You were there too.*

THE MATERNITY WARD IS FAMILIAR FROM OUR WEEK WITHIN ITS WALLS a year and a half ago, but the light is different. It's brighter; the late summer afternoon filters in through the windows at both ends of the hall. I knew it in a darker season. Jenny's room is a few doors from the entrance, which means I do not pass by the room where I first nursed my newborn, where the janitor offered up her diagnosis. I haven't been back to this floor since. None of the nurses looks familiar. I knock softly on the wood-paneled door and Jenny's mother greets me; her father is standing to the left. They are visiting from Italy, and they look the part: elegant, Old World, sophisticated. Jenny is in a blue hospital gown, looking tired, and she winces as she tries to lift herself from the bed, but we all fuss over her and insist she remain seated. Lying in his transparent plastic bassinet is her second child, Vincent. Another boy, wrinkled, beautiful, and blissfully asleep.

Jenny's mother places the baby in my arms. He weighs about as much as a jug of milk. I see his parents in his scrunched newborn features, marvel at the nails on his miniature fingers, coo over the size of his tiny slippered feet. Life is a marvel, and never more so than in these first few days.

I don't stay long with Jenny and her family. I have to get back to packing the half-filled boxes of our life in transition. We need to sell our car, give away our dried goods, and book a plane ticket for the dog before we leave the island. Meeting my friend's second child didn't elicit any stirrings of the earlier dread I felt, only sadness, and some nostalgia. Because I was saying goodbye to him, not hello. Goodbye to his parents, to our baby group, to my home, to this hospital where we spent so many fraught hours with our child in her first months, and to this hallway, seared into my memory for what happened here, and what happened next. I return the sleeping child to his mother, hug them both, and leave the room. After passing through the metallic doors of the maternity ward on my way out, I hear them lock behind me. Even if I'd wanted to turn back, I couldn't. It was time to move on.

CHAPTER 3

The Tribe

THE GIRL IS ON THE PRECIPICE OF ADOLESCENCE BUT STILL VERY clearly a child. She stands still outside the hotel doors, having just arrived, or waiting to leave. A scant few feet lie between us, but she can't see me. I am inside an airport taxi that has pulled up next to her. The windows are tinted. She can't see my wet eyes burrowing into her, soaking her up, imprinting her image on my brain to store there and recall for later use. She can't know how my heart is contracting from the squeeze in my chest, or perhaps from the sharp intake of breath I have forgotten to release since spotting her. Her white hair is tied back into a neat ponytail that hangs halfway down her back. She wears pink glasses.

The raised vantage point from inside the taxi van gives me the impression that I am having an out-of-body experience. The girl is my child, a decade from now. She is a vision from the future, both a stranger and someone whose genetic makeup I am intimately familiar with. She is the second person I have seen with albinism. The first was my daughter. The spell is broken when her mother appears at her side and they join hands, then walk away. I turn to Sadie, now one and a half years old, and unhappily trapped in her car seat. "Mama?" she asks.

"Yes, I'm here," I answer, though it feels like I have been some-where very far away.

Andrew, Sadie, and I had arrived in St. Louis, Missouri, that July morning and it was already blazing hot. It is a much different sun from the cloud-shy one we have come to know. The glint off the city's famed Gateway Arch is blinding. The streets of the downtown core where our hotel hovers over Busch Stadium have very little foot traffic: there are plenty of cars but few people. I am accustomed to barren winter streetscapes, piled high with snow, the temperature so far below zero that skin freezes, but I have never seen the reverse—streets empty because of the heat. It is baffling to imagine hundreds of children and adults with albinism navigating this scorching city over the next four days, here, as we are, for the fourteenth biennial NOAH conference.

Last night I had turned to Andrew and said, "Let's cancel this trip." Yes, he agreed, it might be too much. We waffled, but our suit-cases remained packed and propped by the door. In the early light of morning, we silently acquiesced and hefted the luggage into the trunk of the car, then set out for the airport.

I am not shy, and I am familiar with conferences from my aca-demic life. I do not mind a room filled with strangers wearing name tags. It is our sameness that frightens me. My intense scrutiny on Sadie's genetic condition loosened in the months following her first birthday. I am afraid of losing ground.

Sadie learned to walk at around thirteen months, and while I nervously waited for dire vision-related problems to arise—issues with depth perception, inability to navigate in new spaces, problems moving from carpeted to wood floors—it became clear that she wasn't living in the darkness I had envisioned when the doctors suggested she would be legally blind. Her pink glasses, now a fixture on the brim of her button nose, won't ever correct her vision, but they aid, in slight degrees of perception, how she traverses her world. Going to this conference will give me a glimpse of what lies ahead, and I'm not sure that I am ready. I've only just caught up to the present.

Our room in the Millennium Hotel in St. Louis is on the eighteenth floor and towers so high above the city, it feels like we are still on the airplane. I begin to unpack and the space quickly fills with the usual baby detritus (stuffed toys, rubber soothers, and the ubiquitous orange fish-shaped crackers) plus the accoutrements of albinism (black nylon shade covers for the car seat and the stroller, a bottle of SPF 65 sunscreen, three hats, and one pair of baby-sized sunglasses).

Andrew amuses Sadie by holding her up to the window. "Look at all the kids with albinism in the pool," he says to me. I join them in staring down at the hotel courtyard. I had never considered swimming with Sadie in an outdoor pool, but here at the blister of high noon a dozen platinum-haired children are defying the sun. The three of us stand watching the floating specs of white like exhausted desert travelers might stop to ponder a mirage, wondering at its possibilities.

That night, the opening ceremony takes place in the lower ballroom of the hotel: red-carpeted, ceiling dripping chandeliers, and, if you squinted and looked into the crowd, a sea of white. There is the familiar din of hundreds of voices, accompanied by the inaudible swish of white canes sweeping side to side across the floor. Ethereal teenage girls drift by in groups, giggling, recapping two years' worth of stories. Pigmented parents and grandparents, called "pigmentos" at these events, chase after white-haired toddlers. Organizers of all shades rush purposefully through the masses carrying clipboards. Boys coast toward the games room, bored by the adult chatter, looking for stimulation elsewhere. At least four continents are represented in this room. It is a multicultural meeting, but the races are hard to decipher. The elderly, white-haired from age or genes, sit quietly and wait for the speeches to begin. Andrew and I stand at the back, corralling Sadie, who runs from one end of the room to the other and back again.

In the moments before the ceremony starts, the attendees busy themselves arranging their various visual aids to better see the podium. Three people at one table use monoculars. Futuristic and old-fashioned at the same time, these are not unlike what people once used at the opera and resemble mini-telescopes. Younger adults and kids use their iPads, smartphones, and camera screens, modifying the technology, using the zoom function not to frame a photograph but as a lens through which to view the details of life. It is a live illustration of visual aids and the varying levels of eyesight in albinism.

Andrew scans the crowd. He doesn't say anything when I catch his eye. Later that night, he tells me he'd been wondering, *Which one is Sadie going to be? Is she going to be the young person with the cane, or the one walking freely around? Will she need a guide dog?* When I notice a person with a white cane in the hotel lobby, I suppress a threatening torrent of tears. I'm ashamed to admit this, but until now, I didn't know exactly how difficult my daughter's vision might be for her. Or maybe I knew all along, but I never confronted the fact until arriving here.

NOAH's executive director, Mike McGowan, takes the stage and the room quiets. I have had a few email exchanges with Mike this year, learning that he is from Chicago, and that he had worked as the director of information technology for the chief judge of Cook County, Illinois, until his retirement. He has been running these conferences with an army of volunteers and one paid staff for eight years now. He told me that he has reached the age where having white hair is not unusual (he is fifty-three) so he no longer hears "Hey, albino!" from passing cars.

"The way that people within the community deal with the term 'albino' is different," Mike tells the crowd early in his welcome address. "Some people are very comfortable with it, and others, because of the pejorative or hurtful way it has been used, can find it very offensive. It could be the equivalent of an ethnic slur or a racial slur. I'm not the political-language police. I just want you to know that you could be hurting the people around you."

I bristle when people refer to Sadie as an albino but not because I am offended. The term suggests that she belongs to a different tribe than my own, and this strikes at the heart of what divides us from one another. Sometimes I forget that we are two people: I had neglected to mention her when booking our flights for this trip, which caused huge complications on the way here.

Our familial connection is not as obvious to outsiders. When I am caught alone in the elevator with a couple not attached to the NOAH contingent, it's clear they're reeling from walking through the hordes of white-haired patrons in the hotel foyer. Shaking her head, the woman catches my eye as we rise slowly toward our destinations. "They sure have beautiful babies," she says. Without my child, nothing in my appearance suggests I belong to this clan. Still, I take the compliment. I smile back. "I know," I say. "I've got one."

When she was a baby, people often remarked on how Sadie looked like me, but the comments stopped when she turned one and began wearing her glasses full time. I see her inherited resemblances—my nose, the shape of Andrew's eyes—but to outsiders, like the woman in the elevator, she looks more like the other children at the conference than me. Even I find Sadie's Houdini-like disappearing acts all the more frustrating in the sea of matching ivory-haired toddlers. This superficial resemblance is what prompted early scientists and anthropologists to see albinism as an ethnicity, as a group of people belonging to the same tribe.

ON THE FIRST MORNING OF THE CONFERENCE, I AM STANDING IN LINE to drop Sadie off at the NOAH-organized daycare, a service that allows parents to attend sessions and focus on why they are here. The crowd is bottlenecking at the entrance to the nursery and I am standing alone, holding our place while Andrew searches the crowds for Sadie, who has disappeared again. I turn away from the line and am startled when I catch sight of a familiar pair of eyes.

It takes me a moment to realize that I am looking at myself. I stand framed by an ornate mirror: a pigmento mom with a run-of-the mill non-hairstyle and the hollowed eyes of the unrested. A jersey shirt is tied around my waist like a belt, the only indication that there was, at one point, a waist there to be cinched. Bags hang from both of my shoulders, packhorse-like. One hand rests on a rickety umbrella stroller.

She looks unbelievably overwhelmed, this harried mom, harassed by life, terrorized by the baby's cries at expected and yet never regulated intervals throughout the night. I observe myself with a mixture of horror and fascination while the world buzzes around me, until the line shifts and I step out of view.

After I drop Sadie off at the daycare, a woman, blond-haired, pigmented, approaches me.

"I heard you're from Newfoundland," she says. Her name is Lori McDonald and she's lived in Ontario for the past six years, but her daughter, Rebecca, who is now eight years old and has albinism, was born in the same hospital as Sadie. Like my unusual newborn baby, Rebecca drew attention from across wards. "They all wanted to see the baby with the white hair," Lori says. "She was stunning. She just stood out like a little angel."

It was not until the second day that the pediatrician on rotation hovered over Rebecca for an unsettling amount of time and then asked permission to take her away for an examination. When the doctor returned, she asked to speak to the parents alone, clearing their room of the family that had gathered there during visiting hours.

"Your daughter has albinism," the doctor told the parents, the head nurse at her side, ready to lend support.

Upon hearing the news, Lori started to cry. Her husband, Tony, was silent. "It was just such a shocking diagnosis," Lori says. "It was almost like the floor opened up and swallowed us in."

Then the pediatrician looked at Lori coldly and said, "Why are you crying? It's not like she has Down syndrome."

"That stuck with me, and I'll probably never forget it," Lori says. "I understand medically what she meant, now that I have Rebecca— she's living, you know, a happy, normal life. But in that moment, they were telling me that my child is going to be ridiculed and handicapped for the rest of her life, because that's all I heard."

I encountered this doctor's sentiment, toned down and couched in comfort, from family and friends when we relayed the news of Sadie's diagnosis. People often responded by telling us that "it could be worse." But couldn't everyone's life be a shade worse? And *how*, I wondered, could it be worse? What form does worse take? I think they meant that I should be happy she is not disfigured, or that her intellect won't be affected, or that her condition is not degenerative or fatal. I am relieved that my daughter isn't suffering and that her disorder is stable, but I'm uncomfortable comparing her with children afflicted by more severe medical issues. "It could be worse" is a pat phrase, and we say it all the time. In our case, it was mostly intended as a means of comfort, and I'm sure I've said it to plenty of people. In these kinds of social interactions, when an illness, or a genetic condition, or any-thing unexpected, rears its head, we look for silver linings. All we can do is value the concerns and grief inherent to each situation, whatever the degree of severity. That's the best we can hope for.

ON THE HOT CITY STREETS, WE SEE OTHER MEMBERS OF OUR TRIBE—
flashes of white disappearing into the revolving doors of a department store, through a restaurant window; and tonight on our way
to dinner, we'd followed a gaggle of platinum teenagers setting out
for the evening. Sadie remains asleep in her stroller while we eat at
a hipster farm-fresh burger joint. In a misguided impulse, I order
dessert. Sadie wakes in a howl. Furious, her neck cramped, her surroundings unknown, she steams her glasses with tears and kicks her
faded blue sneakers in a rage against Andrew as he lifts her into his
arms. I watch them leave, but I don't follow. The server delivers a
bowl of organic ice cream with new-age ingredients and I ask for the
bill. Then I eat. In hurried gulps, I plow through the cold sweetness.
Sadie's tantrum drew stares, and my own glutinous solo performance also garners attention. I feel watched. I've felt watched since
we arrived. Curious onlookers know that we belong with the others
roaming the streets of St. Louis. The others. I scrape the bowl clean
before paying the check.

I AM SURPRISED THAT A GATHERING LIKE THIS CAN HAPPEN WITHOUT
media scrutiny—no small write-up in the local paper, no quirky
report to round out the nightly television newscast. This is not always
the case. Groups of people who share a genetic condition have long
caught the attention of the popular media, particularly in the height
of the sideshow days and more recently in the reality-television arena.
I come across an article about a family of four, all of whom have albinism, visiting New York City in 1900. The Pittsleys were not celebri-
ties, just regular tourists, but their genes landed them on the pages of
the local paper. "It is our first visit to New York, and had we known
how conspicuous we would be, I doubt very much if we would have
come, much as we wished to see the city," William Pittsley tells a

reporter for the *New York Morning Telegraph*. "In Freetown, where we live, there are so many of our family that no more attention is paid to one of us than to any other person. Here it is entirely different and we are followed wherever we go by small boys and older loafers."

Pittsley was purportedly the head of a New England albino colony, which garnered nationwide attention in the fall of 1895 when a local news story was picked up by the wires and syndicated in papers across North America. The Pittsleys were insular and clannish, the article reported, and they lived in a "lonely part of the woods or out of the way end of a township." Their numbers ranged from fifty to two hundred, though the reporter also suggested that the clan was petering out and dispersing, so they were difficult to enumerate with accuracy.

It is likely that, owing to intermarriage, which wasn't unusual in the late nineteenth century, the Pittsleys had a high occurrence of the genetic condition within their family. Today, a small cemetery sits on the outskirts of Freetown in Bristol County, Massachusetts, named for the Pittsley family and populated by the remains of their kin. It is overgrown and out of use. A lane runs from the scattering of headstones to a house on the side of the highway, which, a quick white pages search turns up, is owned by Wayne M. Pittsley. The surname is still common in the region, and there may still be carriers among them, but there's been no mention of a white-haired clan for a century now.

Stories of albino colonies feature in contemporary legends across the United States. They crop up in Nebraska, New York, Pennsylvania, Missouri, and, with frequency, in the state of New Jersey. According to Mark Sceurman and Mark Moran, the publishers of the Weird NJ, a website, newsletter, book, and television series that chronicles supernatural geographic locales, the most notorious clan lives near Clifton, on the banks of the Passaic River. The publishers claim they've received hundreds of letters from fans detailing visits to the alleged village. It is typically described as a cluster of homes on a remote stretch of untamed landscape and almost always on the final stretch of a dead-end road.

Teenagers from nearby communities visit the colony, dubbed Albino Village, cutting their headlights and honking their horns to provoke the angered residents from their homes. In the parlance of folklore scholarship, these teens are legend trippers: young people engaging in a rite of passage, placing themselves at the fringe of control to peer at the possibilities.

The abundance of tales associated with this region is likely because of the Weird NJ publications, and in the case of Midgetville—a supposed colony of people with dwarfism in Norwood Terrace, also situated on the banks of the Passaic River—residents actively blame the two publishers for the harassment they endure at the hands of thrill-seekers. I enjoy a breezy email conversation with Mark Sceurman until I confess my ambivalence, as the mother of a child with albinism, toward these tales. Despite my repeated attempts to contact him after this, our correspondence goes cold.

Intellectually, I understand the attraction of legend tripping, but something about the antagonism, vandalism, and inherent conflict in these midnight confrontations feels personal. I contact folklorist Dr. Bill Ellis, professor emeritus of English and American Studies at Pennsylvania State University, whose work on contemporary legends and legend tripping helped define the area of study, and I ask him why teenagers engage in these rituals, and why they might target a specific genetic condition.

"These different types of colonies of others, it seems to me, [are] more symbolic than real," Dr. Ellis says. "You're doing this not so much as an external journey to physically put yourself in danger but as an internal quest where you're going to a part of your personality that you don't fully understand and that is a place where some of your most primal fears are located. I think psychologically legend tripping, which is especially popular among adolescents and young adults, is a way of developing psychological defenses against things many people intensely fear, and one of these is the fear of death, and I think another is the fear of the other."

Dr. Ellis goes on to explain society's fluid notion of the other and points out that currently this fear is defined ethnically (Latino drug gangs; Al-Qaeda) but that in a previous generation it was defined in a religious sense, as with the satanic cult scares of the early 1980s. Before that, medical differences were feared, and legends were geographically linked to institutions—for the mentally ill or for tuberculosis patients, for example.

"Maybe what we're seeing is a kind of survival in scattered places from when otherness was defined primarily in a medical sense," Dr. Ellis says in reference to the albino colony tales. He has seen variants of this legend where the protagonists are not albinos but melon-heads, which is a derogatory term for people suffering from hydrocephalus, a water buildup in the brain with varying levels of severity, the worst being death.

Legends do not unfold in the ambiguous landscapes and eras most often associated with folklore. The narratives are chameleon-like and adapt easily to local settings and known characters. The stories are a response to fear, and the trip is a means of asserting control over the unknown territory of the mind. The legends scare me because they hint at a harsher, more ignorant, world than I have encountered thus far; a world populated with detestable teenagers driving their parents' cars, lurking in the dark, taunting people for their perceived differences, and daring them to prove that they exist.

AT THE NOAH CONFERENCE, WE ENCOUNTER A DIFFERENT BREED OF teenager. Several young people wear red, white, and blue Hawaiian leis to advertise that they are part of the Ask-a-Teen-with-Albinism program. This means that you can approach them and ask questions about what life is like for a high school–aged person living with albinism. Lauren Berglund, a fifteen-year-old from Storm Lake, Iowa, is one of these volunteers. Lauren lives with her parents and eleven-year-old twin brothers, one of whom has OCA1 type B, like Lauren. She is very fair, but her hair is honey-colored, not white like it was when she was born. She has slowly developed pigment, and even a few freckles, over the years, which can happen with people who have the type B variant of the condition. Lauren attended her first NOAH conference when she was seven years old and has not missed one since. I am too shy and shell-shocked to approach Lauren in St. Louis. Instead, I call her six months later with my list of questions. She graciously accepts my tardy request.

The first questions I have are about vision. She tells me that she uses a cane to navigate outside and in unfamiliar interior spaces. I ask her about distance vision.

"Just a sec," she tells me, "I'm going to find my mom and see how far I need to be from her face to see her eye color." (Turns out, she needs to be three inches away to see that her mom's eyes are blue.)

I am curious to know about the relationships she has formed at NOAH conferences: there are at least four married couples whose courtship bloomed through these conferences, and most met as teenagers. I ask about romance, and she laughs and brushes off the question. For now, or at least as far as she's willing to disclose, Lauren's connections remain platonic.

"Did you find you connected with the other kids? In a regular way?" I ask her.

"Yeah, in the regular way that you make friends with other kids, but you always have those special things that you can all agree on or that you've all been through before," she says. "I actually have one friend I made at that first conference who I keep in constant contact with, and I'm excited to see her at every conference. Her name is Katelin, and she's in Wyoming. She's close but so far away."

"Is she one of your closest friends?"

"Oh yeah, like, we can talk about anything, and nothing is off-limits between us. It's nice because you get the normal friendship aspects and then the aspects of a friend who just understands and can relate to everything."

"So you look forward to these conferences, then?"

"Oh yes. For sure. I actually have a countdown app on my iPad that gives me the number of days until the next conference. Now through Facebook we can communicate a bit more and see what's going on in each other's lives, but as soon as one conference ends, we are counting down to the next one. Like, yeah, I'm going to check my countdown right now to see how many days until the next one."

The line goes silent while she checks the counter.

"Four hundred and seventy-one days," Lauren announces, sounding a little disappointed.

"Oh dear, that does make it seem far away," I say.

"Eighteen months? Yeah." She laughs. "It goes by fast, though."

It is a long time to wait for those fleeting few days to materialize, and I understand Lauren's yearning in a way. I remember how as a teenager I would cross off the days of fall and winter on my calendar in anticipation for when I would head north to my job as a counselor at a summer camp. It was the place where I felt my real life existed. I wasn't miserable at home. But there was something delicious in the longing, and in having something to long for.

Lauren's life between these events, I am happy to learn, is fairly pleasant, if not without challenges. She is a sophomore but is taking junior courses to prepare for college, where she plans to study "something in pediatric medicine." Her schoolbag is a little heavier than her peers' bags because she carries her iPad, laptop, and extra-large-print algebra textbook, all of which facilitate her classroom work. Her worst experiences are encounters with mean-spirited strangers on public transportation. "They think that because I can't see them, I can't hear them either," she says.

In contrast, she finds that her newer school friends do not acknowledge her visual impairment. "They're so nervous to ask because they don't want to offend me," says Lauren. "But I won't get offended if you ask me. I want to answer your questions and educate you." In elementary school, the young kids were freer, not afraid to ask questions, but now her peers are more reserved.

Just before we hang up, I ask Lauren what advice she might give to my daughter as she gets older. She considers this for a moment.

"I would tell her to never give up. You got to just keep trying, and you'll more than likely find a way to make it work." She pauses, then says it again: "Never give up."

THE TERM "BULLYING" IS CONSPICUOUSLY ABSENT FROM ANY OF THE conference session descriptions, though some of the titles hint at this hot-button topic: Dealing with Negative Comments from the Inside Out; Stares, Smirks, and Shout-Outs; Building Self-Esteem in Your Child. I avoid these talks because I feel they apply to parents of older children. So I am unprepared when the first bullying incident happens only a few months after the conference, at a drop-in kinder-gym for children under age five.

A three-year-old boy circles my daughter like a hornet and then strikes—his little fingers claw at her face, ripping Sadie's pink glasses from her nose. I interfere, sternly shooing him away. His mother rushes over apologetically. "I'll watch him," she says before she returns to her seat and settles back into conversation with her friend, gesticulating wildly and obliviously. The boy runs around us, homing in on his prey, and he strikes again. I step between him and Sadie, but he circumvents me so that I have to snatch his arms to keep him from grabbing the glasses again. I can feel his tiny bones and his speedy pulse. A five-star alarm rattles in the recesses of my cranium.

Immediately, I realize what I have done. Disciplining a stranger's child is frowned upon at best, a punishable offense at worst. I drop his hands and glance to where his mother sits. She is still engaged in her hand-weaving conversation, unaware of the drama unfolding between her young son and an adult. My grip won't leave marks on this boy's arms. I am the one who walks away with battle scars.

I am unsettled by this incident and wonder if my reaction was typical or overblown. I ask social worker Sheila Adamo how she might interpret my behavior. Sheila has four children. Her oldest son, Joey, who is a freshman in high school, has albinism. She served on the NOAH Board of Directors for eight years, and now she facilitates some of the organization's workshops, discussion groups, teleconferences, and programs for parents of children with albinism. She gave the talk on dealing with negative comments in St. Louis, and has hosted plenty of parents' workshops over the years, where, she says, they discuss incidents like one I described.

"My hunch, in your case, is that this had less to do with albinism and more to do with being mama bear because someone was clawing at your kid's glasses," Sheila tells me. "Or maybe it was an over-the-top response because you have to deal with it a lot. Right now you're in the heart of the comments phase because the outside world feels they can say anything to you as long as your kid's a toddler or younger."

I wonder how this scenario might change a few years down the road, so I ask Sheila about her son's experiences at school.

"Joey did struggle," she says. "What I experienced with bullying is exclusion. It's a new phase of bullying. It's not very obvious. I think the visual impairment makes that even more challenging for kids with albinism because it's hard to read social situations, and you know, he really struggled in junior high and grade school—who to approach, talking when no one is listening, people turning their backs when he comes into a room. There would be a bunch of eye contact going around that he can't see but I can see. You know, that kind of stuff."

The nuances of an eye roll, a smirk across a room, a raised eyebrow, a turned back. These small but important gestures are lost in the space in between Joey and his peers. The intricate social world of the lunchroom and hallway is as crucial and as complicated as algebra.

"That's kind of heartbreaking," I say.

"Yeah, that was the hardest stuff for me to see," Sheila says.

I remember the prickly sensation of discomfort on my skin. That age of hurt and disillusionment. I also remember the kids on the fringes who simply couldn't find a way in to high school's social knot. They were either invisible or hyper-visible, their appearance advertising difference and otherness. "We had two really weird albino brothers at our high school, but they were just odd, it had nothing to do with genetics," a friend tells me in a misguided effort to calm my fears. I wish I could believe her, but I don't. People with albinism are not inherently weird, but they can be treated that way, and over time, wouldn't that affect how they navigate their world? Maybe it wasn't the brothers' weirdness that my friend detected; maybe it was their armor.

Parents of kids with an obvious genetic condition are concerned about playground bullying years before their children enter school. Sheila leads NOAH's Rapid Response Team, which allows new parents of children with albinism to speak to an experienced parent over the telephone or via email. They receive up to seventy-five calls per year, and bullying always comes up in these conversations.

"It is something that everybody worries about," Sheila says. "You know, you have a child who looks somewhat different, and I think it's human to be confronted with your expectations earlier than a normal parent. I used to worry a lot, and I wish I could get that time back, so I always try to say to the parents, 'Things will be fine. Love your child,' just so they can enjoy these stages and they're not overcome with what may or may not happen in ten or fifteen years."

When I had called a member of the Rapid Response Team, I was equipped with a list of about twenty questions I had written on the front and back of a recipe card. I didn't ask about bullying. It's not that I hadn't envisioned future tormenters; it's that I couldn't bear articulating my concerns and getting a response. Sadie was only three months old. Asking about this seemed deterministic. But, of course, I thought about it.

Sheila points out that if the child does experience bullying, parents like us are armed and ready.

"I like to take the positive side and say that parents of kids with albinism often get snapped into reality quicker than the other parents," she says. "So, in that way, we're more prepared."

I AM WEAVING THROUGH THE LUNCH CROWD WITH ANDREW, BOTH OF us balancing plates of food and coffee mugs on trays, searching for a place to sit in the ballroom. We find two empty chairs at one of the round tables near the stage. I fall into conversation with the woman next to me, but she grows distracted by the people setting up the silent auction. She turns to her husband and motions toward the activity, and he excuses himself from our table. "We have something to add to the auction," she says, sounding exasperated. Moments later her husband returns carrying a stuffed white gorilla the size of a Smart car.

"There's two of them," the woman tells me, shaking her head woefully. "My sons won them at Cedar Point," she says, referring to the big amusement park in Ohio. "I have two sons with albinism, so they chose two white gorillas."

"Ohio?" I ask. "How did you get them all the way here?"

"He had to strap them to the roof," she says, gesturing to her husband, who has returned to the table. "They were tied, well, sort of back to front. Do you know what I mean? People were honking at us, taking videos. I am pretty sure we're on YouTube."

"Yeah, some joker tells me, 'Hey, buddy, this is a family park' when I tied them on, but, aerodynamically, that's the only way it would work," the husband says, shaking his head. "We normally get 400 miles per tank, but with the two of them tied up there, we only got about 250."

He looks over his shoulder and glares at the leering white animal, separated from its twin and now being prepped for bidding in the silent auction. "They took up the whole hotel room," he concludes, rubbing his eyes with fatigue, as if to suggest the two gorillas also keep the family awake as they cavort wildly through the night, snout to backside.

I'M NOT SURE WHAT SADIE DOES OVER THE TWO DAYS THAT HER PARents attend meetings, socialize, and sit in hushed darkness listening to stories. I am allowed to preview the nursery, but I can't visit during the day. I know that there are eight folding cribs lining two walls of the room and a stash of plastic toys arranged neatly behind them. When I drop Sadie off both mornings I see that her playmates are mostly white-haired, and some of them also wear the indestructible plastic glasses that need to be special-ordered from a company based in France. After her first day at the nursery, Sadie is wild-eyed and wound like a top. She spins out of control—until she's strapped into her stroller on the way to dinner and immediately goes slack. The volunteer who hoisted her into my arms at the end of the day shook her head and laughed. "Did great. No sleep." Again, at the end of the second day, the same volunteer hands over my pudgy, exhausted toddler with a knowing shrug. "No sleep."

Sadie bonds with a small girl named Elizabeth, year and a half older than her, who also has albinism. Like Sadie, it is Elizabeth's first conference, and they met at the back of the room during the newcomers session. Elizabeth's white hair frames her face in a page-boy cut, and she wears sparkly pink shoes that light up when she walks. Over breakfast one morning, the two girls frolic on the carpeted floor, posing for pictures side by side, leaning into one another and mugging for the cameras. At one point, Elizabeth whispers in Sadie's ear. What does she say? The words are lost on the snap-happy adults surrounding them, but later, looking back on these photos, I think of Lauren and Katelin and imagine Elizabeth telling Sadie, "Nothing is off-limits between us." I picture the two of them at future meetings when they are five and six, eleven and twelve, and fifteen and sixteen. Quickly they will transform into the otherworldly teenage girls who float around the ballroom in packs. What secrets will they tell then?

On the final night of the conference, a space is cleared in the ballroom to accommodate a dance floor. About twenty kids swoop and glide to the music being played over loudspeakers. The silent auction spans the length of the back wall, and a steady stream of people are posing for photographs with the giant white gorilla that had caused such strife for the couple we met at lunch.

Andrew buys us each a beer and we drift toward the front of the room. When the song changes, we are suddenly caught in a crush of people. At first I can't place where I have heard the tune, but then I recognize the chorus. It's "Born This Way" by Lady Gaga, an eccentric American pop star whose message of acceptance resonates with this crowd. The dancers throw back their heads and sing along emphatically. We are carried into the fray, and their emotion is catching. Sadie wriggles out of my arms and onto the floor, a whorl of dancers encircling her. The scene is beautiful and defiant, fragile and elegant. A buzzy energy fills the room. There is a feeling of release, as if we've all been set free.

I see Mike McGowan at the edge of the chaos and go over to introduce myself—we have never met in person. Months later, I'll tell him about how Andrew, Sadie, and I almost didn't go to the conference, and he'll laugh and tell me that he felt the same way back in the mid-1990s during his first NOAH meeting. He had told his wife, "If this thing turns out to be a bust, what I'm going to do is call you on a pay phone and then have you page me and I'll say that I've gotta go to work." He'll tell me that he never needed to be paged, and I'll know exactly what he means.

Lori, Tony, and their daughter, Rebecca, waited eight years before attending a NOAH conference, but Lori says that now they will never miss it. "The fact that Rebecca met other children her age who look like her and who had the same difficulties as her, you know, it meant more to us than anything," she told me. "I would sell my house if I had to, to get her to every single one of the conferences."

We will travel great lengths in parenthood, physically and psychologically. In a way, going to the NOAH conference was like taking a legend trip. Like the teenagers cutting their headlights and drifting into the territory of the other, we flew right into the heart of our fear. Like the beleaguered cottagers dwelling in their storied landscapes, the conference attendees we encounter in St. Louis are regular people trying to get on with life despite its challenges.

I step back into the undulating crowd and find Andrew and Sadie. We dance and twirl, sometimes in the company of new friends, sometimes just the three of us. Being here, immersed, it is difficult to remember that it is a temporary world, one that will unravel tomorrow morning as suitcases are packed and people check out of the hotel, dispersing across the continent, across oceans, and, in some cases, clear across the world. Mostly these people live as solitary flickers of white within the darker pigmented realm.

Eighteen months ago, I couldn't have imagined this ballroom scene, or myself in its midst, and the prospect would have saddened me. Now, I understand why previous participants described this conference as a kind of family reunion. You don't choose your kin; it's a relationship orchestrated by DNA. As with my extended family, I don't necessarily share politics, ideologies, lifestyle choices, or geography with the people in this room, but we know each other in ways no one else can.

CHAPTER 4

Pigment

IKPONWOSA ERO ALWAYS KNOWS WHEN IT'S ABOUT TO HAPPEN. SHE'LL be sitting on a bus, or in a waiting room, or at a coffee shop, and she'll feel someone staring. Then the person will approach her and ask about her ethnicity. I.K., which is what her friends call her, tells me this when we meet for coffee in December 2012 at a café in Vancouver. When she describes this scenario, I imagine a middle-aged woman, Caucasian, with short hair and glasses and maybe a fanny pack. The woman will say something to I.K. like, "I'm sorry to bother you, but my husband and I were just talking and we can't figure out your ethnicity."

"I'm black," I.K. usually tells such women. But they never stop there because that doesn't satisfy them.

"You must have a white parent, then," the interrogator will say.

Both of I.K.'s parents are black. She doesn't have a white grandparent. She doesn't have any white ancestry, as far as she knows, anywhere in her gene pool.

"I have albinism," she'll say.

You might think that the stranger would muster an embarrassed apology and wander off, but it's at this point that she'll often start to play it cool. "Well, how fascinating! Harold? Harold! Come over here and meet this interesting woman! Turns out we were both wrong!"

I.K. has curly yellow hair that frames her face in a symmetrical bob. Her features are African, but her skin tone is closer to that of a Caucasian person. She wears stylish thick-rimmed glasses to correct what she can of her vision. She's pretty, sophisticated, and approachable, which is probably part of the reason strangers ask her such personal questions about her ethnicity.

This inadvertent ambassadorial role can be exhausting. Most days, I.K. smiles and plays the part, laughing to make the inquirers feel comfortable. She is well-spoken, a recent law school grad with a stacked résumé who carries herself with confidence. She was born in Ibadan, Nigeria, and immigrated to Victoria, British Columbia, with her mother and siblings in 1996, when she was fifteen. Her parents told her she would need to leave home before she became an adult. They worried that her genetic condition would prevent her from finding employment in her native country. In the mid-1990s, Nigeria was suffering under the weight of a succession of dictatorships, and human rights violations were rampant. The future looked bleak, so her family sought asylum in Canada.

I first saw I.K. in a departure lounge at the Toronto airport back in July when we were waiting for our flight to St. Louis. By chance, Andrew and I sat with her over lunch on the second day of the conference and I mentioned that we'd been on the same plane. "Oh, really?" she'd asked, then smiled and waved her hand toward her glasses. "Sorry, I wouldn't know—low vision."

We talked about life in Victoria while we ate. I told her we'd be moving there in a couple of weeks, and that it would be a big change from Newfoundland but, I conceded, it hardly compared to I.K.'s move from Nigeria.

"What was that like?" I ask her.

"I was one of the only black girls at my high school besides my sisters, and I was white," she said. "People didn't really know what to make of me."

IT TAKES TEN HOURS TO FLY ACROSS THE COUNTRY, AND WE ARRIVE IN Victoria just after midnight. We have too much luggage to fit into any of the taxis waiting in an orderly line outside the airport. Someone calls a van. Sadie is cranky, having roused from sleep when we touched down. Her wails pierce the night. I can smell the ocean. The air is damp.

We're staying in a sabbatical rental in Oak Bay, a neighborhood that has strict bylaws against clothing lines and forbids people from renting out basement suites. The sidewalks are clear of garbage. You can be fined for tying your dog outside the grocery store. The city runs on staid order. It's a bureaucrat town, with a small traffic blip around four o'clock that dies down within an hour.

Victoria sparkles: the spit-shined sidewalks, the dimpled light on the ocean, the white sailboats moored at the marina, the red-brick facades of the quaint downtown. Endless expanses of green space foster urban deer herds, which roam the streets munching on the well-manicured lawns and noshing on the contents of flower beds as if they were at an all-you-can-eat salad bar.

We move into a rental house in the community of Fairfield, and one morning I am charged by a doe when walking our dog. We escape, running madly as I dig through my purse for the keys to the front door while my shaggy mutt races by my side, the sound of hoofs hitting the pavement behind us. It's like a scene from a horror film as I repeatedly miss the lock because my hands are shaking. I don't look back. When we're safely inside, I peer out the window and lock eyes with the mother deer, who is standing on my lawn. Defiant and unafraid, she's letting me know I'm on her turf.

71

Victoria is ethnically diverse, but this is not immediately apparent in the faces we see at the farmers' markets, grocery stores, and playgrounds, or by the beach. We are newcomers here, but we look like every other couple in their thirties carting around a young child in our neighborhood. Even Sadie's stroller is the same brand and color as all the others lined up outside the local community center on Thursdays when parents attend the drop-in playgroup with their kids. I can't say for sure that all the people inside are white because I've never managed to get there early enough. By the time we roll up, the sign on the door always reads FULL.

Outcast, Sadie and I spend these mornings at the beach. It is calm along the water, compared with the Atlantic shoreline we've come from. Sadie toddles right into the water in her pink rubber boots, and spends hours digging with a little plastic shovel. She fills her pockets, shoes, and even her diaper with sand. She has words now, though she speaks in a language that only her parents understand. In the past I'd marveled at how a mother or father was able to interpret the seemingly nonsensical sounds of their child. It appeared to be a hard-won skill, and I was surprised to find that it came naturally.

We are slowly rebuilding Sadie's medical world, contacting the local pediatric vision services and CNIB, meeting our new ophthalmologist. I tried finding a family doctor but without luck. "Yeah, I've been on the list for five years," the receptionist at a medical clinic tells me when I inquire if her employer is taking patients.

"You've been on your employer's wait-list for five years?" I ask.

"Yep," she answers.

We go to a walk-in clinic near our new house, and the doctor is irritated by my long list of referral requests.

"Does she really need a dermatologist?" he asks. "I mean, presumably once she needs a dermatologist, the damage has already been done, right?"

"You mean we should hold off until she gets skin cancer?"

He shrugs. "I just don't think it's a big deal."

Maybe not, I think, *but surely writing a referral isn't a big deal either.*

I'm not sure how much of these visits Sadie understands. Her role during my tête-à-tête with doctors is to open and close the garbage can, pull the tissue off the examining table, and check the doorknob to see if she can escape. She usually makes a good impression on the medical professionals, but her charms were lost on the surly physician at the walk-in.

We learned early on that the most challenging appointments are with the ophthalmologists, and Andrew will usually take a morning or afternoon off from work to join us for these events, which can run hours long. It involves an initial checkup, then a dilation of the pupils, which makes Sadie look like a cartoon character as the black practically envelops the blue of her irises. Then we wait for the follow-up exam. Rather than a chart of letters, Sadie identifies a series of images decreasing in size on a large computer screen: duck, star, circle, and crescent moon (which she sees as a banana, when she sees it at all).

During my first few months on the west coast, I occasionally think about I.K. and wonder what it must have been like for her when she arrived here from Nigeria as a teenager. She left Victoria after high school, earned her undergraduate degree at the University of British Columbia, and was just finishing her last year of law school at the University of Calgary when we first met. She's been working part time with Under the Same Sun since 2009 as an intern, researcher, and adviser. Her family lives in Vancouver now, and when she was home for a visit, I'd asked to meet her because I was interested in hearing the rest of her story. Partly because I'm curious, knowing Victoria, the city I.K. first lived in when she arrived in Canada, as I do now, and also because I want to keep growing Sadie's web, the group of people from whom we might seek guidance and inspiration as she grows older. I.K. had struck me as the kind of person you'd want your daughter looking up to.

When I meet with I.K., we chat about St. Louis and goalball, a sport favored by the low-vision crowd, and then I ask if she would mind telling me about her early experiences in Victoria.

She says her first memory is of feeling cold. She arrived with her family in September. I.K. didn't know the temperatures would continue to drop, or that Victoria happened to be one of the warmest places in Canada during the winter. That year, the city suffered a freak blizzard that saw three feet of snowfall within two days. The "whitemare," as it was quickly dubbed, caused power outages and immobilized the provincial capital, which sees a few flakes every winter but nothing that sticks around for long. The army was called in. I.K. and her siblings had been excited to see snow, but the novelty quickly wore off.

The weather was a challenge, but high school was I.K.'s largest hurdle. One of the most hurtful aspects was that the students didn't bother to ask about her condition, which is the same issue Lauren, the teen from Iowa, mentioned when we spoke. What was worse for I.K. was that most of the kids didn't talk to her at all but called her names as she passed by. Stage whispers of "white nigger" trailed her down the hallway. "What's a nigger?" she asked a friend, having never encountered the hateful racial slur in Nigeria. "It's not good," the friend replied.

The comments that people make about my daughter in public, either directly to me or as they pass by, are never racially charged, and certainly nowhere near the vile term I.K. heard at high school. However, Sadie's appearance does prompt questions about our ethnicity. Rather than "What are you?" people tend to ask, "Where did her hair come from?" It's an important distinction. Sadie's ethnicity, while often wrongly pegged as Nordic or Swedish, is not questioned in the same way that I.K.'s origins are. I think this is because we're Caucasian.

"Everyone looks at me through a white lens, but I'm not white.

I'm a black girl who looks white," I.K. says. "Sometimes when I've been spending a lot of time with my extended family I forget, and I scare myself when I see myself in the mirror. I forget I have this skin tone," she says, laughing. Her humor is genuine but belies the challenges she faces. It can be a liminal existence when how you look and your identity are at odds.

"It's so hard to be white among black people. To be born into a race with color, without color. When Caucasian people have albinism, the comments and the fixation is on the hair color, but for Africans, it's everything. It's our hair, our eyes, our skin."

"You two look so alike when you're wearing your glasses," our local librarian comments one morning when Sadie and I wander by en route to the kid's section. I thank her, a small thrill rising in my chest because this happens so rarely. When Sadie started wearing glasses, people stopped saying that we looked alike. Her white hair set us apart, but her glasses further disguised our phenotypic link. No stranger has ever told Andrew his daughter looks like him. Even though she has the shape of his eyes and his tall lean frame. Still, he isn't asked if his child is adopted, and no one has mistaken me for the nanny, which is what occasionally happens to parents of color who have a child with albinism.

I'd read about these experiences in a personal column written by Garcia Lee Waldorf in NOAH's parenting handbook in the section that focuses on families of color. After her son was born, she overheard the obstetrician joke that "someone must have been messing around with the mailman." Waldorf, who is African-American, was perplexed until she saw her baby's pale skin. She goes on to describe instances where strangers asked if her son was adopted, if she was the babysitter, or if he was even her child.

Carl Washington, an African-American parent of a fourteen-year-old boy with albinism and an eleven-year-old girl without, addresses these interactions with unrelenting optimism. Carl is a business developer and manager in the high-tech industry in California. We speak on the phone, and I ask if he's faced any persistent questions in relation to his son's albinism, specifically because his family is African-American. He says that, no, he's faced scattered queries and stares, but it isn't the norm, adding that humans are inherently curious and so these encounters leave him unfazed.

"That's what makes the world so exciting," Carl says. "It's so diverse."

For him, interactions with strangers are an opportunity to inform and educate. "I always tell my son that it's a good way to meet people," Carl says. "It's a great conversation piece."

Then he tells me something that changes my perspective on intrusive questioning.

"The way you react to these comments reflects who you are and how you feel," Carl says. "When my son was younger, any time I had a negative feeling about a comment it was because I didn't know what my son was going to encounter as he got older, and I was fearful about that."

From the beginning I understood that how I reacted to comments would set the tone for Sadie, but I hadn't looked at it as a reflection of my identity, how comfortable I was with difference, or with myself. The interactions that leave the deepest scars are the times I've behaved badly, been flippant, evasive, or rude. As Carl points out, these reactions are rooted in fear.

"We don't overprotect our son from people questioning him," Carl says. "We do the opposite, try to get him out there."

Carl concedes that his son, Ennis, might stand out in a group that is purely African-American, but that the family hasn't had an overall negative experience. His son is outgoing and has learned to face social challenges gracefully, which is a credit to how he was raised. Carl and his wife don't treat Ennis as if he is different from any other kid, or put limitations on him, and they encourage his interests, even when it means his traveling across the country on his own to attend space camp.

"Everybody is abnormal in some sense, [but] some abnormalities are more visible than others," Carl says. "It's just a fact of life. We're not perfect people."

SOMETIMES I WONDER WHOSE HAIR SADIE HAS. YOU INHERIT YOUR hair color from your parents, but also how it falls, curly or straight, and if it's coarse or thin. When I try to imagine her with Andrew's dark brown hair, I am never able to achieve a mental image in my mind. Even if I switch it for my own mousy blond, I can't quite make it fit because it doesn't suit Sadie. She is the way she is, and that's how I see her and love her and want her to stay.

At the NOAH conference, a researcher from the National Eye Institute, a division of the National Institutes of Health, announced that it was looking for individuals with OCA1B to take part in a trial involving the drug nitisinone, which may increase melanin production. (Sadie has OCA1B and A, but is under eighteen, so she wouldn't qualify.) The drug has been approved by the FDA to treat a different condition, and its effects on people with albinism are as yet unknown. The objective is to understand whether nitisinone could improve vision by increasing the pigment levels in the iris. It may also boost melanin production in the skin and hair.

To date, this drug has been tested only on mice with albinism, whose white coats turned the color of dishwater during the trial. It was also administered to pregnant mice whose fetuses had albinism.

The eyes of people, and mice, with albinism develop differently in the womb, and all human eyes continue to develop in the early postnatal stages. The role that pigment plays in low vision isn't well understood, but it is thought that administering this drug in utero and directly after birth could significantly increase visual acuity in people with albinism. Although the baby mice were born with darker coats and irises than their control-group counterparts, and no corresponding congenital issues, and the adult mice seemed to tolerate the drug well, how the increased melanin production might manifest in humans isn't known. For that, the researchers need about five volunteers. One of these potential test subjects is Alex Carrillo, a nineteen-year-old who lives in rural California with his parents. I met Alex through NOAH. He's Caucasian, with a big smile and a puff of curly yellow-white hair. He'd taken part in an earlier, less invasive trial run by a different set of researchers at the National Institutes of Health. When we spoke over Skype he was considering the nitisinone study. I admitted to Alex that after seeing an information video on the trial, I was wary of the premise and the side effects.

"When I was watching that clip, they showed the mice that they had done these trials on. There was a beautiful white mouse, and then there was the mouse that had undergone the drug therapy with nitisinone, and he was a sort of muddy color," I said. "The drug had turned the mouse's coat into a color that really wasn't as palatable, and I'm wondering what will happen to people. I mean, it could very possibly change the way you look."

"The scary part is that they really don't know how it's going to work," Alex says. "They don't know how skin or hair pigmentation is going to change, if it will be blotchy or even, so that's one reason that keeps me from wanting to do it."

"To be honest, it sounds like magic to me," I tell him. "But I have to wonder if it's good or bad magic. The intention is good because, of course, the real purpose and benefit is to improve eyesight. But, I mean, how would you feel if your hair changed color? Would you care?"

"I think it could be kind of neat. When I first heard about this drug, I thought it was to cure albinism indefinitely, entirely. After speaking to the doctors and doing all the research, I understood that it could happen but it's not what they're aiming for," Alex says. "I thought, well, even if it worked, I wouldn't take this drug full time because I don't want to."

"Why wouldn't you take it full time?" I ask.

"Because albinism is part of who I am, and I've grown up with it," Alex says. "Even if I could change it, it's like, nah, I'd rather not."

"That makes sense; I see what you mean. In our case, it would be a decision my daughter would make on her own when she's old enough. For me as a parent, I get really defensive and kind of weepy if people suggest I dye her hair. I just think it's so beautiful and it's a part of who she is, and I feel like that would send a message that there was something wrong with her, and that's not the case," I say. "At the same time, when she was born, if we'd heard about a study like this, we would have found it really hopeful. But, as you said, it becomes a part of who you are, and you don't necessarily want to change that."

Andrew is torn when I ask him about the nitisinone study. We sit on the couch in the living room one night talking it over. It's a hypothetical question for now but may be a real possibility in the years to come. In the early days, shortly after Sadie's birth, he'd done research, looked for studies like this one. As a scientist he'd had faith in exactly this kind of research making a difference for his newborn daughter. Seeing her grow, adapt, and thrive has changed his perspective.

"I would think taking this drug is a good idea in terms of vision and sun protection, but then—" He pauses. "It gets really muddy. She is Sadie. Everything about her, her coloration and her humor, that's all part of her."

"Better vision and sun protection would improve Sadie's life," I say. "But does it come at the cost of changing how she looks, and does this change who she is?"

"Isn't that superficial?" Andrew asks. "My hair is going gray, is that me changing? Phenotypic traits are important and related to self-identity, but we are more than how we look."

"But how we look is part of who we are," I say, and point out that a lot of the positive attention Sadie receives from people is directly related to her difference. Lori, the mom I'd met at the NOAH conference, told me that her eight-year-old daughter, Rebecca, loves having albinism because of all the compliments she gets on her hair. As Sadie and Rebecca grow older, however, this kind of scrutiny might not be as welcome, particularly during the difficult teen years.

"I don't know, I guess the real issue is what might motivate Sadie to take a drug like this," I say. "If it is because she wants better vision, or because she wants to change who she is."

I am buoyed by this study, the fact that people are focusing on this rare genetic condition that I carry in my cells. Maybe it will help my daughter's vision. If I could improve Sadie's eyesight without any harmful side effects, then why not do it? At the same time, part of me wants to accept people with albinism the way they are and not try to mess with cellular development. Just as I'd told Alex, I have ambivalent feelings about dying her hair, thinking it would send a message. What would her taking a drug for pigmentation development say?

The nitisinone therapy is most successful if administered early. Would I have administered drugs that altered my newborn baby's amino acids to help her vision and pigment develop? Maybe back when we were scared and looking for a cure, but, like Andrew, I don't think about this anymore.

This debate isn't unique to the albinism community. People with achondroplastic dwarfism are divided on the issue of limb lengthening, and the people within the Deaf (with a capital *D*) community are equally ambivalent on cochlear implants used to improve hearing, some likening it to a form of cultural genocide. Proponents of Deaf culture see themselves as having a linguistic difference rather than an impairment. Deaf culture has been recognized since the early twentieth century and likely grew out of segregation from the mainstream. A cultural identity can take root when a group is separated from the world, extolling its belief system and practices in a language that is lost on the hearing. These procedures—limb lengthening, pigment augmentation, and hearing implants—are developed to improve lives, not devalue them. It's the messages that these purported improvements carry that I struggle with. It suggests that these bodies, the way they look or function, are faulty and therefore in need of fine-tuning.

One way of approaching the issue of acceptance has been through art, something photographer Rick Guidotti has achieved within the albinism community. Guidotti, a former fashion photographer whose models are now mostly people living with genetic conditions, gave the most moving talk I attended at the NOAH conference. Midway through his career, he'd tired of the banal beauties featured in his haute couture shots. *Who says this is what beauty looks like?* he wondered. In 1998, he'd walked by a teenage girl with albinism on his way home from his studio. He abruptly turned around. She was stunning, radiating a kind of beauty he'd never seen or noticed before. His interest piqued, he sought out photos of people with albinism online and in medical texts, but found the images incongruent with the teenager he'd seen. These were grim, unflattering shots of people who looked ill. Not one of them was smiling.

He contacted NOAH, explained his fashion photography credentials, and asked if the organization might assist in finding him models with albinism. Wary of exploitation, the organizers initially declined to help. But over time, Guidotti's enthusiasm wore them down.

81

His first subject was a teenage girl named Kristina, a tall beauty, her white hair straight and long. He used the same setup, language, flattery, and encouragement as with his high-fashion models. Kristina had walked in with heavy shoulders, clearly afflicted with low self-esteem. Throughout the shoot, with Guidotti's exuberant reassurance, her confidence grew. It was transformative for the teenager and for Guidotti. That same year, he founded his company Positive Exposure, through which he's photographed hundreds of people with albinism worldwide, as well as those with a host of other genetic conditions.

Today, the NOAH community sees Guidotti as a kind of celebrity. It's not hard to understand why. He is magnetic and a wonderfully locquacious and witty speaker. His talk at the St. Louis conference was standing-room only, and the audience laughed uproariously until, with a flourish, he finished with an emotional anecdote and everyone cried.

Guidotti doesn't offer pigment, or longer legs, or the ability to hear. Instead, the people who pose for him are afforded dignity, a sense of respect, and, most important, acceptance for exactly who they are.

I NEVER MAKE IT TO OUR LOCAL PLAYGROUP ON TIME. WHEN THE weather gets cold and we have to abandon the beach, we start going to the kinder-gym up the road. Sometimes we get turned away, but mostly we're able to make the cutoff in time for Sadie to tackle the obstacle course and zip around on the scooters with the other kids. Today, she spends most of her time inside the bouncy castle, struggling up the steep ladder to the top of a near perpendicular slide. ("That thing was designed by some twenty-year-old who was not a mom," a woman standing beside me remarks as we wait for our kids to come tumbling into view.)

Through the mesh I can see Sadie making her way slowly up to the top of the slide while bigger boys pass her and trample her fingers—still chubby from babyhood despite her elongating frame. She is tall for her age—almost two years old—but these kids are closer to five, and, of course, she sees less.

She disappears as she rounds the corner and waits her turn for the slide. I bite my lip, dip and sway, weaving through the other parents to get a better view of my child. It is a structure made of air. What could possibly go wrong? I have a mental checklist that ranges from practical (glasses smashing into face) to implausible (broken neck).

Worrying an object is an inadvertent act. To worry over a child is much the same. It is an involuntary, repetitive action. It is a dull ache rather than an acute pain.

Before speaking with Carl I'd felt that people of color with albinism faced monumentally different challenges than the Caucasians living in North America who share this genetic condition. I still think there are specific issues, like those I.K. mentioned relating to ethnicity, but I believe that we—the parents at least—are more alike than different.

Like Carl and his wife, I.K.'s mother refused to see her daughter's difference as a limitation, pushing her to perform on stage. "She made me overconfident," says I.K. "Some people find it irritating."

About a year after our visit, in September 2013, I.K. represents Under the Same Sun at the United Nations Human Rights Council in Geneva and addresses the forty-seven intergovernmental delegates, imploring them to take a stand against the violence toward people with albinism in sub-Saharan Africa. She speaks with confidence and poise. Her mother's encouragements clearly paid off.

Curious for her opinion, I send I.K. an email and ask if she would consider taking a drug like nitisinone to augment her pigment. In her response, she says it's not something she would seek out. "To change my appearance will erode a deep sense of my identity and dignity," she writes. If the drug were also able to correct her vision, however, she'd face a difficult choice: "I, like most people with albinism whom I've met, and who have matured in their appreciation of their nature, would like improved vision but not changed appearance," she says.

When I last spoke with Alex, he was undecided about whether to participate in the trial, waiting to read the safety concerns listed in the consent form. What he'd been more preoccupied with was attending the Albinism Fellowship of Australia conference in Sydney. He said his parents don't want him to go alone. I asked if this was because of his low vision, or because they were his parents.

"Both," he answered.

Alex will be leaving home soon. He plans to attend college and study medicine, maybe focus on psychiatry. I understand why he is straining against his parents' concern. Still, I empathize with his mom and dad. We're still far from Sadie's college years, but her struggle for independence began around the time she learned to sit up. I worry about her on the playground, on stairs, near busy roads, and in water. Her vision concerns me, but there's so much else to fuel my anxiety. I've always had a large capacity for fear.

When I worked as a camp counselor in northern Ontario over the summers of my teen years, I never let the campers in my charge dive into the lake. Never. Not off the dock, where it was deemed safe, or along the shoreline, certainly not from a cliff's edge, and, ridiculously, not off the diving board, designed for that very purpose. I had trained as a lifeguard—twice because I had failed my first set of exams—and the fearful possibilities (from belly flop to paralysis) were seared into my brain, always floating close to the surface, face down.

I wonder, watching Sadie struggle out from the knot of children at the top of the bouncy castle slide and fly face first (which is not allowed) toward me, if this dull ache might subside with time. My mother continually assures me it won't. It's just something I'll need to manage and learn to live with.

It can be difficult for parents to let go. It's hard to watch your child take those first tentative steps down the board, the initial leap straight up, then a quick touch down before diving off, head first, into the black waters, and all you can do is hold your breath, knowing that if you don't let her dive, she'll never have the chance to soar.

TWO

EXPLORATION

CHAPTER 5

Adam

How do you forget a story?

First you unravel the plot. Implode the narrative into a jumble of fragments, splintered scenes, imperceptible objects, and unmapped locales. Then address the protagonist. Erase them physically, and then rub out their essence—obliterate their shadows and wipe their imprints clean. Next, remove the minor players, the bit parts, and the walk-ons. Send them into the woods, the water, or the mountains. Send them to a place where your mind can't unexpectedly wander into their path.

The stains of our own stories are the hardest to scrub: the trace of the bad decision; the smear of shame. These memories worm their way through all the mind's layers, and even when they lie dormant—whether for a short spell or a lifetime—this doesn't solve the problem. Even if you can't access these stories, they can always access you.

Sometimes you run into a story, and while you might not be acquainted with the characters, and the geography is unfamiliar and rendered unimaginable, the details smash into you with enough force to leave you whiplashed and bruised. I heard a story like this in February 2012 when Sadie was fourteen months old. Still reeling from the emotions of new motherhood, I tried to forget the details as soon as they hit me.

I had listened in a distant and removed way. I couldn't imagine the setting the way I usually did when hearing stories or reading novels; the way houses and landscapes that I've known morphed slightly to become the backdrops for the characters to inhabit. The story I couldn't forget is about a boy named Adam Robert Tangawizi. It takes place in rural Tanzania, a country I've never visited, a landscape that has no form or shape in my imagination. I'd been speaking with Peter Ash on the telephone, interviewing him for an article I was writing that included a section on witchcraft in Tanzania. He was in Vancouver, and I was listening from across the country in Newfoundland to his quick and certain succession of facts about the challenges and the violence against people with albinism living in East Africa.

I had been taking notes until he told me Adam's story. Then I rested my pen because the details were extraordinarily tragic and I didn't want to capture them in my notepad for fear that they might escape. I didn't want to think about the story again, and I didn't plan to retell it either. This is because it meant something to me, on a deep, almost unreachable level. There was a comparison between this boy's life and my child's life. Had my daughter been born in East Africa instead of Canada, she might have a similarly brutal survivor's tale.

In the months that followed, I relented, sharing the narrative with a select audience, and writing an abridged version in the article I'd been working on. When I occasionally spoke of the atrocities in East Africa and was challenged by my listener, I countered with Adam's story. It was a grisly swat at their skepticism. It was an effective weapon. Once I set the story free, I realized it had the ability to silence critics, to provoke thought, to incite fury and also agony. So I changed my mind. If this story wields power, if it might be the catalyst for change, then I'll remember and retell it, and hope that it marks the beginning of the end.

It was late afternoon on October 14, 2011, when the stranger appeared. Adam was corralling his father's cattle in the bush, watching over the cows as they grazed. He was a wiry tween, turning twelve the next day. The stranger, who'd sprung up suddenly in the tall grasses, called to him and waved him over toward where he stood a few paces away.

"I have a hat to give you," the man said, holding out his offering for Adam to see.

Adam has low vision and can't see very far. He was born with golden skin, and his eyes are a buttery hazel. His neck and forehead have grown wrinkled from exposure to the sun but despite this he appears younger than other boys his age. People call him an albino, or they call him a ghost, or "zero-zero," meaning that he is nothing at all.

"I do not need a hat. I have one already," Adam said to the man.

"Bring your cattle over here," the stranger said. "This is where the green grass grows."

"No, this grass is fine," Adam told him. "There's no need for me to come there."

Adam was rattled by the stranger. He had heard the stories about people with albinism being butchered and their body parts sold to witch doctors to use in powerful potions. This stranger could be a poacher, a witch doctor's henchman. To people like him, Adam's body is a sum of its parts. It is a gruesome arithmetic: a femur, a hand, a finger, each had a price.

The stranger might see Adam as a piece of meat to barter and trade. He might see Adam with X-ray eyes, boring through his pale skin to his precious bones, which miners might use to divine gold in the nearby hills.

Adam felt certain the man was going to hurt him and so he hurried home to where he lived with his father, stepmother, and siblings. His older brother, Salum, also has albinism. He was sixteen then and taller than Adam. On that day, he was visiting his grandmother in a nearby village.

When Adam arrived home, he was shocked to find the stranger from the bush sitting at the kitchen table and speaking with his father.

"This man tried to attack me," Adam whispered to his stepmother, but his fears were dismissed and the stranger was invited to stay for dinner.

"Make a fire in the cow-dung pit," his stepmother urged, and Adam complied.

The stranger joined the family around the fire. The stepmother served stew. Adam ate nothing. A sudden rain interrupted the meal and the diners scattered toward the house.

Adam was at the threshold of the door when the weight hit, immobilizing him. He knew it was the stranger. The man held Adam still with his body and pinned his arm against the door frame, using the wood like an upright butcher's block. With a thwack the stranger drove his machete into the flesh and bone of Adam's left shoulder, but he got the angle wrong, slicing it lengthwise. He tried a second time, but again his blade slipped to the right, opening a vertical wound that ran half the length of Adam's arm. The cut was deep but it didn't amputate. Covered in blood, Adam slid to the ground. Now he was helpless, on his back. The man's weight pressed him into the earth, and this time the shiny blade landed widthwise across Adam's arm, just below his elbow. The man was trying to dismember him. In his final attempt, he brought his knife down across Adam's palm. The bone cracked and the flesh gave. Two fingers and his thumb were wrenched forever from him. Adam screamed and called for his father, for anybody, to save him. No one came. In that sickening moment it became clear he must save himself. With the last of his strength, Adam pitched forward into the bulk of the man and bit the crotch of his pants. A weight was lifted. A flashlight shone, then disappeared. Bushes rustled and then there was silence. Where was his father? His stepmother? Lying in a pool of his own blood, Adam slipped into unconsciousness.

In the hours that followed, the police arrived and took Adam's father and stepmother, along with two other relatives, into custody to question them about the attack. Not to question them as the traumatized guardians of a slaughtered minor, but as the perpetrators of the most heinous of crimes: filicide. According to one news report, Adam's stepmother confessed to knowing about the crime, saying that the "original deal was 'attack without killing.'" Whether this quote was fabricated or true, it doesn't matter. Adam's stepmother and father were released from jail because of insufficient evidence and will never stand trial.

After falling unconscious, Adam was delivered by ambulance from his rural home to the nearest hospital in the city of Geita. Once there, the doctors stopped the bleeding, disinfected his wounds, and dressed them, saving his life. Days or maybe weeks later, he was roused from his gurney and placed gingerly in a wheelchair, a nurse lifting his feet and tucking them neatly into the footrests. His lips were dry and cracked, his voice was soft. His irises darted back and forth under his drooped eyelids. His wounds were freshly bandaged: white gauze wrapped the gashes across his arms and wound carefully around the stumps of his missing digits. He was wheeled through an outdoor corridor where people sat in groups. Some turned to stare as he passed, others whispered, and yet others lowered their eyes. Then his chair was turned and parked in front of a reporters' scrum. The journalists were poised with notebooks and pens, some had recorders, and there was a video camera pointed directly at Adam.

"Tell us about what happened to you," they said. "Tell us your story."

When Peter described Adam's attack to me, I had trouble understanding the context.

"Capitalism and witchcraft are a dangerous combination," he explained.

"Is money enough to motivate these gruesome murders?" I asked.

"Once you believe that someone is not human or equal to you, you're able to do all kinds of things to them," Peter said. "You believe they are a curse, or an evil spirit, and that you can get rid of this evil and make some money."

Adam's father and stepmother never considered Adam human, and saw the financial gain worth their son's pain and possible death. It's not a pardon or an excuse but a shaky explanation of what moved these people to commit an unforgivable crime.

On paper, the story shares key character roles and plot movements with some of the European folktales I studied in my graduate degrees. There was an evil stepmother, the attempted murder of a child, and the devil disguised as a traveling stranger. In particular, it reminded me of "Maiden without Hands," a tale about a pious daughter whose father sells her to the devil in return for endless wealth. She dons a white dress, washes herself, and draws a circle of chalk around her body. Because of these measures, the devil finds that she's impenetrable. He's thwarted a second time when she's purified by her own tears. "Cut off her hands so she can't clean herself," he instructs the father. Wary of losing his newly acquired wealth, the father complies. Her tears wash her bloodied stumps clean and the devil, reaching his quota of attempts on the third try, must retreat. The girl leaves home, she wanders through the woods in her white dress, she meets and marries a king, and she grows new hands, silver and shiny. Despite the devil's malevolent interventions, she eventually lives happily ever after.

I'm drawing from the Grimms' version, first published in the early nineteenth century, but this tale stretches back to at least the thirteenth century, with variants recorded in Russia; Eastern and Western Europe, including Great Britain and Ireland; Latin America; and French Canada. Scholars have heaped analysis on this tale, from feminist to psychoanalytical perspectives. The chopped hands might symbolize female repression, a punishment for masturbation, or, most perplexing, a castration.

In my own reading, the principal issue is betrayal. I can't grasp why parents would mutilate their child to secure their finances. I imagine the pious girl extending her arms so that her father might chop off her hands, and when the blade comes down, she understands that her father's love was limited, if it ever existed at all. Just as Adam must have known, in that moment when his father didn't heed his call for help, that he was entirely alone. The maiden can never look back on her childhood, the times when she sat on her dad's knee and he read her a story, or held her hand when they walked together, without the sound of the blade whistling in her ear and reminding her of how he'd betrayed her when she needed him most.

Under the Same Sun has shared Adam's story with the media and through its own publications to help promote awareness. It knows the details will stick in the listener's craw. It's hard to turn away from a child so cruelly betrayed by his parents. Also, the story has a happy ending. The hero, Adam, survives and even gets a new hand, not silvery like the maiden's but a refabricated version of the original. For this, he must journey halfway around the world to the Pacific

Northwest, and this is where my path collides with the protagonist of the story I'd tried to forget.

I MET ADAM IN DECEMBER 2012, ABOUT A YEAR AFTER HIS ATTACK. HE had arrived in Vancouver a few months earlier. From his seat on the plane, he looked down with wonder at the expanse of the Atlantic Ocean. "Still Lake Victoria?" he asked his travel companion, Dr. Patrick Bulugu, the Geita physician who first treated him. "No, that is the sea," Dr. Bulugu told him.

During Adam's rehabilitation earlier that year, Peter Ash had flown to Tanzania and visited him in the hospital. When he asked what he could do to help, Adam said, "I'd like to go to school."

For this, he would need to write, have the ability to hold a pencil. The attack had left his dominant hand useless. Peter and his team came up with a solution. Adam would travel to Canada, where he could undergo surgery at Vancouver General Hospital—something that would happen on a quiet night, physicians, nurses, and other staff donating their time and skills to help rebuild his hand.

In the hospital's operating room, the sight of the instruments sent him into a frenzy. Cold, shiny, and metallic, the tools instantly conjured the machete in his mind. He had traveled the curve of the globe, but he couldn't shed the demons. In the nights after he arrived, he would wake suddenly, yelling into the darkness of the hotel room he shared with Dr. Bulugu. He took shelter in the closet, fearful that the stranger might return for him.

The physicians are friendly, careful, and kind. They remove a toe from Adam's right foot and attach it to the bone of his mangled hand with wires, then fuse the muscles, tendons, nerves, and blood vessels. For two weeks Peter sits at his bedside in the hospital while Adam slowly heals.

He spends the next three months in physiotherapy, adapting to his new hand and learning English. There is no common language at the primary school he attends. He speaks Swahili. Most of the other kids speak Arabic or Urdu, but classes are conducted in English. He relearns to write by carefully balancing the pencil across his palm and curling his new thumb and remaining fingers around a thick wad of tape wrapped at its base.

By the time I meet Adam in early December, he's able to write his name. I'd taken the early morning ferry to Vancouver to meet with Peter, and the Under the Same Sun's director of operations, Don Sawatzky. I'd been considering a trip to Tanzania since attending the NOAH conference five months ago, but it was more an idea than a concrete plan. I'd had a few conversations with Don on the telephone but wanted to meet with both men to learn more about what is happening in sub-Saharan Africa and to ask their advice on who I might meet with and what regions I might visit, should I decide to put my tentative travel plans into action. Today I would have lunch with Peter and Don, and at the end of the school day, meet with Adam.

The office is in Surrey, a suburb of Vancouver. It's an uninspiring setting on this low-ceilinged, drizzly day, wrapped in fog and populated with the usual chain restaurants and strip-mall stores of suburban North America, flanked by grim multistory high-rises. At the restaurant we sit in a dark wooden booth next to the window that overlooks a parking lot. Peter sits across from me, Don beside him, and Amadou Diallo, a third Under the Same Sun (UTSS) staff member, sits to my left. Amadou, who has albinism, was born in Guinea but spent most of his childhood and young adulthood in Côte D'Ivoire. After suffering a violent hate-fueled attack in his early twenties, he fled to Europe, where he lived precariously, hoping to be granted asylum. Now he works at UTSS as the advocacy officer for francophone Africa and is waiting for his refugee claim to be processed in Quebec.

"The potions that the witch doctors make out of the body parts of people with albinism cost thousands of dollars, so who do you think is buying this stuff?" Peter asks me over lunch.

"I'm not sure who buys the potions," I admit.

"Wealthy people," Peter says. "Powerful people like politicians and businessmen. Which is why putting an end to the poaching will be so difficult, because the people who run the country are the same people who support the trade."

I consider this for a moment. I had thought that the killings proliferated because people in power were afraid of the witch doctors. This is partly true. What I didn't know was that they were full participants in this grim process of supply and demand. They are the consumers sitting at the top of the food chain.

Peter is a tall man and wears glasses with orange-tinted lenses. He's an imposing presence and an astonishingly fast talker.

Don, who has salt-and-pepper hair and wears thick-rimmed dark glasses, had been his professor at college, and the two men, along with Peter's wife, Debbie, had grown close. When Peter founded UTSS, he called Don and asked him to help tackle this human rights issue. Don didn't hesitate.

UTSS has two main goals: advocacy and education. It supports students with albinism across Tanzania, with more than three hundred currently within their fold. It investigates and publishes reports on crimes against people with albinism throughout Africa, and uses awareness campaigns to demystify the genetic condition in Tanzania and other countries. The NGO has had a tremendous impact since its founding in 2008, and it is now the main source of information and support in regard to the witchcraft-related crimes. The organization's second office is in Tanzania, and employees there have direct contact with the children they support, and are often some of the first officials on the scene following an attack. Both Peter and Don travel to

East Africa several times a year. The work is taxing and emotionally draining, particularly when they deal with violence against minors. "It's really painful," Don concedes during one of our telephone conversations, "to see these little children who have been tormented so deeply."

Many of the victims are young because they are vulnerable, easy targets. They can't fight back. But there is another more gruesome reason: young flesh and bones are purportedly more powerful and thus more desirable and worth more money.

IT'S GETTING DARK WHEN ADAM ARRIVES AT THE CLOSE OF THE SCHOOL day. He scampers into the boardroom and takes a seat at the head of the table, to my left. I shake his new hand and it feels small and clenched in my grasp. Adam has thin yellow hair cut short to his scalp. He is wearing DKNY eyeglasses with a stylish purple stripe that runs along the temples. He is stretched and gangly, as pubescent boys tend to be, and he is fidgety and excited. He lets out a series of husky giggles when I ask him questions, which surprises me. I'd seen a local news segment about his reconstructive surgery and in it he was withdrawn and frightened, his voice barely audible and his eyes downcast. He'd looked smaller in those clips, wearing blue pajamas, limping, with his hand and foot bandaged. I'd expected a broken little boy but was met with a goofy kid. I hoped to hear Adam's story firsthand, translated by Dr. Bulugu, and ask him the details that I'd imagined.

"How is your writing?" I ask Adam.

"Good," he answers politely.

"Where's your special pen?" Peter asks him. "Why don't you show Emily? Write your name."

Adam concentrates on the task, gripping the pencil tightly, the thick band of tape scrolled an inch from the nib acting as a crutch for his newly reformed hand. Slowly, he scrawls his name across the sheet of paper. When he is finished he begins to draw, looking up occasionally to answer my questions.

"I want to ask you about when your hand was hurt, and your shoulder," I say to him. "Do you remember your parents being there with you?"

"Yes." He nods.

"Did they help?" I ask.

Adam rolls his eyes, and a throaty giggle escapes.

"No," he says. Then he turns to Dr. Bulugu to qualify his answer in Swahili.

"He says that they helped him after the attack by raising the alarm, but not while he was being attacked," Dr. Bulugu says.

"Did you know the man who attacked you?" I ask Adam.

"Name?" he asks.

"Did you know him before?"

"I know his face but not his name," Adam says, then goes back to his drawing.

I don't know if he means that he'd known the man from earlier that day, or earlier in his life, but I let it rest. I'd wanted to hear his story firsthand but suddenly the details don't matter. What matters is that he survived and that he is here in front of me. He isn't a label, a victim, an albino, he is just a kid. A kid who had a really terrible thing happen to him but who has made it out the other side. He has a hard time sitting still, he likes drawing and going to school, and he gives one-word answers to long-winded adult questions, like any kid would.

"Adam, did you know that Emily has a child with albinism?" Peter asks.

"I can't believe I forgot to tell you that," I say. I'd been so focused on Adam that I forgot to tell my own story, the main reason I'm here. "Here, I'll find a picture to show you. They're all of Sadie." I scroll through the photo album on my iPhone. "Oh, look, here's a video of her," I say, and we both lean in to the screen to watch.

"See her white hair and her glasses?" Don asks Adam, and he nods.

Sadie is not quite two years old in the video, which is shot in our kitchen in Victoria. She is wearing a green dress and showing me, with some urgency, that the sun has come out. Halfway through the recording she pauses, then turns to the camera and says, sadly, "The sun's all gone."

Adam laughs. He shyly nudges his drawing my way and I ask if I can take it home. He nods. He's drawn a baobab tree, native to Africa, inspired by a photograph on the boardroom wall, and a house with a series of people lying in their beds. I instantly read into the image—the people are on stretchers in a hospital—but Adam truncates my analysis by informing me that it's a parking lot.

"Parking is a big deal in Canada, this is true," I say.

"Yes," Adam says and giggles again.

In a few moments we are in the common room, where a small crowd has gathered to say goodbye to Adam and Dr. Bulugu. They fly back to Tanzania tomorrow, arriving in time for the Christmas holidays. Adam will join his older brother at boarding school in Dar es Salaam, where the pair will be safe and where they can earn their high school diplomas. Earlier I'd asked Adam if he wanted to go home and he nodded emphatically. I was surprised he didn't want to stay here, but his longings were made clear by the way his eyes lit up when he whispered the name of his country.

A box of Timbits is passed around. It's time for me to leave so I shake Adam's hand and thank him for speaking with me. I tell him that I hope we can meet again. He smiles, but I'm not sure he understands or even hears me. It is distracting, the party, the friends, and he is the center of the celebration. It is his night.

ON THE HOMEWARD-BOUND FERRY, A ROVING GANG OF BOYS RACES UP and down the aisles, appearing at random intervals, plotting boyish plots, whispering conspiratorially among themselves, separating, reuniting, hiding, and then reappearing. "We aren't allowed to go into any enclosed spaces on the ferry unless you really have to go to the bathroom," one says to the other two, repeating the edict of some absent guardian. "You are allowed to go into the bathroom."

They are probably approaching twelve or thirteen, the tipping point of childhood when these elaborate games of chase recede into memory. They are balancing between boyhood wildness and teenage aloofness. They would be Adam's peers if he'd been born here. By tomorrow Adam will be on a plane heading back to Tanzania. I think of Amadou's parting words from earlier today as I watch the boys make yet another lap down the aisle. "Your daughter is fortunate to be born in Canada."

I imagine Sadie asleep in her crib as I speed toward her across the dark water. I think about how I will slip into her room when I get home and check on her, watch her for a few moments, listen to her slow sleepy breathing, as I've done every night since she was born. I can't get home fast enough. At the same time, I'm planning my next voyage. This one will take me farther away, beyond the parameters of what I know and find comfortable. I've decided that today won't be the last time I see Adam. I want to put his story into context. I need to understand how people live with this fear, and how they manage to overcome their challenges under the weight of constant threat. I want to know what I can do to help. I want to go to Tanzania, and I want to bring my daughter with me.

CHAPTER 6

"I'd Want a Gun"

THE PREMATURE DARK OF A WINTER AFTERNOON SETTLES OVER OAK
Bay Village in Victoria. Christmas lights are strung cheerily between
lampposts and stretched in a canopy across the road. I'm running
errands: library, grocery store, bank; check, check, check. And still
half an hour to spare before picking Sadie up from daycare.

The whir of the espresso machine and the jet-engine milk frother
form the backdrop to a few moments of stolen reading time. This
Italian bakery has a cerebral selection of periodicals, as varied and
class-specific as the pastries, artisanal breads, and fancy coffees on
the menu. A latte. A *pain au chocolat*. A *New Yorker*. The *Paris Review*.
Looking up from the magazine pages, I spot a small boy, about three
years old, carefully devouring a galette at the table opposite mine.
His father, hair gelled, pea-coated, eyes encircled by dark-rimmed
glasses, sits at his side. I smile at the boy and throw an elongated,
knowing, conspiratorial nod in his father's direction. My warmth
goes unreturned. The father gives me a clipped smile and looks away.
Embarrassed, I quickly realize my mistake. I am alone, without my
child. This man thinks I am a broody hen leering at his chick, or
worse, directly at him.

Red-faced, I lower my eyes and focus on my magazine. *Just who am I*, I wonder, *when I am not a mother?* Of course, I am always a mother, but without my child's physical presence, my peers can't recognize me, and I find this strange. In other stages of my life, it was easy: a backpack, a street address, the shoes you were wearing, or the bumper sticker on your car. Small signs of belonging that were imperceptible to the uninitiated but immediately recognized by your kind.

If I travel to Africa this spring without my child, how will people know who I am? Of mothers and their children, novelist Rachel Cusk writes, "When she is with them she is not herself; when she is without them she is not herself; and so it is as difficult to leave your children as it is to stay with them. To discover this is to feel that your life has become irretrievably mired in conflict, or caught in some mythic snare in which you will perpetually, vainly struggle."

I am caught in the teeth of this snare as I consider traveling with Sadie to Tanzania or leaving her behind. When it was just the glimmering tip of an idea, when traveling to Africa was a hypothetical scenario, fun to muse over because there was nothing to lose, I asked a parent of two children with albinism if he would take his kids to Tanzania. It was at the conference in St. Louis when Andrew and I stopped to chat with the co-founder of a US-based NGO about his work in East Africa. It was a casual conversation about a monstrous subject: dismembered children with albinism in Tanzania. The man looked like how I imagine a character from a Jonathan Franzen novel would: youthful with crow's feet, wearing a casual plaid button-up, baggy shorts, probably drives a Volvo. He talked about how he and his wife started the charity after his kids were born with albinism and the atrocities in Tanzania came to his attention. He'd visited Africa multiple times since.

"Would you take your kids?" I asked him.

He hesitated. "We think about that a lot," he said. "Not yet. But if we did, I think I'd want a gun."

"I'M COOKING MY BRAINS OUT," MY MOTHER SAYS WHEN I ANSWER MY cell phone. "We're having a dinner party later."

"We're in the car," I tell her. Andrew, Sadie, and I are heading to a beach a few hours east of the city.

"That's nice. Anyway, I've been looking at the Under the Same Sun website," she says. I can hear water running in the background and the clang of pots. "I've been reading about the people with albinism being killed in Tanzania. So you can't take Sadie there."

I sigh and turn around to look at Sadie, snugged into her car seat. "Going to the ocean," she says, then tosses her board book to the floor. "Fell down," she tells me mournfully. I hold the phone to my ear with my shoulder while I grope the car floor for the dropped book—a careworn copy of *There's a Wocket in My Pocket*, by Dr. Seuss.

"She will just have to stay with Nana," my mother continues. "It's just too scary, and she's just too little to travel all that way anyhow."

"We'll let you know," I say. If we don't bring her with us, I will need to rely on my parents and Sadie's paternal grandparents. I can't be rude or curt or rail against their voiced concerns, because I might need them.

I can't reach the book and Sadie begins to wail.

"Pocket! Pocket! Pocket!"

"I have to go," I say to my mother.

Andrew says nothing. He isn't worried about Sadie's safety the way my mother is, and the way I am. He feels that we can look after her, protect her. He doesn't think we'd need to "bring a gun." His fears are not about killings and witch doctors; they are about sleeplessness, screaming fits on the plane, and managing our sun-shy toddler in the harsh glare at the equator. He's also less concerned than I am about leaving her behind. They've been separated before during his field seasons, and they spent five weeks apart last spring. It was hard but not impossible.

His silence has me trapping strangers in long philosophical debates about my quandary. I make appointments to meet with friends of friends who have worked in East African countries. I send long, convoluted emails to acquaintances with knowledge of Tanzania, soliciting their advice. I ask each person if I should bring Sadie on our trip, and I am always disappointed with the answer I invariably get: "Ultimately, it's up to you." It is clear that my husband feels the same way.

We drive on in silence.

At China Beach we park the car and realize we've forgotten to bring the child-carrier backpack. Sadie will need to walk the steep half-mile down to the water. Despite the cloud and forest cover, I slather her with sunblock and fasten a pair of dark sunglasses across the bridge of her nose. It's a densely forested trail with a steep drop on one side. Sun spots light up moss and lichen. We descend about two hundred steps and reach a clearing through which we can see the beach and a line of surfers skimming the breakwater. I stop to read a warning posted on a tree. There has been a co-occurrence of cougar and wolf prints recently, which marks a behavioral change, or an increase in cougars, or worse, bolder cougars. CHILDREN AND SMALL ANIMALS ARE PARTICULARLY VULNERABLE TO ATTACK, the sign reads. I look to the soaring cedars above our heads and shiver. Just because you don't see the danger doesn't mean it's not there—a lurking threat that can alter your life's trajectory with one strike.

EARLIER THAT FALL, I'D SAT WITH MY FRIEND MEGHAN ON THE BACK deck of my tony sublet and talked about the possibility of visiting Tanzania. This was two months before I met Adam and the trip became more of a reality. Before the idea crystallized. We were watching Sadie chase Meghan's son, Max, around the manicured yard. The house was an old yellow beauty in the topiary-mad district of Oak Bay, Victoria's wealthiest neighborhood. It was where we got our bearings over six weeks while searching for a more permanent home. It was a surreal utopia. I wasn't working, the sun shone daily yet the UV levels weren't staggeringly high like they are elsewhere, there was always a farmers' market, the beach was close by, and we shopped in the nearby village where busy stroller-pushing moms hustled their children from ballet to soccer to the library and back home again.

Meghan has lived in Victoria for seven years, but we grew up together in an Ontario town without stoplights about two thousand miles from here. At summer's end, when we were both eighteen, she drove west in an overstuffed wood-paneled station wagon with three of our friends. The plan, to live and work at a ski resort, seemed shaky and unsure to me. My own route eastward to university felt more concrete if less adventurous. Part of me wished I could cram myself into the station wagon, and part of me knew I'd suffocate under the weight of the crowd.

In late August of that year, Meghan's parents held a goodbye party for everyone on their back porch. It felt like it was marking the end of something significant. I was already nostalgic for our shared childhood in that town, riding bikes over the country roads in summer and lurking around the arena during hockey games in winter.

"Are you nervous or sad about leaving?" I had asked.

"No. I'm ready to go," Meghan answered. It was years before she came home to visit, and she never lived in our town, or province, again.

I am a decision waffler, but Meghan has always been clear-eyed when facing small—or large—choices. I wanted to channel some of this strength, so while Sadie toddled after Max in the garden, I asked her opinion.

"We are thinking of going to Tanzania this spring," I said. "If we do, we might bring Sadie. What would you do?"

"I wouldn't bring her," Meghan said.

She'd been set up. I'd already told her the background and gruesome stories, and had built up the dangers. I'd told her about my conversation with Don Sawatzky at Under the Same Sun earlier that week: "It takes about thirty hours door to door," he said to me over the phone. "To be honest, I probably wouldn't bring her. I'd consider waiting until she's older."

When I solicit advice from other people, I omit some crucial details to see if I might get a different response. I don't mention witch doctors or how people with the same condition as my daughter are being murdered, their body parts traded and bartered on the black market. I don't say that these white-skinned Africans are called ghosts because people believe they never die, or that pregnant women turn from them, afraid they will curse the baby in their growing bellies. Leaving out these frightening narratives, I ask my friend Anna, who is intrepid and strong-willed, for her opinion.

Anna and I spent several summers hitching rides with strangers over both land and water when working as counselors at a summer canoe-tripping camp. We smoked cigarettes in a porta-potty while the children in our charge wandered off into the woods, or lingered near open water. On our days off, we crashed drunken parties hosted by strangers in the closest town and used badly matched fake ID to gain access to grimy hotels and dimly lit bars.

Now we have kids and live on opposite sides of the country. The last time I was in a bar it was daylight and there was a high chair at the table.

"We are heading to Africa this spring to learn more about the beliefs surrounding albinism there," I write to Anna in an email. "Should I bring Sadie? What would you do?"

"Yes. Bring Sadie," she responds. "Take lots of pictures and get immunized and bring drugs and revel in what I'm sure will be a life-changing opportunity. First of all, how could you leave Sadie? Second, what an amazing contextual layer. Learning with and through her. Third, if something less than perfect happens, she'll never remember, but no matter what, in ten years she'll wear it like a badge of honor."

How can I deny my child this badge of honor? Anna is right, Sadie won't remember any perilous situations should they arise. This is a major part of why I want to bring her now, rather than wait until she's older, as so many people have suggested. At two, she won't be cognizant of how the atrocities relate to her identity. As a toddler she is free of the facts—the parcels of information that interfere with life as much as inform it. She would meet other small children with albinism there, and she would see them as playmates, not define them by the challenges in their lives—heartaches I can no longer look past and which, in time, she likely won't look past either.

It's my friend Rachel who gives weight to my wildest fears. Rachel, who once looked at me wide-eyed across a yellowing motel room above the downtown bus station in San Diego and said, "Our mothers would hate this place." We'd collapsed in peals of laughter. She was possibly concussed from the windowsill landing squarely on her skull during a failed attempt to spy on our fornicating neighbors—a john and his date. Our mothers would most certainly have hated that place, but for us it was just part of a summer-long adventure up and down the Californian coast when we were nineteen. I was less fearful then. I think I would hate the motel now too.

"I'm scared of the witch doctors," I confess to Rachel when we speak over Skype. "I'm scared they will somehow know I am coming and that I'm bringing Sadie. It's not that I believe in witchcraft, but I'm afraid not to believe at the same time. Because the magic isn't real, but their power is."

"I would be afraid of that too," she says. "It might be like delivering this tiny perfect package directly to them."

FIRST IT WAS AN HOUR, AT THREE MONTHS, READING THE ENTIRE NEWSpaper at a coffee shop on my birthday.

"Can I join you?" a chatty acquaintance asked when he spotted me at the corner table.

"No," I answered uncharacteristically, and realized that motherhood had already changed me. The hour was mine, to be guarded ferociously, protected. Then it was a night, a dinner, and a glass of wine. A weekly knitting class. An afternoon of work. A weekend in Montreal. Then, at eight months, it was the eleven hours a week of babysitting while I taught a class at the university.

I'd physically stumbled through lesson plans at school and infant care at home, wrenching my two selves apart, afraid of delving too deeply into either world for fear that one might inadvertently break through into the other. I couldn't exist in both places at the same time. *Don't think about the baby*, I'd instructed myself, afraid of leaking breast milk while lecturing to semiconscious undergrads. When Sadie turned one, I began spending three days a week in a windowless office, where I wrote my dissertation. It astonished me that I was able to exist, to focus, to move back into the life I'd left behind at childbirth.

Perhaps that's a part of labor's agony. Beyond the physical pain there's the knowledge that this is the first separation of mother and child, the first step toward the child's eventual, inevitable autonomy. Maybe this is why it's so hard to push the child out and away from you. Sadie took forty hours to emerge. "That's a whole workweek," a friend observed. From the beginning, letting go, pushing away, has not been my forte.

It's a constant negotiation, an ongoing dialogue, a long-stretching push and pull of time spent with her and time spent apart, and neither state feels entirely certain.

Now, the map of Africa is laid out before me. It's a bulbous drip, a vast blank canvas. To know her, I feel I must go there. But to keep her safe, do I need to leave her behind?

I think about Sadie's world now. How different it looks from how I'd imagined it when she was diagnosed at three months. How she navigates her landscapes with half the sight I have, and how she does so with astonishing precision. How she will retrieve a toy dropped on the chaos of a Persian carpet by feeling for it with her hands. Or she won't pick up the toy at all, having moved on to the next amusement. Our home is strewn with the detritus of the very young: bits of crayon, rubber balls, puzzle pieces, and plush toys—material, inanimate matter, and yet infused with meaning and encapsulating all the days that lead away from the beginning.

Sadie is two and a quarter now. She likes stripes. ("You have stripes on your forehead, Mama!" she says to me.) She likes avocados and the color yellow. She prefers to wear mismatched socks, especially if one is yellow. She sleeps with eight stuffed animals, whom she refers to as "the guys." Her hair has grown long past her shoulders, but she will not tolerate ponytail holders, even if they are yellow. Her glasses are one size bigger than her infant pair, and a darker shade of pink. Her white eyelashes are so long that they brush against the lenses when she blinks. She lies still while we rub sunblock into her skin two to three times a day. She doesn't wear T-shirts, or shorts or sandals, and she has almost never left the house without a hat on her head. On her feet she wears pink-and-black high-top Converse sneakers or orange rubber boots.

She is a first-rate mimic and an accomplished medic: "Elmo has pink eye. He's okay, but he cannot go to daycare today." She will not reason but is amenable to bribery. She prefers men to women. She continues to be keenly interested in Max (who has just turned five), but her best friend is a two-and-a-half-year-old boy named Elan. When he switches daycares, she feels the loss deeply.

A FEW DAYS PAST CHRISTMAS, WE VISIT A TRAVEL CLINIC. IT'S post-holiday quiet in the hallway outside the office. A miniature Christmas tree twinkles and blinks on the counter, where we wait to speak with the receptionist. Sadie, in my arms, yanks a candy cane from one of its branches. A smooth-haired young woman in scrubs steps out to greet us. *She looks like someone you might meet at a youth hostel*, I think. Someone who knows her malaria from her dengue fever and has the remedy for both in her dusty, well-worn backpack. She has a light tan. Probably from her last trip to the continent, I surmise hopefully. Andrew and I fill out green medical history forms detailing what we can remember of our vaccinations while Sadie, a whirling dervish of sticky destruction, ransacks the magazines. We hand in our cobbled-together medical history to the pretty nurse, who, I think, probably spent last year traveling Southeast Asia if not touring Africa.

She passes our forms to a stern, matronly woman with short gray hair and glasses. The woman's fuchsia sweater hints at playfulness, but her pearls and upper-crust British-sounding accent override it. She introduces herself as Mrs. Keen and whisks us down a back hallway.

"I was prepared to give one consult today," she says when the three of us settle into her tiny office. Sadie is immediately drawn to an assortment of international travel souvenirs arranged on a low-lying shelf. She tosses a small antique globe like a rubber ball and then focuses her attention on a collection of delicately carved statuettes that look, optimistically, like they come from Africa.

Mrs. Keen reminds me of the schoolmarms who ran the British-style boarding school where I suffered out grade nine in a tie and knee socks. She is unflappable. Sadie begins to scream when Andrew pries a wooden carving from her grasp, and Mrs. Keen produces a box of crayons and coloring paper from her desk drawer with a Mary Poppins–esque flourish.

"Do you travel a lot?" I ask.

"Not enough!" she says, avoiding my foray into chitchat and launching into her lecture. It is immediately clear that Mrs. Keen knows travelers' health risks with a level of intensity that would outdo the best of the backpackers.

"Now, what is this?" she asks, tapping the map on her computer screen.

"Lake Victoria!" I say, feeling chuffed.

"Not a toe in Lake Victoria," she says, waggling her finger in front of my smug face.

A snail that releases parasitic flatworms into the water lurks in the lake. In the medical literature these worms are described as "water-born larvae that penetrate intact skin" and cause schistosomiasis (also known as bilharzia), a disease that can affect the bladder, liver, and spleen, among other important organs. An image of Sadie breaking free of my grasp and dipping her feet into the zombie snail–infested lake plays in a loop at the back of my mind while I listen.

"Now, on to rabies. This is especially problematic for young children," Mrs. Keen says, nodding toward the door Sadie and her father recently exited through. I grow distracted thinking of the suffocating affection my child visits on the family dog, and how she approaches strange animals with vigorous enthusiasm when other children would be hesitant and nervous.

"No typhoid vaccine is available currently," Mrs. Keen continues. "There's been a recall, and we have no idea when the new batch will come in."

"So we will just risk getting typhoid?" I ask.

"Yes."

"And is the risk high?"

"Very."

Some of the health sites I visited online offer advice to travelers to Tanzania that borders on preposterous, cautioning against the contraction of human plagues that have been extinct in the West for a century. "To minimize risk, travelers should avoid areas containing rodent burrows or nests," one site cautioned. "Never handle sick or dead animals," warned another.

It prompted me to research what outlandish behavior visitors to Canada are warned against engaging in. Quite a lot, it turns out. A disease called Q fever is "reported among goats in Newfoundland, the corresponding human illness reported among those travelers who ate goat cheese from such goats, or touched a goat placenta." There is also a warning regarding trichinellosis, which is common in northern Canada, the result of eating infected walrus or polar bear. I suspect that my chances of plunging my arm down a rat's burrow in Tanzania are about as high as touching a goat's placenta might have been when I lived in Newfoundland.

The most frightening issue is also the simplest: traveler's diarrhea. Mrs. Keen advises me to get a prescription for the super-antibiotic ciprofloxacin.

"Can Sadie take Cipro?" I ask. I know small children aren't supposed to take antibiotics, but surely in a pinch it would be fine.

"Absolutely not," she answered. "If she gets traveler's diarrhea, you will need to be airlifted to Nairobi."

"Kenya?"

"Or Europe."

"Europe is eight hours away," I say.

She nods. "So Nairobi is a better choice."

I understand that, in her line of work, Mrs. Keen must offer the least risky option, which can sometimes also be the most extreme. I think we could find medical attention in Tanzania, and yet I can't ignore or erase the information I've been handed here in this office. It will weave itself into the fabric of all my worries and rear its head in an ugly I-told-you-so at the height of any panicky situation.

Sadie lasted less than five minutes in the small office, despite the offered crayons. If this is an indication of how well she might travel, it doesn't look good.

Mrs. Keen comes to the end of her rattling consultation, looks up from the computer screen, and meets my bleary eyes with a stern gaze. "Now, I must tell you that there is one very big problem with traveling to Africa—"

I lean into her pause, swallowing, readying myself for the big reveal. Here comes the nugget of wisdom from the sage traveler, the doyenne of communicable disease. Here comes the deciding factor, the X, the absolute black and white. I nod, indicating readiness to receive insight.

"Once you've been there, you will want to go back."

CHAPTER 7

Into Africa

IN THE WEEKS LEADING UP TO OUR DEPARTURE, I AM STARTLED INTO
movement. I begin to run. This is not an unusual activity in Victoria,
where we live. Any given Saturday the city looks as if it were host-
ing a geriatric triathlon. The elderly population hits the pavement,
running and cycling, and also swimming in the pools across the city
(some, shockingly, in the chilled waters of the Pacific). In spring,
under the weighted branches of cotton-candy blooms on our street,
alongside the gutter streaming pink with dropped blossoms, I too
begin to run. I run down an ocean path where I can see my destination—a locked shed on a spit of land—propelling myself in a gangly
forward-moving mass.

The first time I started running I was doing it to catch up. I was
turning thirty-one and my life was sliding backwards. Like Alice in
Wonderland, the only way to keep a reasonable pace was to run. I
was back in school while my friends were moving paces ahead in
careers and family making. I spent more dinner hours at the Ship, or
Erin's Pub, in downtown St. John's, than at my kitchen table. I had a
part-time job entering data from notecards into a giant spreadsheet,
helping to digitize the folklore archives at my university. It was an

important but menial task that I carried out while listening to radio podcasts, often getting lost in the story. Because of this I had to keep returning to where I'd started; I kept making mistakes. It was a lot like the rest of my life. So I ran.

I am a lousy, no-good runner with an awkward gait and bad form. I give up easily, and my efforts rarely yield a proper sweat. In all the years that I have been running, a sporadic five, I have never run more than three miles at a stretch, the pithy basic unit of any race, and mostly I barely make it to three.

My in-laws can run marathons on a whim. My brother-in-law has completed the Ironman triathlon twice and yet I chug along huffing and puffing like a steam engine, or a commuter train that makes frequent stops. Unlike my betrothed family, rather than running as a pastime or in the pursuit of health, I run when I am desperate. I run away. I run, like Alice, to stay in the same spot when I feel like my solid earth is crumbling beneath me.

The fears planted by the consultation with Mrs. Keen festered into a sore I couldn't heal. In the days after we met, I was struck by images of my baby girl shivering with typhoid fever or in the grip of stomach cramps from a food-borne illness. The health-based concerns overpowered even my anxiety about the witch doctors and their powerful reach. I couldn't shake the sense of foreboding, no matter how hard I tried to change the channel in my mind.

I am traveling across the world soon, and I am leaving my baby behind. The decision provided no comfort, no relief, and no closure. I think that leaving Sadie, and the trip, are dangerous mistakes, but too many plane tickets have been booked to cancel now—two sets of grandparents, and one aunt will be flying to Victoria to care for Sadie, and Andrew will be flying to Dar es Salaam with me. We will be gone for almost three weeks. Although I'd initially planned to go alone, I'd been spooked by two recent news stories out of Tanzania that featured Canadian women. First, a volunteer worker from Ontario was murdered shortly after her plane touched down in Arusha. Next, a woman from Vancouver was hunted down at her hotel in Mwanza (a city on my itinerary) and her life threatened by a local gang wanting to lay claim to the building she'd erected to house a Montessori school. From the photos that ran alongside the news stories I could see that they were both blond and white and looked out of place in Tanzania, like I will. Andrew booked time from work in May to accompany me. A lot of people have interrupted their lives because I set this plan in motion. I can't stop this machine however much I would like to. If I don't run, the ground, my life, might swallow me.

WHEN YOU HAVE BEEN ANCHORED FOR YEARS, YOU UNMOOR SLOWLY, rocking gently away until, quite suddenly, the line snaps and you find yourself adrift, floating and looking down startled at what you left behind.

First, we arc over the Gulf Islands: drops of green edged by the royal blue water of the Pacific Ocean. Then we are jostled over the white caps of the Coast Mountains, with Mount Rainer, an isosceles triangle with its perfect point, towering in the distance. We circle the Rocky Mountains before landing in Calgary and watch them recede when we take off again. We glide over the wide-open prairies and the cracked ice surface of James Bay, then clip the northern tip of Labrador. In darkness we trace Greenland's southern shore. A morning, afternoon, and evening have elapsed back at home, and we are somewhere over the Arctic Ocean when my parents are putting Sadie to bed—bathing her, dressing her in stripy pajamas, and reading to her from the books that line her dresser. Their verses jingle-jangle through my mind in a loop: *Good night stars, Good night air, Good night noises everywhere.*

Light follows quickly on our jet stream and it's a new morning when we land in Amsterdam. From there we skirt the Croatian coastline before slipping quietly into Africa—first Egypt with our nose toward the equator, then Ethiopia, Kenya, and finally, Tanzania. We touch down at Kilimanjaro in a rocket of rain. The cabin immediately dampens when the door opens. The passengers—hikers, backpackers, aid workers, a group of college students—shuffle toward the wet black exit and disappear into the night. The plane takes off again and, forty hours from when we began our journey, we touch down in Dar es Salaam.

The night before we left, as we set the final pieces in order before bed, my mother hovered. She admonished our hotel choice in Dar es Salaam, having overheard our discussions on price. The word "motel" in the name of our lodgings had her believing we'd chosen cheap and therefore dangerous sleeping arrangements.

"You don't want to end up murdered in your hotel beds," she said. Murder is too dramatic, though. Dying in a car crash, maybe drowning, contracting a little-known but deadly tropical disease are more realistic fates.

The next morning, we had waited at the front window for the taxi that would take us to the airport. My parents were asleep in our room. Sadie, asleep in her crib. I'd stood over her in the dark for a moment, watching her chest rise and fall—her white eyelashes resting above the apples of her cheeks, her mouth set in a half-smile—before turning away and shutting the door behind me. A fingernail moon hung over the city and there were few shadows in the blue-gray light of early morning, the threshold between night and day. I've known this hour's many faces: wobbling home in the dregs of a wine-soaked night; nursing my crying infant back to sleep; and on this morning, in the first tentative steps of a long journey.

THE FLOORS AT JULIUS NYERERE INTERNATIONAL AIRPORT ARE SLICK with rain, puddled, cracked, and uneven. It is almost midnight. There's a crush of men in white shirts at the door. We are ushered into a white car by an illegal taxi driver, a tourist extortionist, and he whisks us into the city, blanketed by night. Approaching major North American cities, even minor towns, there is an assault of lights— empty office towers lit from stem to stern, lampposts lining the high- ways and downtown streets, blinking digitized billboards. But none of this spark and flash exists here, in one of the world's fastest-growing cities. A metropolis slated to reach 5.6 million people by 2020. The hotel lobby, dark as mud, illuminates only when we step inside.

The next morning, Dar es Salaam doesn't wake up so much as it explodes to life at first light. Straddling the equator, there are scant daylight hours. The call to prayer tickles my dreams and gently prods my subconscious. The mosque is so close to our hotel that from our bed we can hear the service, sometimes obscured by the squeak and whir of the failing air conditioner.

Outside, the teeth-sucking staccato of the water and nut sellers alert passersby of their wares. Sharp and rhythmic hissing, tongue against teeth, it's a distinct language. Others shake the change in their palms like maracas, each beat a slight variation of the last. Personalized, the sounds are their calling cards. Inside, an endless stretch of soccer matches plays on the TV in the hotel lobby.

We step across the city on gravelly mud roads and the odd paved one, and are hit by heavy rains before noon. Flash floods follow, envel- oping whole sidewalks and streets. We walk through the Kivukoni Fish Market, where women sit in groups dressed tip to toe in cloth *kangas*, looking like they're socializing but, in reality, running the show. The air is thick with smells from the sea. We are the only tour- ists, or at least the only white people at the crowded market, and teen- age boys follow us through the stalls trying out their English words:

"Hello! How are you?" The vendors don't bother with us; what would tourists do with flounder? Fish is not a souvenir. On our way back toward the hotel, we walk by an open culvert, water gushing into its gaping mouth with the force of a hydro dam. It would be easy to fall into this hole, stepping out of the way of a *dala dala*, cyclist, or car, and right into the throat of the body-sized cavity, to be sucked down into Dar's gut.

Dar es Salaam is like a Jackson Pollock painting. At first glance there is only chaos, nothing recognizable, nothing ordered, but slowly patterns appear as your eyes and mind adjust and you find your way around the canvas, discovering rhythm, detail, and beauty in the scribbles that initially seemed to be an uncalculated mess.

We walk by a young man with albinism on our first morning; he's wearing a poor-boy cap and carrying a satchel. A student, maybe. Our arms brush and I turn to him in shock. By the day's end I've seen two more pale-skinned Tanzanians: a child and a snappily dressed businessman. Africans with albinism mainly carry the OCA2 gene, whereas most people of European descent carry the OCA1 gene, like Sadie. The prevalence of OCA2 worldwide is about one in twenty thousand, but here in Tanzania it is one in two thousand. Some hypothesize that it is closer to one in six hundred.

The numbers manifest on the streets and in the cultural vernacular—derogatory labels for people with this condition include "ghost," "zero-zero," and "*mzungu*." The first two I am already familiar with, having learned Adam's story; the last one I come to know quickly.

"*Jambo, mzungu!*" people call when we pass them on the street. I think this could mean "Hello, foreigner," but the direct translation is "Hello, white person," and it's not exactly pejorative in our context. It's more greeting than the insult it is intended to carry when directed at people with albinism. I always respond. I'm friendly, open to conversation. Andrew is cautious. People sense this and they don't approach him in the same way. Despite my relaxed social attitude, I am nervous about leaving the hotel alone.

"I saw two foreign women walking alone today," I tell Andrew. "Maybe I could go out on my own too."

"*You* saw two women," he says. "But maybe four started out."

He's joking, of course. Truthfully, very few people had harassed us on the street, only the vendors who had something to sell. I haven't had so much as a leer in my direction from the men on the crowded sidewalks. My fear is rooted in culture shock, something I've downplayed in the past but which is confusingly real this time around.

I find it hard to cross the streets near our downtown hotel. There are no traffic lights, seemingly no speed limit. It's difficult to make out the street signs, when they appear at all, and the map provided by the hotel has been photocopied into near oblivion. I worry that if I were to leave on my own, I'd never find my way back.

On our second night, we plan to eat at a restaurant a few blocks away and ask our hotelier about walking after dark.

"Oh, it's perfectly safe. Just don't bring anything valuable with you," she says, then turns to me. "And take the earrings out of your ears."

We take a taxi.

WE SPEND THE NEXT WEEK THIS WAY, SLINKING THROUGH DAR'S CON-gested streets by taxi. We are in constant motion, as we have been since we stepped out our front door and traveled the globe's curve to arrive here. I've been traveling since I was Sadie's age, and my dreams crowd with airport corridors and train stations. There is comfort in this movement, but also a nagging fear that it's unnatural to fling yourself across the earth this way. It's a thought I've had since overhearing a story at my maternal grandparents' home when I was a child of nine or ten.

My grandmother's octagonal kitchen table was where her extended family gathered during happy hour. The women sat in the chairs drinking martinis and talking while the men drank Scotch and watched television just a few paces away. The women's voices competed with the polite clapping and subdued cheering of televised golf, and together this made up the backdrop of evenings throughout my childhood summers. My four half-siblings were much older, and I spent most of my cognizant younger years as an only child. It was a balance of intense focus and obliviousness. One child is quiet and easily forgotten in the cacophony of adult chatter. I was drawn in by the women's stories as much as I was repelled by the men's sporting events.

On one of these late afternoons, my mother told a story she'd heard about a British traveler ascending Everest. He'd been barreling ahead despite his Sherpa's advisement of a day of rest, annoyed by his guide's refusal to follow suit. When the two men rejoined a day later, the British traveler had berated the Sherpa for his perceived laziness. "Be careful," the Sherpa warned. "You need to rest to allow your soul the time to catch up with you. If you don't, your soul might never rejoin your body."

When I look for evidence of this scrap of overheard conversation, I follow a trail of contemporary legends. Some reference the British mountaineer, but in other variants the protagonists are wealthy Americans trekking in the jungles of Brazil who want to forge ahead but are warned by wise locals about moving too quickly for their souls to catch up. In yet another variant, Americans on safari in Africa are warned by the sage guide to slow down and wait for their souls to rejoin their bodies. The settings vary but the protagonists are interchangeably American or British.

The account of the lost souls worried me as a well-traveled child, and stays with me into adulthood, as I set up and deconstruct my life in cities across Europe and North America. I can see now that the legend casts the exotic other in the role of simple sage, a soothsayer with a metaphorical message. I understand the lesson this legend is teaching us and its appeal to citizens of the West since the Industrial Revolution ramped up our ability to travel far and wide and, most important, fast. As a child I found the story unsettling. If a soul has trouble keeping pace during a strenuous mountain climb, my own soul was surely lost forever. I worried about the distance I'd traveled and fretted about my poor lost soul wandering the Burgundian hills of France, or Miami's beaches, or worse, stuck on the shoulder of Highway 401 somewhere east of Toronto, looking for the person who'd carelessly forsaken something so important.

Over another happy hour decades later, I ask my parents about the legend, expecting the tale to have vanished, as ephemeral stories do within greater life narratives. Instead, they both know it immediately.

"Jakob Amstutz told Mieke that story," my mother said. "He was a Swiss philosopher who taught at the University of Guelph. And it wasn't Everest; it was a different mountain in Tibet." Mieke, who is an artist and my mother's closest friend, had been mentored by Jakob when she was a student.

"He said he was climbing with Sherpa guides, and they reached the summit and started heading down the other side," my dad says. "The philosopher wanted to hurry down, and he felt the animals were rested and ready to descend, but the Sherpas said they needed to wait for the animals' souls to catch up with them."

"No, no, it was the Sherpas who were waiting for their own souls to catch up with them," my mother says.

Variations persist in this retelling, and details are lost in time. I ask Mieke about the Sherpas and she tells me that Jakob Amstutz heard it from Carl Jung, who'd heard it from Walter Evans-Wentz, the American anthropologist who'd published an early translation of

The Tibetan Book of the Dead. Ultimately, the teller's details are extraneous to the narrative because the truth is in the story. It is a mindful warning: slow down or risk losing yourself.

My triathlete brother-in-law told me that rest is an important part of an athlete's training regime—that you cannot absorb the benefits of your workout without this period of repair. Like the soul, your body's fitness slips quietly away if you don't wait for it to catch up with you.

Now that I am here in Tanzania, for the next twenty days I will run this race, run as fast and as long and as hard as I can. Then I will fly home and quietly resume my life as a mother. I will rest and stay still for as long as I can and hope for my soul to rejoin my body.

CHAPTER 8

Undercover

IN THE MILKY FOG OF MY DAUGHTER'S FIRST WEEKS, SOMETIME AFTER her grandfather had examined her and relayed his findings, I typed the word "albino" into an Internet search engine. Within the first page of results were gruesome headlines involving maimed children. Babies, like my baby, murdered for their whiteness.

The new moms in my peer group were scanning articles on sleep remedies and colic. While they were learning how to care for their newborns through advice posted on parenting forums, I was learning about executions, dismemberments, and disturbing human rights crimes that in some way related to me, my family, and the makeup of my DNA. The images that accompanied these stories contributed to my husband's desperate silence in the first few weeks of our daughter's life. The murders and attacks happened in a far-away place, and we could live unaffected by these atrocities. It might have been easy to let the details slip quietly off to the periphery of my mind and then disappear, to be eclipsed by the ordinariness of my life. Except for the connecting line, a tiny genetic switch, alive in my cells, expressed in my child. It was a distant tale, but it wasn't entirely foreign.

By the end of 2013, the number of crimes against people with albinism in Tanzania totaled 128—72 people were murdered, 39 people survived an attack, and there were 17 gravesite violations. Across sub-Saharan Africa another 54 people with albinism have been killed, and 116 attacked. Some of these crimes are because of a cross-border trade in human body parts between Tanzania and nearby countries. Under the Same Sun, which tallies these statistics every two months, believes these numbers are modest. They don't include unreported incidents, or any crimes prior to the first documented police case in 2006. The official UTSS position is that these atrocities have been going on "for time beyond memory."

Two months before we arrived in Tanzania, there had been a spate of violence in the north and west of the country. Four people with albinism had been attacked over the span of two weeks, from late January to mid-February. The first victim, a seven-year-old boy named Lugolola Bunzari, from Tabora Region, died from his injuries, which included gashes across his face and limbs and being partially dismembered. His grandfather was also killed while trying to protect him. Then, about 250 miles south, in Simiyu Region, villagers fought off armed men attempting to kidnap a seven-month-old boy with albinism. A few days later, there were two incidents in the southern region of Sumbawanga. First Maria Chambanenge, a mother of four, was attacked in her bed. A group of five men, including the woman's husband, pinned her down and severed her arm from her body. Two of her children were asleep beside her when it happened. Four days later, two men using machetes attacked a ten-year-old boy named Mwigulu Matonange, from Rukwa Region, while he was walking home from school. He survived but lost his left arm.

Following this string of attacks, United Nations high commissioner for human rights Navi Pillay issued a press release condemning the gruesome killings. "These crimes are abhorrent. People with albinism have the right to start living, like anyone else, without fear of being killed or dismembered," Ms. Pillay said. "I urge the Tanzanian authorities to strengthen their legal response to such crimes and increase their efforts to bring perpetrators of attacks and killings to justice."

To date, only five people have been prosecuted and charged in relation to more than one hundred incidents. Five years ago, these crimes went unreported. They didn't appear in police files or in the local and international media. It was the work of a former BBC journalist named Vicky Ntetema that directed the world's attention toward the human rights violations in Tanzania. She almost lost her life in the process. Today, Vicky works as the executive director at Under the Same Sun, a post she's held since 2008, when Peter Ash asked her to helm the local chapter of his then-fledgling NGO. It was after reading Vicky's report on the plight of people with albinism in Tanzania that Peter booked his first plane ticket to Dar es Salaam. "I had heard about discrimination before, but not ritual killings," he told me when we spoke in February 2012. "I felt I had to go there to find out more and get a sense of the magnitude of these crimes."

When I relayed stories about the atrocities in East Africa to colleagues, I sometimes sensed they felt I was exaggerating. I consulted one scholar, who asked, "Are you sure this is even true?" A second academic corrected me when I used the term "witch doctor." "Traditional healer," she said, nodding as if I were complicit, as if we were both acknowledging my politically incorrect slip. But the truth was that I didn't know this sanitized moniker because I'd never encountered it in news reports. Looking back, I do remember thinking that the term "witch doctor" sounded antiquated upon first learning about the situation in Tanzania, but as I read hundreds of reports in academic journals and the popular media, it had slowly normalized. Which is an example of why language is so powerful—and also can be so hard to change.

"Witch doctor" is an ethnocentric term that British colonizers ascribed to a person who practices traditional medicine in Africa. There was no role like this in Western culture. In Swahili, these practitioners are called *mganga*, and their aim was to diagnose and cure the ill through a combination of herbal and spiritual remedies, but the early Europeans deemed them, in name and practice, witches. Further confusing the matter is that a major part of the purported witch doctor's practice was to exorcise evil spells cast by people who can only be described as witches. Laws were passed forbidding all forms of what the English perceived as magic but which did not discern between good or bad, writes anthropologist Granville St. John Orde-Browne in his 1934 paper presented to the International Congress of Anthropological and Ethnological Sciences: "To the African, such a standpoint must be most bewildering, since ... [it] regards the physician and the poisoner as equally reprehensible."

Dr. Simeon Mesaki, a professor at the University of Dar es Salaam whose scholarly work focuses on witchcraft in Tanzania, likens the witch doctors who are committing crimes and preying on vulnerable people today to quacks in Western medicine. He writes that "in every society there are charlatans who prey on the gullible and distressed for gain. Thus it is important to distinguish between the genuine majority and the spurious few." The United Nations Human Rights High Commission, as well as the international media, uses the terms "witchcraft" and "witch doctor" in relation to the crimes in Tanzania, and so I will also continue to use it, but with the acknowledgment that it is not a blanket term that applies to all practitioners of traditional medicine in East Africa.

Westerners are often accused of promoting a barbaric and exotic image of African countries, and no group more so than members of the press. This is why Vicky, a Tanzanian national, is an interesting case. She spent two decades away from her home attending boarding school and university and had the resulting starry-eyed gaze that affects many diaspora. The homeland becomes a mythical place, a geography of longing, and every step taken is toward the eventual return. Vicky earned an MA in journalism from the Belarusian State University in Minsk, in the former Soviet Union state of Belorussia (now Belarus) and an MSc in software engineering from the London School of Economics and Political Science. In 1991 she was hired by the BBC.

She harbored dreams of working as a reporter back home, but her cv was always tossed. "You're overqualified," the newspapermen told her. "You have an MA, and most of the editors you'd be working under don't even have a degree. You see the problem?"

Her break came when the BBC expanded its Tanzanian bureau in advance of the 2005 general elections. Vicky applied for and won a two-year reporting contract to work out of Dar es Salaam. "The image I had of Tanzania before I left when I was very young," she says, "was different from the reality"—a sobering realization after all those years spent yearning for home.

IT TAKES US TWO TAXIS TO REACH THE UNDER THE SAME SUN OFFICE. When Andrew was describing our destination to the first driver, I wondered if we even had the order correct. Was it the street name or the district that Andrew repeated emphatically? We drive for twenty minutes and then the car stops and the driver confers with a banana seller. Then, after another ten minutes of touring dusty roads, we idle in a parking lot while the driver has a conversation with a Masai warrior. He was employed by the adjoining hotel to guard the cars from theft, as far as I could tell, or he was a parking attendant. The Masai was wearing the traditional tartan fabric, beads, and headdress that I'd seen on other warriors throughout the city. He seemed a little bored, welcoming of our distraction. He pulled out his cell phone to consult someone while we waited. Then he shook his head. The driver turned to us and also shook his head, then dropped us off at the nearby Hilton Hotel in Oyster Bay. Since we had an hour to spare before needing to find another taxi, we ate lunch in the lobby, watching the white clients in business suits stride by in groups, carrying clipboards. I recognized a few people from our flight. When our meal arrived, I noticed that there was a tomato and some lettuce on our sandwiches.

"Should we be eating this?" Andrew asks, reminding me of the traveler's edict that food must be cooked, peeled, boiled, or left untouched. I look around at the shiny marble floors and the chandeliers and the baby grand piano.

"It's probably fine," I say.

THE UTSS OFFICE IS DOWN A DUSTY POTHOLED ROAD IN A QUIET DIStrict of high-gated buildings that house international and local aid organizations. A security guard checks our identification and the contents of our backpacks before we enter the foyer, where a fan oscillates and a wall-mounted television is tuned to Al Jezeera. The secretary has albinism, as do many of the staff members who wander by and introduce themselves. It's not a prerequisite to be hired here, but unlike with many employers in Tanzania, having albinism gives you an edge on the competition.

Vicky approaches and greets us warmly, then shows us to a second-floor boardroom. She is wearing a white-collared blouse under a mauve suit jacket and a matching long skirt. Her curly hair is pulled back and she wears thin wire-frame glasses. She looks like a Western NGO director. But Vicky is a chameleon. A few months ago, I'd seen photographs of her at a ceremony where she'd received the 2010

Courage in Journalism award from the International Women's Media Foundation and she had looked more like the Tanzanian women I'd seen these past few days on the streets of Dar es Salaam, wearing a dress made of block-print fabric, a beaded necklace, and earrings, her hair shaped into a crown of dense curls that haloed her face.

Vicky's ability to shape-shift had served her well when she posed as a businesswoman and visited a dozen witch doctors in northwest Tanzania to glean details for the July 2008 BBC report on the attacks against people with albinism in her country.

It's chilling to watch a clip of her surreptitiously filmed meeting with one of the witch doctors. In her businesswoman persona, she asks unbelievable questions, such as "What are the legs good for?" and "How much for the leg and the hair?" Finally, Vicky asks, "If I can't bring you these body parts, can you help?" The film is choppy and grainy, the witch doctor is a slippery dark shadow, but his answer is clear: "There are always ways. We do have albinos in this area, and it is possible to get hold of parts for you."

The speaker is callous and confident, suggesting that it's an easily accomplished task for which there would be no repercussion. An hour after this undercover interview, Vicky started receiving threatening phone calls and texts.

A rooster crows repeatedly from a neighboring yard as we settle around a long, narrow table. I've asked Vicky to tell us the story of her undercover reporting—what drew her to that point and what happened next. "That is a long story," she says, laughing. "So I will tell it to you in the shortest way I can."

Six months before going undercover, Vicky had an epiphany at a press conference for disability rights in Dar es Salaam. It was December 2007 and word of the attacks on people with albinism had reached local media. A man with albinism took the podium and announced that he would donate his body if scientists could prove there was lucrative magic in his bones. A lot of people live in poverty in this country, he said, and perhaps this would help. Vicky stood in the crowd, shocked by his statement. "I thought, *This person is desperate*. It's not something that one would just get up and talk about, say[ing] that you will volunteer your body. I thought this person has reached a place where he thinks there's no help."

Up until the press conference that day, no government official or leader had stepped forward to condemn the killings and attacks on people with albinism. They weren't being acknowledged by politicians, and the president remained silent on the matter as well. At that point, Vicky had heard from credible sources in the northwestern part of Tanzania that four people had been murdered, two graves robbed, and that several people's body parts had been stolen, just as petty thieves might steal a purse or a wallet. *Why aren't the people in power doing anything about this?* she wondered. Then came an even more disturbing thought: *Does this mean that the Members of Parliament, the government, believe in witchcraft?*

"And that's when I realized that people with albinism in Tanzania are being discriminated against and also are facing quite a lot of challenges," Vicky says. "Before then, I didn't know."

Throughout her childhood years in Tanzania and while studying abroad, she believed that her country was free of discrimination, a peaceful place. When the killings revealed something different, it forced her to reexamine her own society. She felt compelled to find out more because she's a reporter and it's part of her life's work, but also because she belonged to the culture within which these atrocities were taking place.

"I wanted to dig deeper into the whole issue of the plight of people with albinism, the atrocities, the stigma, and the discrimination," Vicky says. "I wanted to know why they were a target."

When she pitched the story to her BBC editors, they were initially hesitant to assign it to her. The details were so gruesome and outland-ish that they wondered, like my colleagues, if they were rumors or tall tales. But Vicky was convinced that the information she received from residents in the northwestern part of the country was sound. Once her employers relented, she needed to find a way in.

"From that time, I started seriously investigating," Vicky says. "But I had to go undercover."

Vicky donned the persona and appearance of a businesswoman and consulted with a series of witch doctors in the northwest of Tanzania. Her intention was to expose these practitioners as fakes in an effort to thwart the body-part trade.

The sessions with the witch doctors cost between $20 and $100 (US), though the fees for potions using the albino body parts are much higher—it was $2,000 for a potion made of ground internal organs.

If the consultations weren't so grim, they'd border on comical. One witch doctor pointed Vicky toward a chicken and instructed her to share her problems with the bird. Another told her she must dance on a series of graves to revive her spirit, which was broken because she was already dead. They described imaginary enemies and told her that she'd been bewitched by invented relatives. What they weren't able to do was conjure Vicky's true identity or mission. It was a local policeman she had conferred with at the outset of the investigation who tipped off the last witch doctor she interviewed.

Within an hour Vicky began receiving text-message threats to her cell phone. A group of men were dispatched to search guesthouses in the town of Magu, where she was last seen, but she'd moved on to the larger city of Mwanza. Then a phone message.

"What have you done now?" the caller asks. "Watch your back."

The report ran on July 21, 2008. A few months earlier, President Jakaya Kikwete had stepped forward and publicly condemned the witchcraft killings. Around the same time, he elected Al-Shymaa

Kway-Geer, the country's first MP with albinism. The killings weren't abating, but at least they were being acknowledged. Change is expected to be slow. So slow that when I first spoke to Peter Ash, he told me that it was unlikely he'd see a resolution in his lifetime.

This is because witch doctors have a powerful grasp on the nation's psyche. A 2012 Pew Research Center survey on religion and public life indicated that 92 percent of Tanzanians believe in the existence of witchcraft. At the same time, most Tanzanians are religious, with one-third identifying as Christian, one-third as Muslim, and the remaining third ascribing to indigenous religions. Belief is malleable and interpretive, and one value system doesn't necessarily cancel the other. The study doesn't elaborate on whether the respondents might condone murder in association with witchcraft.

The threats intensified in the days following the broadcast. Two witch doctors visited the Dar es Salaam BBC office looking for Vicky. She pretended to be another reporter and threw them temporarily off her scent.

"After that, I locked that door and I was trembling," Vicky says. "Then I called London. I was all alone that day, and I said, 'Guys, this is the situation.' So I was told to lock the doors when alone, but also I was told to leave the country."

Vicky filed a follow-up story for the BBC chronicling the threats, reporting from an undisclosed location. She was frightened and worried about her family but, she wrote, "even if I die today, those involved will have been exposed."

The security guards at her apartment complex fled under pressure and she moved to a hotel, then another, trying to elude the men who were tracking her. Vicky fled to her mother's house, taking several modes of transportation and unusual routes in an attempt to avoid being pursued. When she arrived, she began writing another report but the lights went out. It appeared that someone, presumably one of the men who'd been following her, had tampered with the electricity. After this, Vicky left the house, realizing that her presence might be putting her mother in danger. (Her mother, a religious woman, was concerned for her own safety but felt that God would protect her from any harm.) After she left, a taxi that Vicky never ordered arrived to collect her. The driver claimed he was employed by the government and that he'd find her with or without her mother's help. Vicky's mother called her daughter's cell phone and gave her one directive: Run.

Vicky says the mysterious taxi driver was the final straw. She could no longer live under threat. "That day I had to leave the country."

WHAT SOMETIMES HAPPENS TO JOURNALISTS TASKED WITH CHRONIC-ling injustice is that they cross the threshold from reporters to activists. Their job is to siphon information from a source, share it objectively, and move on to the next story, but for some the weight is too difficult to bear. Their hearts sag. They can't let go because the story feels unresolved, which it tends to be for reporters covering difficult topics. Whether they are writing about war, human rights crimes, poverty, or famine, a feeling of responsibility creeps in and takes hold. The problem is that when reporters shift in this direction, they become liabilities. They are no longer objective. They are fighting for a cause they believe in. They put themselves in danger. As Vicky demonstrated, these reporters will die for their cause. This is a problem for publishers, and this was an issue for the BBC when, after eighteen months of exile, Vicky returned and again began investigating witchcraft in Tanzania. She was told by a police official that if she continued, her life was at risk.

"This is activism, not journalism," her employers told her. "You can keep your job, but you can't stay in Tanzania."

"I want to see the end of the atrocities against people with albinism," she responded. "I think it's my duty to continue with what I've started."

She tried taking a sabbatical, but in the end, she knew she couldn't leave this issue behind. Her only choice was to resign from her job at the BBC. "It was very difficult for me to walk away from my journalism career because I had dreamed of following that path from the age of three," Vicky says.

After she left the BBC, Peter Ash asked Vicky to run UTSS in Tanzania. Through it, she could continue what had become her life's mission. She doesn't work as a journalist anymore, but a major part of her job is to investigate and file reports, which she then shares with the media. "We find the data," she says. "But it's their story now."

I ask her if it's difficult to see other writers' bylines on her reporting work, but she doesn't see it this way. "I am happy that they keep the story alive," she says. "What I am doing now is a calling."

WE'VE BEEN SO ENGROSSED IN VICKY'S TALE THAT WE HAVEN'T PAID attention to the time. The sun is starting its rapid descent, and I don't want to be out long after dark. We make arrangements with the UTSS education officer to visit Adam and his brother at their new school in a few days. Then we talk about our upcoming journey to the northwest, where we plan to visit one of the schools where UTSS funds many of the students. We say goodbye, and I know I won't see Vicky for a while, probably not until the next NOAH conference. I hope that she stays safe and that no one is following her home at night or tampering with her electricity or killing her pets. I don't say this because it seems macabre but I hope that she can soon live without threat. Although the more I learn, the less I think this is possible.

THE NEXT NIGHT, I BEGIN TO HALLUCINATE DURING DINNER. WE ARE IN a restaurant in the Kisutu area, which is a bit leafier and more relaxed than that surrounding our hotel a few blocks away. I'd noticed a man with albinism eating on the restaurant's patio when we entered. Now, from where I sit, I can see a pigmented man on a bicycle who has come to a stop behind him watching him with interest from the street. The man with the bike catches me staring at him and he begins to gesticulate wildly, pointing exaggeratedly at the man with albinism, mimicking how he's eating his rice dinner. I worry that he is warning me, trying to tell me something. That he knows I am here to ask questions about witch doctors. It is a preposterous thought, I know, but my logic has dissolved into sweat. Andrew's back is to the action, and he's enthusiastically tearing into his jerk chicken.

"This is really good," he keeps telling me, though his words barely permeate the surface of my brain. I am too frightened by the man on the bicycle and gripped by the unearthly movement of my stomach. I am beginning to lose rationality, and I know this because I also feel that the man gesturing at me is the American actor Morgan Freeman. He cannot be the American actor Morgan Freeman. He has a bicycle. Would Morgan Freeman be riding a bike around Dar es Salaam? No, a look-alike, surely. More pressing is the reason he is pointing at the man with albinism and why he is connecting this man to me.

I try to eat a few of the plain noodles I ordered but can barely choke them down. I curse the fancy hotel and its shiny floors and its fresh sandwiches. Maybe it was the juice I drank at breakfast. Maybe it was the lip of an unclean drinking glass. But I think it's more likely that I ate something I shouldn't have at the Hilton (lettuce and tomatoes) because the surroundings reminded me of Miami and I let my guard down.

"We need to go," I tell Andrew and then run to the washroom.

I am peripherally aware of the mopeds zinging by us, and the crowds, and which streets we take to get back to the hotel. Mostly I am concentrating on placing one foot in front of the other. Back in our room I stumble into the bathroom and slide onto the cool tiled floor. It's a relief to be in private, away from the man on the street and whatever his intentions were.

The air conditioner above the window alternately chirps and gallops, shaping my lucid dreams. First I am in a barn filled with swallows' nests, watching horses race through a crack in the wallboards. Next I am back in my hotel room, a repairman hammering methodically in the background, perhaps fixing the broken air conditioner. For hours I lie across the cool red tiles of the bathroom floor in a sweat, violently ejecting fluids. When there's nothing left, the sickness wrings my entire body like a wet towel, squeezing out the final beads of liquid. Every thirty minutes I hear a knock at the door and Andrew pokes his head in to check on me and ask if we should call someone for help. "Not yet," I answer, and each time I wonder who we would call.

While I lie on the bathroom floor, Vicky's story flits through my mind in pieces. The dark shape of the witch doctor in the grainy video, her disguise, the men at her office door, how she'd reached London safely but learned that her six puppies had been poisoned and left to die as a warning. I think of Vicky at her mother's house and how the lights went out, but how she was able to escape, all the while knowing she was being stalked. The men who came to her office, threatening. How they followed her. The story churns in tandem with my stomach.

Near midnight I try to swallow an Imodium and an antibiotic with a glass of water but my body rejects both pills with spectacular waterworks. It is hot in here but I feel cold and clammy. I know if I can swallow a Gravol I might have a chance of keeping the other pills down. I prop myself up against the wall while I unscrew the lid of my water bottle and then pop a tiny orange pill from the foil of the blister pack. I feel the order is important—nausea first, treatment second. I swallow and then lie carefully back on the tiles. My breathing is shallow and my eyes are wet. I wait. Moments pass, or maybe even an hour, and I feel a subtle shift. I reach for the water bottle on the floor beside me, toss the other medication into my mouth, and swallow quickly. For the first time tonight, I believe this will pass. It is in this moment that I allow my mind to wander into "What if?" territory. I think about my small daughter and wonder what she is doing. It is evening in Victoria, she will have just come home from daycare. My sister Robin would be arriving that night. They would be eating dinner shortly, or maybe they just finished. Spaghetti, probably. My mom always makes spaghetti.

When we'd emailed to arrange our meeting, I told Vicky how tormented I was to leave Sadie behind. A mother of two grown boys, she understood my concern and answered kindly.

"Sorry about leaving your daughter behind! Temporary separation has to occur at some point in life because of our community responsibilities."

What if Sadie had been here while I was so sick? What if I'd been alone with her? Who would have cared for her while I writhed and hallucinated on the bathroom floor? Then I think with a shudder, *What if she'd been sick like this? Or worse?* I banish the thought as my stomach knots, threatening the sense of calm I'd finally landed on. Why dwell on this? Sadie is not here, and for now I am profoundly grateful.

CHAPTER 9

Albino United

WE ARE STANDING IN A DUSTY FIELD A FEW PACES FROM OCEAN ROAD in Dar es Salaam watching a group of young men practice soccer. They gather here six evenings a week. The uneven earth is swampy at the edges and occasionally long grasses brush the players' legs as they run drills. Some of them are barefoot. Player number 9 wears one shoe. Brown and fraying, the soccer ball has lost its black spots. The players arrive each day at around 4 p.m. as the sun descends and the glare and heat fade into dusk. The team has thirty players and most of them have albinism. They participate in fifteen matches a year in the professional Tanzanian soccer league, which is remarkable considering many of them are legally blind.

This is Albino United, a soccer team founded in 2008 by a group of young men who met through the Tanzania Albinism Society. It was the same year that Vicky Ntetema's investigative report on the mutilations and murders of people with albinism aired on the BBC, and a year after the first public acknowledgment of these atrocities by an elected official. The men got together and talked about what they could do to change their collective fate. How could they end the killings? How could they convince people that albinos were the same as everyone else? How could they end the relentless stream of discrimination? What is more powerful than witchcraft?

"Through that meeting we decided to form a soccer team and use it as a tool for educating people, creating awareness, and joining people with albinism together," said Saidi NDonege, a founding member, player, and current team leader.

I'd met Saidi in the lobby of the Heritage Motel in Dar es Salaam earlier today. He is thirty-three years old and his face, arms, and hands are spotted like a cheetah's coat from sun damage. He speaks in a gravelly voice, closing his eyes and rocking forward when asking questions. He wears a green Adidas shirt, and a black-and-white John Deere baseball cap. He works as a carpenter when he's not playing soccer. Saidi was accompanied by Jacob Mwinula, the team captain who is also a founder and the group's only university-educated and English-speaking member, which means he's tasked with translating our conversation. Jacob facilitates requests like mine—to meet the players, watch a practice, take photos—which have trickled in over the years from media organizations across Europe and North America.

I'd written to him months before, telling him about Sadie, about our trip, and about my desire to understand the beliefs concerning albinism in Tanzania. Jacob writes emails using only capital letters, which gives his messages a sense of urgency, as if he were shouting to make himself heard over the din of fiber optics. When we met, I was surprised to discover that he was soft-spoken, sometimes withdrawing into silence while he scanned his smartphone or mulled over a question I asked. He is twenty-five years old and recently graduated with a law degree from the University of Dar es Salaam. He had just come from court on the day we met and was wearing a crisp white shirt with a mauve-edged collar, dress pants, and shiny black lace-up shoes, a getup that prevented him from participating in the practice hours later.

"Why soccer?" I asked.

"Soccer is loved by so many people," Jacob said. He shrugged as if the answer were obvious. Soccer is a powerful ally, a revered and intrinsic aspect of Tanzanian, and African, culture. Like religion, the game has a belief system, rules, and a moral code to which its legions of followers adhere. The players felt that if they could weave their message into the practice of this renowned sport, it was possible they might be heard.

FIFTEEN PLAYERS ARE ON THE FIELD TODAY; HALF ARE ABSENT BECAUSE they can't afford the bus fare or because they are in school. The players range from teenagers to men in their thirties. They are sinewy, fit, healthy soccer-playing boys with sun-related lesions on their heads, arms, and hands. A gangly boy, one of the youngest, steps eagerly toward me, stops inches from my face. His eyes are closed against the late-day sun; he cracks a wide-open smile. He tells me his name. I tell him mine. Neither one of us can pronounce or retain the jumble of sounds that we call our own and so we just laugh and hold hands. Then he runs back to rejoin the practice.

The boys razz each other, slapping one another on the back, laughing when players get splattered with mud. Their conversation carries through the drills and continues when the team divides in half to play a practice game. The younger players look to their seniors for instruction, and it's easy to see how this mentorship role might extend beyond the field.

They see each other almost every day of the year. They are like family. The camaraderie that builds among members of a group is layered here. Younger players see their older selves in the upper echelons of the team: they see men who are employed, engaged to be married, raising children, educated. They see smart and organized men who founded a team that garners international attention for its innovative approach to fighting discrimination. What they see is a version of their imaginable futures.

When journalist Steve Bloomfield interviewed war survivors who played on Liberia's amputee soccer team, some said the game saved their lives. The sense of belonging buoyed their tortured spirits. One player described it as a kind of psychological counseling. For men who'd lost limbs in the country's brutal civil wars, the physicality of the game opened a door they'd thought was permanently closed. The same is true for the members of Albino United. Before the team was founded there wasn't a single player with albinism on any of the leagues' eighty teams. Men like Jacob and Saidi introduced new ideas of who soccer players could be.

Being a part of the team fosters confidence, and feelings of belonging and self-worth, but playing for Albino United is like playing for any other soccer team: it's about the game. It's about the adrenaline on the pitch when facing down one's opponents, the competition, the goal scored, the battle waged, the losses balanced precariously against the wins.

"Last year we played in the fourth division," says Jacob. "There are only four divisions in Tanzania, and you have to work your way up to the premier league. There are about twenty teams in the fourth division, and we are expecting to remain there this year."

When Jacob says this I expect him to look forlorn, to shrug his shoulders in defeat or give a wry smile, but he doesn't. Albino United plays about fifteen matches per year, and encapsulated in each of these events are the dramas, hopes, dreams, and persistence of the team's collective lifetime. Winning the game is always possible, and it seems that knowing this is enough.

To the right of the field a group of young men has gathered under the drooped limbs of a baobab tree. I peg them as fans.

"Do you know the people under the tree, are they here to watch?" I ask Jacob.

"They are street people," Jacob says. "They are always here. They live under that tree."

"Do you have fans who come to watch your games?" I ask.

"We have a lot of supporters who come to see us," he tells me.

Albino United draws big crowds when it plays a match, but the stadiums aren't filled only with fans. There are skeptical hecklers who deny that the players have talent, jeering from the sidelines at the group of men who can't see much past twenty feet but nonetheless make up a professional soccer team.

"In 2010, we played in Mwanza, and there were more than two thousand people there watching us, and they came because of Albino United," Jacob says. "It was their first chance to see people with albinism playing football. They came there to see whether we could play. They didn't believe it, you see? But we played and we won that match."

This was a particularly significant victory, as the majority of the violence carried out against people with albinism in Tanzania happens in the lake region, the districts in and around the city of Mwanza that line Lake Victoria. If the team hopes to spread awareness, it's in this region that it's most badly needed.

Not everyone on the team has to have albinism, which was an important decision. "We cannot segregate ourselves," Jacob says. "We decided that people with albinism and black people should play together so that everyone can see that we are the same, and that there is no difference."

The team coach, Mohammed Mbarak, is one of the members without albinism. He circles the field on his bicycle calling out encouragement and following the back-and-forth movement of the players.

He wears a green-and-blue-striped golf shirt and jeans, and he's a little chubby. He carries himself with humility and emanates an air of kindness. Mohammed has been with the team for five years. When he's not on the pitch he works as a barber and also runs a restaurant. He takes a break from directing the players to introduce himself, and I ask him why he wanted to coach Albino United rather than any other team in the division.

"I started as a player and I liked working with these people, so I decided to coach the team," he says. "I love them," he adds without sentimentality, then picks up his bike and loops back to where the team is clustered in a knot around the ball.

The rains left vast sections of the field swampy wet. In some areas, the water is ankle deep, but the players splash through. Black cranes and white cattle egrets flap around the edges of the pitch, readjusting their positions when the game rolls into their turf.

"Look at all the water," I say to Andrew.

"Good mosquito habitat," he quips.

I look glumly down at my bare legs and see two mosquitos hovering around my ankles. Malaria. I think of the DEET spray I'd pragmatically packed in my luggage, and picture the little green bottle sitting unused on the bathroom counter in our hotel room. I imagine Mrs. Keen at the travel clinic back in Canada shaking her head. I can almost hear her exasperated sigh and see the whites of her eyes as she rolls them skyward.

Encircling the field is the golf course, and beyond that the downtown skyline. Dead ahead, unseen over the lip of a hill, lies the ocean. The huddle of men under the shade of the tree stands to our right. Behind us, brush, overgrowth, and greenery. There is constant foot traffic in this seemingly abandoned patch of the city. I lock eyes with a man who is wandering into the tangle of leaves and vines and notice that he is carrying a machete. Earlier I asked Jacob if he ever feels scared, and he said only in his native city, Mwanza, where attacks are frequent.

"Here in Dar es Salaam at least we can say that we are safe," he said.

I feel rattled by the man, despite Jacob's claim. My fear is shaped by stories that always include a stranger, bushes, a knife, and a pale target. Later at the hotel, I describe the machete-wielding man to Andrew, who hadn't noticed him because he'd been busy shooting photos of the team.

"I did see a lot of guys hauling coconuts out of the bush," he says.

I think of the hundreds of small coconut stands that line Dar's streets. I'd conjured a killer out of a fruit seller. What did he see when he looked at *me*?

Earlier that day, back at the hotel, I had showed Jacob and Saidi the small collection of photographs I brought from home. The pictures were dated, most taken a year ago. Sadie, one and a half, wearing a green dress and in her grandmother's arms in Georgetown, or squished into a chair with her cousins Gabby and Jordan. A family shot with my parents when she was six months. Sadie on the artist Mary Pratt's red chair at Christmastime in St. John's just before she turned one. Jacob looked with polite interest, but Saidi pored over each photograph. Holding the images close to his face, he scanned slowly and with purpose, as if he were searching for something in the background.

"Who is this?" he asked of the other people in the photos. He would nod and chew over the answer and then proceed to the next shot and ask again. He went through the pictures several times. When he finished, he looked up at me and Andrew.

"I have some questions I would like to ask you," he said.

"Of course, yes," I stumbled. "I've been doing all the asking, please, whatever you want to know."

"What was the perception in Canada when your child was born with albinism?"

Andrew and I looked at each other.

"The doctors didn't realize that she had albinism when she was born," Andrew told him. "We learned slowly, later."

"What was your reaction?" Saidi asked.

"At first we were sad and scared," I said. "Mostly because we knew nothing about it."

"We were worried about her," Andrew said. "But we aren't sad anymore. Now we know that our daughter is just like everybody else."

Saidi nodded, accepting our answers. It skimmed the surface though, and I think he could divine this from the photos. What was our reaction? What happened next? We had our DNA sequenced and we were coached through the process by experienced counselors; we made appointments with medical specialists, some of whom were totally unnecessary; we got our tiny daughter eyeglasses that cost $400; we attended a conference to learn more and meet with other parents and people with albinism; and we make adjustments all the time to ensure our daughter has everything she needs, and a lot of what she probably doesn't need.

Saidi. Sadie. A vowel of difference but a world apart.

"Now that you know us albinos in Tanzania, know about our challenges, what are you going to do?" he asked.

"We will tell people about you, about your challenges, about your success with Albino United," I said. I searched for something else to say but didn't want to offer what I couldn't deliver.

Saidi nodded, then said something unexpected: "Now you are the mother and father of all albinos."

THE SUN STARTS ITS DESCENT AND SIGNALS OUR DEPARTURE. JACOB gathers the players to a small hill on the edge of the field to say goodbye. We stand awkwardly and say a few words of thanks, which Jacob

translates into Swahili, and then we hand out our patriotic parapher-
nalia, which, in its dollar-store plasticity, looks garish and brightly out
of place in this urban wilderness: red-and-white Frisbees, lanyards,
and hacky sacks with the Canadian maple leaf plastered across them.
I give Jacob the soccer ball I'd deflated and carried in my backpack.
The boys clap. The coach stands and speaks emphatically to us: "Love
your daughter, and she will do anything she wants."

One of the players bicycles to the road and hails a taxi for us. The
car lurches over the pocked earth and comes to a stop by the street
people—who are mostly children and who watch silently as we wave,
then step inside and close the door.

Our taxi slinks along Ocean Road. The sun casts its magic-hour
light over the beach, where hundreds of boys play soccer in the sand. It
is a choreographed dance, miles long, the players in constant motion
as they weave and sway in pursuit of the ball, sometimes launching
it off their heads, knees, and chests. More graceful than aggressive,
more fluid than forceful, the game is a common language in which
men like Jacob and Saidi have discovered their voice.

CHAPTER 10

Mount Everest School

MOUNT EVEREST SCHOOL IS THREE STORIES TALL AND BUILT IN A U-shape around a sandy courtyard. The exterior outdoor hallway that joins the classrooms is swept to a shine, and the walls are freshly painted in a deep turquoise mimicking the color of the Indian Ocean, which lies about a mile away. Signs posted on trees read SPEAK ENGLISH!—English being the language of instruction, though most of the teachers and students speak Swahili. The sound of children practicing vowels in unison drifts out of an open classroom door. Little girls with buzz cuts and wearing matching yellow T-shirts and blue skirts walk hand in hand, stopping to stare and giggle when they see me and Andrew sitting on a bench outside the principal's office. Eight yellow, snub-nosed school buses are parked in the dusty lot adjacent to the main building. There is a soccer pitch down a gentle slope, and boys in shorts and maroon T-shirts are playing a match. Large trees provide shade between the field and the courtyard.

We are here to visit Adam and his older brother, Salum, who are both pupils at this school, and waiting for Omary Mfaume, Under the Same Sun's education liaison, to return from speaking with the principal. Omary is tall, and he wears a black-and-white-striped button-down shirt, jeans, sneakers, and a tan fisherman's cap to shade his face from the sun. He is in his early thirties and lives in Dar with his wife and young child. Like many of the nonprofit's employees, Omary has albinism. Squinty-eyed, with a wide smile, he'd greeted us affably at the UTSS office this morning before showing us to the waiting car.

We'd driven north, parallel to the ocean, sometimes inching forward in jigsaw traffic jams, sometimes racing along the inner lane, passing *dala dalas*, cattle, bikes, and slower-moving cars. For the entire forty minute ride into Dar's suburbs, there was a steady stream of people walking along the shoulder of the road. The roadside was a long succession of market stalls where people sell coconuts, mangoes, papayas, tomatoes, and nuts, as well as mosquito nets and phone cards. The logos of the country's mobile networks, Vodacom and Airtel, were splashed across the umbrellas that shade the sellers and their wares. When we were about halfway to the school, the driver pointed out a young woman with albinism. Her hair was braided and pulled back, her cheeks were a fiery red. Her eyes were closed despite the fact she was walking inches from oncoming traffic.

Omary returns with the principal. She is around forty years old and is a mixture of warm and stern. She seems like someone you'd want to obey and please.

"Yes, you will see Adam, but it will be a wait," she tells us after we shake hands.

We will wait for almost two hours, but I like that she isn't willing to pull Adam from class to suit our schedule.

We sit in the open-air foyer and chat with Omary. He tells us that we will be meeting with four boys today. I brought gifts for Adam and his brother; I hadn't known about the other two. I show Omary the bag with two sets of colored pencils, sketchbooks, and the Canadian flag pencils fitted with special gummy holders to help with Adam's grip.

A quiet moment on December 27, 2010, the morning after my daughter, Sadie, was born. Soon after this, nurses and other medical professionals came from across the hospital to see her. TONY URQUHART

The first photograph of Sadie wearing her glasses, taken on Christmas Eve 2011, two days before she turned one. ANDREW TRANT

Sadie and her new friend, Elizabeth, play together at the National Organization for Albinism and Hypopigmentation (NOAH) conference in St. Louis, July 2012. EMILY URQUHART

The Albino United soccer team practices in an empty lot in Dar es Salaam, May 2013. The majority of the members have albinism and low vision. ANDREW TRANT

Albino United player number 9 wore only one shoe on the day we visited the team. Despite lacking funds and supplies, the team practices six days a week. ANDREW TRANT

Omary, Adam, Kevin, Mwigulu, Salum, and Andrew on the day we visited Mount Everest School, outside Dar es Salaam, in May 2013. Both Adam and Mwigulu were recovering from attacks by poachers, having been targeted because they have albinism.
EMILY URQUHART

Handing out UV-proof hats to some of the girls at Mitindo Primary School in western Tanzania, May 2013. About ninety pupils with albinism attend classes here. ANDREW TRANT

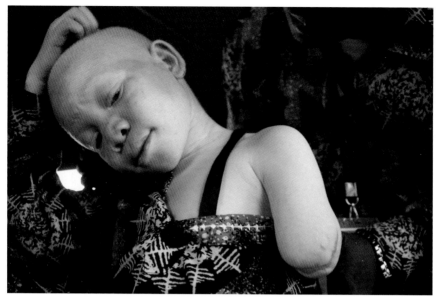

Mwigulu Matonange, photographed while attending a summer camp organized by Under the Same Sun in July 2013. Shortly after this experience he began to communicate again.
DON SAWATZKY/UNDER THE SAME SUN

My grandmother, Maryon Morse Urquhart, is the baby in white at the center of this photograph, taken in the backyard of the family business, Morse & Son Funeral Home, in Niagara Falls circa 1908. The other two children are her brothers. The adults are the children's nanny (far right), a neighbor (back row), and two unidentified women who appear to have white hair. When my father showed me this photo in August 2013, he had no solid information about these women but thought they could have had albinism.
GEORGE MORSE

Seeing this image for the first time in summer 2013, I was certain that the young woman on the far right had albinism. She is holding my great-uncle Ronnie; the other two children are my grandmother and her other brother, Wesley. The second adult is the children's nanny. What I didn't know then was how or if the young woman on the right was connected to my family. GEORGE MORSE

Family portrait taken in Victoria, BC, spring 2014. DEAN KALYAN

Sadie, at three, Easter 2014. EMILY URQUHART

Sadie and her dog, Owen, mugging for the camera in 2014. EMILY URQUHART

Arthur and Rosella Spencer of Niagara Falls, circa 1905. Four of their five daughters had albinism. COURTESY OF THE MORSE FAMILY

"That's okay, they will share," Omary says. "They love each other."

When the boys round the corner, they come as one unit—Salum is in the lead and Adam takes the rear. Two smaller boys—Mwigulu and Kevin—are packed tightly between them. Kevin is eleven years old, and although he has albinism, his skin is tanned and he has freckles. He eyes us curiously, and when he smiles he shows off two huge front teeth. Mwigulu, who is the youngest, hangs his head. He's downcast and won't meet our eyes. Quickly he shuffles toward Omary, who holds him in a protective embrace for the rest of our visit.

Salum is genial and warm, and happy to see us. Greeting us each in turn, he shakes our hands in the regular way and then again, wrapping his fingers around our wrists, then finally locking our fingers in his, like a secret handshake. He is sixteen and just slightly taller than me. Smiling, he stands inches from my face and holds my hands, his eyes closed against the glare of the sun.

We greet Adam next, shaking his newly formed hand. It looks red and is etched with scar tissue, but his wounds have healed. He is wearing his stylish DKNY glasses, and they are tinting from the UV exposure in the yard. He wears a rosary around his neck, the cross hidden under his T-shirt. In a ridiculous oversight, I ask him if it's a necklace.

"And how is your hand?" I ask.

"Working well," he says shyly in Swahili. "The surgery was a success."

Omary is distracted, examining a festering sore on Mwigulu's head, searching his cropped hair for new sun spots. It is a paternal and private moment, and I turn away feeling like I have intruded. Omary surveys the other boys.

"Why aren't you wearing your hats? Your long-sleeved shirts?" he asks. They grin and shrug.

"It's sports day," Salum tells him. "So we need to wear short pants and T-shirts to play."

He's right, I think. The kids would further stand out if made to wear special pants instead of the maroon T-shirts and blue shorts the rest of the boys wear. My mind flits forward in time to when I will hear this kind of argument from my daughter. I wonder if I will be as reasonable when it's her skin being exposed to the sun's rays.

"Still, you should wear your hats," Omary says. I notice that he's forgotten his own hat in the car.

In a Dar es Salaam–based study on a group of 350 people with albinism, researchers discovered that by age twenty, half of the participants had skin cancer. By age thirty, the number had jumped to 80 percent. "Most albinos in these areas who contract the disease die as a consequence," the authors write. Another unsettling discovery was that among the younger participants in the study, chronic skin damage was evident by their first year of life. When Omary implores the boys to wear hats, it's because he knows this simple act could possibly prolong their lives.

"Do you miss Canada?" I ask Adam.

He smiles goofily, as he did back in Vancouver, and nods.

"When did you arrive?" he asks quietly, this time in English.

"A few days ago. It was a long flight," I tell him. He nods and then suddenly looks hopeful.

"Is Peter Ash with you?"

"No, I'm sorry he's not," I say. "Do you miss Peter?"

"Yeah." He nods.

"I think Peter misses you too, Adam," I say, and he smiles shyly.

"How long have you been at your new school?" I ask the boys.

Omary translates and then answers for them.

He tells me that Salum, Kevin, and Adam have been here for at least four months—since Adam returned from Canada—but that this is Mwigulu's first month at the school. "He came here after his attack," Omary says.

"Attack?" I glance down at Mwigulu, noticing for the first time that his T-shirt sleeve is gaping open where his left arm should be.

"Yes, he is still in bandages," Omary says. "He was attacked twelve weeks ago, and his left arm was taken by poachers." He pauses. "He hasn't spoken since it happened."

My mouth tastes like tin. I swallow. I hadn't expected this. I look at Andrew and see that his eyes are watery. When I'd read the latest UTSS update on the many attacks that happened from January to February, I'd failed to retain the names of the victims. Mwigulu was the ten-year-old whose arm had been hacked off on his walk home from school. It happened only three months ago.

Mwigulu is the broken child I had expected to find when meeting Adam. But Adam had stepped gingerly forward by the time we met, which was a year after his attack. He was shy, but he smiled broadly and often. I don't think this is because the violence he suffered was any less traumatizing than that Mwigulu experienced, but because Adam had the benefit of time. His psyche, like his mangled hand, was in the first stages of healing. Mwigulu, it seems, is still in shock, living with a barbaric and tangible boogeyman. I am struck by the thought that perhaps he is afraid of me and Andrew, strange foreigners here to see him. He is just learning English, and he can't understand me when I bend to hold his remaining hand in mine and tell him, "I think you will enjoy being here at this school. It is beautiful and safe."

I hope to convey in my tone how sorry I am that this happened to him. He is ten but his mannerisms are more like my toddler's than that of a boy in grade four. I don't know if he will be happy here, or anywhere, under the weight of his suffering. But I hope so.

AFTER THE BOYS SAY GOODBYE AND HEAD BACK TO PLAY IN THE schoolyard, the principal returns. She tells Omary that an education official is visiting and that we must wait until he leaves to sign the guest book. We sit in the open-air foyer again and Omary tells us how he'd been to the school last Tuesday to pick up Mwigulu for DNA tests.

"They found a hand that might be his," he explains.

The test would rule out another missing person but, further, the hand might help to identify Mwigulu's attackers based on where and with whom it was discovered. Morbid images parade through my mind. A small white hand. Dried blood. Sealed in plastic. Discovered where? A fridge? A locked drawer in a backroom? I feel dizzy and reach for my water bottle but find it empty.

Unlike Adam, Mwigulu's parents were not involved in his attack. "They are supportive," Omary tells us. They supplied their son with everything he needed—pens, paper, clothing—and traveled the some 550 miles from their home in Rukwa Region to deliver him to this school outside Dar es Salaam. What they couldn't provide, were helpless to provide, heartbreakingly, was safety for their child. They almost lost him. To protect him, they had to let him go.

It is near impossible for me to imagine myself in Mwigulu's mother's position, how she'd lived with such trembling dread, the wide-awake nightly horror, the threat with sharp teeth and a machete that stalked her child, and that could, at any moment, materialize from the darkness. How a parent's ultimate fear—the harm that could come to your child—materialized for her, left her little boy bloody and maimed, nearly killed him. That it happened once means that it could happen again. With no certain means of protection, what else could she and her husband do but let their little boy go? I would send my daughter away too if it meant saving her life.

Mwigulu embodies the stories we read and heard about before traveling here. The raw brutality of his attack was still written on his body. It was so fresh, you could still see his fear. You could almost smell it. His trauma was deeply ingrained. We felt it just standing next to him. He was the saddest person I'd ever met and he was only ten years old.

I'd hoped to cast a cool eye, an academic's lens, a reporter's object-ive take on this issue. It was a preposterous notion. I am a mother and, beyond that, I am a human being. A host of cerebral explanations dissipates into muddy waters.

Tanzanians are not evil. It is humanity that is flawed. Bad people commit unthinkably heinous acts and we can call them poachers, or witch doctors, or henchmen, but "murderer" is the only label that truly fits.

I can only hope that Mwigulu follows the same trajectory as Adam and finds comfort and trust in bonds with adults like Omary and with his peers like Adam, Salum, and Kevin. I hope he plays soccer on the pitch at his school and learns to recite vowels with his classmates. I hope he stays out of the sun and wears his hat and eats well and that at night, when he lies down, he feels safe enough to fall asleep.

After an hour of waiting, we sign the guest book, then climb back into the taxi. The ten-foot-high gates that protect the school com-pound, segregating it from the greater world, open for us and close quickly in our dust trails. The landscape is empty and still, void of the chaos that lines the highway ahead. The dusty, cratered road is flanked by green hills and adobe mansions. The houses are in various stages of construction, but there are no workmen on their grounds and the buildings appear abandoned and ghostlike.

Back in the city, Omary takes us to an open-air restaurant that sells traditional dishes based around *ugali*, a scoop of cornmeal, and accented with vegetables and meat.

"You should order the local chicken," Omary tells us. "It is the nicest."

Looking at the multistory buildings and congested lanes of traffic that surround the restaurant, I wonder exactly how local the chicken is.

Omary shows us how to manipulate the cornmeal in our hands, then make an indent with our thumbs and scoop out the sauces, meat, and okra divided into sections on individual stainless-steel platters. Over lunch we talk about Omary's eyesight, and Omary tells us that he drives in the city but is nervous on the highways. Some researchers believe that people with OCA2 have better visual acuity than those with OCA1, like Sadie, though it's not likely Omary would meet the standards set by the motor vehicle associations of North America or, for that matter, Tanzania. I don't ask if he has a driver's license.

Later Andrew asks me what I would have done if Omary offered to drive to the school today.

"I don't know," I say. "I think I would have just got into the car."

"Me too," he says.

We part ways with Omary after lunch, thanking him for his guidance and time. On the way back to the hotel, our taxi winds into a metal knot of cars so thick we idle for twenty minutes until another driver, or maybe a good Samaritan from the roadside, directs the vehicles, inching them apart, slowly detangling the traffic and setting us free to jerk and grind our way homeward. Along the shorefront, we are stopped again and a rail-thin boy, tough as old leather, hisses "Fuck you" through the cracked-open window. Two of his peers dangle off the bumper of an overflowing city bus beside us, their knees grazing the fender of the cars that follow. They spy us in the back seat of the taxi, leer down at us. I turn away and tuck my bag under my feet, feeling foolish for being afraid of these children while at the same time wondering what gave them such sharp edges.

CHAPTER 11

Mwanza

STONE TOWN IS AN ANCIENT LABYRINTH OF NARROW STREETS CROWDED with loitering children and tiny souvenir shops, their wares spilling onto the sidewalk. Men on mopeds buzz by our heels like hornets. *"Jambo, mzungu!"* people call to us when we pass by. Everyone has something to offer on the island of Zanzibar, where we're spending a few nights to recuperate before continuing on to the northwest of the country.

We'd become immediately lost after leaving the hotel this afternoon, and with both our stomachs in knots, we're desperate to get back. We pass worn shoes collected in a pile at the door to a mosque. Circling back, we see the men spill out into the cramped street post-worship. They retrieve their footwear and gather around a shop with a television set showing an American war flick from the 1980s. Machine-gun fire bang-bangs its way through the alleys. We part the sea of viewers, twice, trying to find our way home. I'm holding a faded crumpled map in my hand, more a diving tool than reference material. We are both on the fringe of parasitic ravages, but I'm rounding the corner. Andrew's illness began early this morning in Dar es Salaam when we walked through the pre-sunrise darkness to the port to catch our ferry.

He'd winced and caved inward while we waited in line to board, and I'd nervously looked around for a bathroom. My gaze landed on a man with albinism, employed as a porter. His skin was scaled and raw from hours spent hefting luggage under the sun. At eight in the morning it was already scorching hot. *He won't live long*, I'd thought.

We find a stone path that spits us out by the ocean and we're able to follow the shoreline back to the hotel. Andrew lies down in a helpless sweat when we get to our room, and he's quickly asleep. The windows are open and a sweet chaotic noise draws me down from the balcony to the small strip of beach that fronts our hotel. About fifty boys frolic in various stages of swim. Grandstanding on the shoreline, older boys teach their younger peers how to backflip and walk on their hands. Boys in the water swim out to the incoming boats and help the fishermen throw down their anchors and remove their motors for the night. The sun sets behind them and the light turns orange. The boys become silhouettes, and it's like watching a shadow play.

Andrew joins me, roused from sleep by the noise. He points to the moon, now a sliver of light in the sky. It's the same fingernail moon I'd seen from the window of our home when waiting for the taxi on the morning we left. It's comforting. The moon, and the warm dusky air. The boys continue peacocking for their parents, who sit on the sandy beach, and for the beet-colored tourists lining the deck of the hotel, but mostly they are showing off for each other. It was a little more than twenty-four hours ago that we met Mwigulu, sorrowful and traumatized, hazel eyes downcast, with an open sore on his head and a phantom left arm. This beach feels like a different planet, rather than an island off the coast. The cacophony of shouts and splashy plays. The joy unbridled and raw. We stay by the water until the sun slips below the horizon and the boys dry off and head home.

The next day, we board the first of many flights on our way to the western city of Mwanza. The only airline employee on the plane is the pilot. It's like riding in a station wagon with wings. I am sitting two rows behind him, but if I leaned forward I could tap the pilot's shoulder. He is white with a Euro-African accent that is hard to place.

"Everyone ready?" he asks. His grin reminds me of boys I'd known but never trusted at university.

I fall into shaky conversation with my seatmate, a world-weary businessman in shorts. He is Dutch and recently moved from Japan to Dar es Salaam to set up a company.

"What is it like living in Dar?" I ask him.

"Chaotic," he answers.

He's trying to distract me with conversation. He'd noticed my white knuckles. In my twenties, I developed a gripping fear of flight. It dissipated over the years, helped by medication that I have since weaned myself from. Now my airborne terror is reserved for special occasions like this one. *Can I maintain this level of anxiety for twenty-five minutes?* I wonder as the propellers whir and the aircraft's needle nose points skyward. The belly drops into air pockets over the Indian Ocean. Once, then again. I look for my airsickness bag and find that the previous passenger has used it, crumpled it, and shoved it back into its hold. I think of our last will and testament sitting under the red button accordion I never learned to play. I briefly think of Sadie as an orphan, and then I don't anymore because I'm afraid the panic will overwhelm me and I'll stop breathing, which is what sometimes happened in the past. Buzzing the high-rises, we glide over Dar es Salaam. We're close enough to navigate the streets and shoreline. I see what I think is the field where Albino United practices. It's high noon. The players won't be there yet; likely it's just the coconut sellers trampling through the long grasses and the kids huddling in the shade of the baobab tree.

On the other side of the world, my mother picks up her grand-daughter from daycare and Serene, our childcare provider, gathers

Sadie's owl-faced lunch pail and yellow water bottle, her coat and her rubber boots. She hands them to my mother and tells her that Sadie's behavior is starting to change, she's being a little difficult. In her understated and quiet way, Serene says, "They've been gone a bit long, I think." Later that night, Sadie wakes and calls for us. "I need them," she tells my mother. "I need them," she says again, fat tears running down her cheeks.

Despite this, Sadie has had a mostly good time in our absence under the dotage of my parents and sister. There have been shopping trips, new stretchy yellow pants, walks down to the beach with the dog, and visits from our cousins, who brought her mounds of Play-Doh. They had dinner at Sadie's favorite pizzeria, where our waiter was surprised to see his top patron with a new crowd of guardians.

My dad has to return home early for his brother's funeral, a death I learn about through a late-night text message. My phone had buzzed sometime after 4 a.m. in Dar es Salaam. *Uncle David has died*, the message read. *We expected it but are very sad.*

Andrew's parents, Mary Lou and Don, arrive in the final week, relieving my mother, who is now completely void of energy. "Nana is very weak," Sadie will say thoughtfully and at random for months afterward. My in-laws bring renewed energy, charioting Sadie around town in her bike trailer, drawing in the sand at Gonzales Beach, and engaging in copious amounts of home baking.

What does Sadie think of this rotating cast of elders? My mother and sister jokingly develop a reality-television show in which Sadie gets to choose her own guardian through a process of elimination. She is the star; the eccentric adult relatives, the supporting cast. This is all pretty much true to life, though the caregivers eliminate themselves as first my father, then my sister, and then my mother leave, to be replaced by my in-laws, and soon, five days later, her own parents, who, I can only hope, will be the ones she chooses when all of this is over.

ON THE MORNING AFTER WE ARRIVE IN MWANZA, WE ARE IN A TAXI speeding so precariously down a highway that I'm remembering the tiny airplane with a kind of fond nostalgia. We're following the Misungwi district commissioner's white Land Rover, and our young taxi driver, whose entire day we managed to hijack, is trying not to lose sight of him. This means that we spend most of our time driving down the middle of the road between the right and left lanes of traffic. Through the windshield, I see cars and trucks coming straight at us. I force myself to focus on the roadside activity—bikes, cows, children, women in elaborate dresses, fruit stands. Beyond this are piles of ancient rocks, tall like church spires, formations unique to Mwanza Region. The sky is dotted with prehistoric-looking birds that have giant wingspans. We first encountered them over breakfast on the hotel terrace this morning. They lurked above, eyeing our eggs. Posted signage warned patrons to be vigilant—these were conniving fowl. They look like they'd been imagined by the nineteenth-century Spanish artist Francisco Goya. They are fantastical, like nothing I have seen in my life, so I have no other point of reference.

Alfred Kapole, our guide for the day, sits in the passenger seat. He's the chairperson for the Mwanza Region Tanzania Albinism Society. He's about fifty years old, wears a navy suit coat despite the heat and a broad-brimmed canvas hat. He is bemused or irritated or protective of us, his foreign charges. It's difficult to know because we aren't able to communicate. When I called him earlier in the morning to arrange to meet, I had to hand my cell phone to a baffled hotel clerk and plead with her to translate. When the call concluded, she laughed, shaking her head.

"He asked me to please be his translator for the day," she said. "He told me, 'I can't understand a single thing this woman is saying to me.'"

We have spent the last five hours with Kapole (which is how his colleagues refer to him) not communicating, at least not verbally.

We'd been at the Mwanza regional commissioner's office waiting to obtain permission to visit Mitindo Primary School, a rural government institution for blind and sighted children, about twenty-five miles away. It is often referred to as a sanctuary for orphaned children with albinism who have nowhere else to go. I was told that about ninety students with albinism lived there. It is primarily a day school, but in recent years, parents had been abandoning their pale-skinned children on its grounds. Two bags of donated UV-proof sunhats sit between me and Andrew, like a fourth passenger in the back seat of the taxi. I originally planned to give them to UTSS, but Vicky urged us to bring them with us to the school. "You'll want something to give to the kids," she said.

Officials are strict about strangers like us visiting Mitindo because of the media exposure in recent years. Reporters and photojournalists from North America and Europe have documented the lives of the children living there. Some of the images are beautiful, but the footage is occasionally grim: the kids look pleadingly into the camera, they aren't wearing shoes, they're often sunburnt. It's exactly these reports that fuel my interest in visiting. That, and the fact these children share a genetic condition with my child, as I explained to the Mwanza regional commissioner earlier in the afternoon, showing him photos of Sadie.

"She's the one in the specs?" he asked, pointing to a photo of Sadie and her two cousins sitting on an armchair in Georgetown.

"Yes."

"She is beautiful," he said, smiling broadly. He was a tall, imposing man in an impeccably tailored suit. He oozed power.

"These atrocities against people with albinism in our country are terrible and should be condemned," he said, shaking his head. "The court system is backed up, and the prosecution of the criminals who carried out this violence is slow."

He granted us permission to visit the school, but only with a chaperone—the Misungwi district commissioner, who was sitting in on the meeting.

WHEN WE TURN DOWN A DUSTY ROAD ABOUT AN HOUR INTO THE DRIVE, I think we must be at our destination. But then we turn down another dirt road, bumping across rutted earth and past chickens and piles of tomatoes, children, small concrete homes with corrugated tin roofs, then we turn again, and again, and each time I think we must be coming to the end of the road, as it looks less and less possible to drive a car down the path, but we keep going, turning, bumping, turning, bottom-dragging over the dry potholes, until we pull up to a set of tall blue gates.

The district commissioner leaps from his car, ready to blaze through this unexpected commitment at the end of his workday. We pass through the gates, and I see about seventy children seated at tables set up in the playground, facing a long, narrow table covered in a blue cloth. Behind it are six chairs.

First we're whisked to the principal's office, a small room off the playground. A map of the world hangs on the wall. The principal wears a white shirt tucked into gray pants. He is short and has longer hair than I'd seen on most Tanzanian men so far. He has a kind face, and looks a little tired around the eyes.

We sign a register, and the district commissioner pushes us onward.

"No wasting your time," he says. "You'll want to be back in Mwanza soon."

But we aren't in a hurry. I'm not sure if *he* wants to get home, or if he's uneasy with what we might see at the school, or if the principal has asked him to make it brief. As we walk toward the kids, Kapole asks us to write our names on a sheet of paper so that he can introduce us, and I realize we will be addressing the crowd.

It's when we're seated in front of the students that I really get a chance to see them. At least fifty kids with albinism are seated at the little desks. One small boy in the front row is about a year or two older than Sadie. The teenage boys directly in front of us make faces at Andrew.

Before we left Canada, a few people predicted we would return with an adopted Tanzanian child. This was always said in jest; in reality, international adoption isn't easily cinched. Andrew and I sometimes talked about this, but we'd never done any research. These conversations were hypothetical, and I know this. Still, when my eyes drift toward the little boy again, I can't stop myself: I imagine him sitting in the fourth chair at our kitchen table, the one that's empty for now, Sadie at his side. The image dissolves but the feeling, maternal, helpless, intangible, remains.

Kapole stands and begins speaking. I don't need to understand Swahili to know that he's educating the children about sun safety. He's pointing to his hat, and then he rolls up his sleeve and points to an open sore that creeps across his forearm like a vine.

When Andrew and I are introduced, we stand and smile, and I say a few words about where we came from, and about Sadie. "Our daughter is two," I say. "And, like many of you, she has albinism. So she needs to wear a hat in the sun, even in Canada, and we brought some hats like hers to share with you."

Then Andrew and I both say *"Asante,"* the only word either of us has managed to learn. The kids throw their heads back and laugh, which makes it pretty clear we haven't mastered our singular attempt at Swahili. They walk tentatively up to the desk, shyly taking the red hats, some trying them on, others embarrassed and holding them in their hands. I lean down and help secure a hat on a quiet little girl's head. She has eyes the color of wheat and a shy smile.

We take some group photos and then spend time meeting the teachers. We give them the school supplies I picked up back home—magnifying sheets and rulers, and about a hundred pencils.

"We need mosquito nets and classroom supplies," the principal tells us. "It would also be nice for the children to have a ball, something they can all share and play with."

As we're heading toward the blue gate on our way out, a young teenage girl catches up with us and tugs on Kapole's sleeve. She's both bold and shy, clear that she wants attention but not sure what to do with it when she succeeds. She is one of the many students with albinism. Kapole hugs her and she giggles happily. A teacher joins them.

"His niece," the teacher tells us in English.

We nod. There is much about this interwoven world we will never know. This is the tiniest slice, this snapshot of life in among orphans in rural West Tanzania. We blow through our visit in a cloud of dust, and quickly it will be as if we were never there. Except we—or at least people like us—come here often. Several independent photojournalists, as well as reporters from ABC and Agence France-Presse, have published stories on the school in recent years.

If the world knows about these children, I wonder, *why do they still need mosquito netting for their beds, and a ball to play with?*

It's the same issue Albino United faced with the press. It wants its story to be told and publicized, but what does it get in return for the scrutiny and the time its members donate? According to Jacob and Saidi, it is promised change, but none has materialized. The reporters are chasing the next story. It's not the journalists' responsibility to affect change so much as it is to share the story. They expose troubling practices. That's their job. Advocacy and awareness are not inevitable; rather, it's the occasional happy by-product of their work. Which is what Vicky recognized when her role shifted from reporter to activist. I still think it's important to tell stories and that they're worth telling. Because amid the dull complacency may be one shining light. Someone like Peter Ash, who has the power and resources to devote toward making a difference, might catch a news report on the television or in the paper. Without the international press, like Vicky's initial report with the BBC, the challenges people with albinism face might never have been brought to the table. Bearing witness is an important role, one that many risk their lives to do.

When we pull up to our hotel, the porter, whose name is Ali, is relieved to see us. He'd asked us not to go with Kapole and the taxi driver this morning.

"You can't communicate with them, how will you even know what is happening?" he asked. We assured him that we'd connected with Kapole through friends in Dar es Salaam and Canada, but we had to concede that he was right. We wouldn't know what was going on—and most of the time, we didn't. Despite the language barrier, by the end of the day, I had a great affection for both the young taxi driver and Kapole. It seemed they'd developed a kind of friendship too.

Kapole is sick with a chest cold, and after leaving Mitindo, he'd asked the driver to pull over at a small roadside pharmacy. He crossed the road to the opposite shoulder, then paused. He wasn't sure whether to recede or advance, or how he might step to safely cross the ditch. This is because he can't gauge how deep it is. It is dusk. I think of Sadie in the park near our house a few months ago. How she seized, suddenly wary of the three-inch drop from the cement sidewalk to the sandy playground. It was late afternoon in winter and slowly getting dark. There were no shadows to guide her, which is often how she calculates depth.

Our driver leapt out of the car. He ran across the road and took Kapole's arm to guide him to the pharmacy, staying with him while he purchased the medicine. Before Sadie was born, I wouldn't have understood Kapole's problem at the roadside, how his low vision was impeding his safe crossing. So few people in my world do understand albinism's visual impairment and how it can't be corrected with glasses. Here in Tanzania, where albinism is so prevalent, people are aware of these eyesight issues. Our driver would know exactly what the issue was and how to help, which he did without hesitation.

A guiding hand on an elbow is a small gesture, but there is something raw, instinctual, and intimate in this act. It didn't look degrading. Rather, it seemed the young driver was showing Kapole a level of respect, which, as the leader of an important organization and as a human being, he deserves. For a man like Kapole, who records and reports on atrocious crimes, whose personal safety is perilous, and whose health is fragile—made apparent by the sores on his skin—I wonder if this kind of interaction is a regular occurrence or mostly absent as he navigates through his days. It's a confusing paradox that in a country where albinism's genetic traits are common knowledge, the condition is so grossly misunderstood.

CHAPTER 12

Homecoming

CLIMBING OVER THE LIP OF THE NGORONGORO CRATER, OUT OF THE mist-settled valley in morning, skirting the cradle of mankind, we begin our long journey home. By noon we are crossing the Serengeti plain. I have known this landscape all my life. In image, in verse, on film, and in the small board books I read to my infant daughter. *Z* is always for zebra, which is almost always photographed roaming in these tall grasses. We left Mwanza three days ago to spend the final throes of our trip on safari. As a biologist, Andrew couldn't conceive of visiting Tanzania without seeing the plains. I'd been interested but was unprepared for the magisterial landscape and roaming beasts. It was like driving through a myth.

This is a bucket-list voyage. We trail the Jeep of a man with his aging father in tow, and over breakfast we see a middle-aged couple who are so overcome with joy their faces might split from the smiling of it all.

Jostling around in the back of a Land Rover on the unpaved roads, we occasionally stop to watch lions nuzzle in the shade of a sausage tree, their keen eyes trailing mixed herds of grazing zebra, giraffe, and impala. We listen to the steady thunder of the wildebeest migration that criss-crosses our path several times a day. We watch elephants bathing their young so close to us that we can hear the water splash. Through this, despite the hippos, flamingos, and wide-open jaws of the crocodiles pointed at the nose of our truck as we cross a flooded bridge; despite the beautiful heartbreak of the water buffalo having just given birth, wildly protecting her newborn from a pack of hyenas; despite the iridescent blue wings of the lilac-breasted roller; despite the orange-pink sun setting over the flat blue land, I am pining for my child. I know there is no sympathy for the sad mother on safari, but, in the final stage of this faraway journey, in the dust and under the wide skies, in the hush of the off-season lodges, I want to go home.

IT IS ALMOST DARK WHEN WE PULL INTO THE DRIVEWAY. IN THE FRONT window I see a flash of white. My baby. My little girl. Sadie, propped up by her grandmother, peering out the window at a dimmed but familiar landscape. She knows the white car and she knows our shapes, lumbering up the walk burdened by luggage. When we push open the door, the dog wags his tail hysterically and winds his way around our legs. Sadie stands to the side, trembling. It is almost two hours past her bedtime. She's wearing the fuchsia and purple party dress I'd bought her last spring. It is getting short at the cuffs, I notice. Her eyes wide, her mouth open, she begins to laugh quietly. At first it's barely audible, a soft *tick-tock* at the back of her throat, but it builds until she throws her head back and howls in a delighted but manic way. We bend to her and she touches our faces, saying, "Mommy, Daddy, Mommy, Daddy" between fits of laughter. In our arms, she vibrates, her little hands cupping our cheeks. I'd expected to find that she'd grown in my absence but she looks incredibly small.

Sadie's reaction to our homecoming is difficult to bear—there is a hum of relief in her happiness, as if she'd begun to wonder if we would ever come back. It's hard to immediately know my role here in the domestic space I'd left behind. It's a disorienting feeling, like looking at your life in a fun-house mirror. You know the contents, and the people, but it's hard to relate to this distorted image, to know where to step, or how to interact with it.

Our two backpacks loiter in the foyer, tilting into each other as if whispering secrets, suddenly foreign, useless, and also dangerous. What horrors lurk within their tucks and folds? I think of the cockroaches, about the size of field mice, scuttling along the corridor of the ship we'd slept in on our last night in Tanzania. It was a listing hulk of scrap metal called the *African Queen*, the former galley and bow redressed as hotel rooms, which were rife with insects and leaks, the windows on eye level with Mwanza's early morning fishermen gliding silently by in wooden kayaks. A bevy of armed teenage soldiers occupied the room next door. We'd woken to find tiny red bites circling our ankles like lace cuffs.

The five of us settle around our dining room table, and my mother-in-law ladles beef stew into the blue-glazed bowls we received as wedding gifts. Here in this stew is our home in the world. In the future, when homesick, I will yearn for this meal.

IN THE GREAT SWATH OF AIRSPACE BETWEEN EAST AFRICA AND THE Pacific Northwest coast of Canada, time stretched and compressed. In the floating hours, we talked. Arbitrary and sometimes important, it was a waking, sleeping, days-long conversation that covered the intricacies of our life before and our life to come. "Let's have another baby," I said to Andrew somewhere over the Middle East. "Is that what you want?" he asked. "I don't know what I want," I answered. We talked about ways that we might get soccer shoes to the Albino United players. "What if we mailed them, would they make it there?" I said. "Why not?" Andrew asked, but I was doubtful. We talked about how Saidi called us the parents of all albinos everywhere. "What can we do to live up to that?" I asked. "You can write about him and the other people we met," Andrew offered. This was true, I would write about them. It wasn't the same as Vicky Ntetema bringing the story to the world, exposing criminal practices within her native country, a place she knew and loved deeply. Maybe, however, I could be involved in the larger process of telling, and in this way I can play a part, however small.

When we arrived in Amsterdam, our bodies cramped and aching, I left Andrew to work on his laptop while I walked up and down the shiny corridors of Schiphol airport. I pored over the souvenir shops, read magazines and newspapers, drank coffee from a paper cup. Then I visited the Rijksmuseum satellite gallery, a boxlike space that hovers over the airport's endless rush. I moved from painting to painting, my bleary eyes surveying the work of the Dutch masters (Steen, Hals, and some of the lesser artists whose names didn't make it into my undergraduate art history courses). Below me, a man played a piece of music on the piano. He was a fellow passenger, not an entertainer. It was a public instrument, there for anyone to practice on. I recognized, in tune only, the music's European origins. Composer and title unknown but familiar to me, in some way, in its cultural composition. Something my father might listen to on the record player in his studio, or have played on the piano at night, under my childhood bedroom, filling my dreams with Beethoven, Bach, and Mozart. I felt close to home there in the gallery, despite the vast geography between me and my house and family.

I remembered how Adam yearned for home when he was in Vancouver last winter. I'd asked him if he was excited to go back to Tanzania and his eyes had flickered to life and he'd nodded emphatically. His desire was absolute. I wondered, back then, why he wanted to return to the scene of such a horrible crime. I couldn't separate the action from the place. But, of course, Adam could. I understand it better now. Where we come from is part of who we are. If we can, we will go home.

In the museum's tiny space, surrounded by images of pink-cheeked women from the seventeenth century, I thought about what pulled me to Tanzania. "I feel like these are my people," Peter Ash had told me when we first spoke a year before. "We have the same DNA." I understood what he meant, that he shares a genetic condition with people who are suffering great injustices, and through this connection he feels a responsibility to help. I also felt pulled toward the center of these crimes, to bear witness on some level, and to try to explain why they happened.

Cultural beliefs are powerful and difficult to change. Fear rules. Cruelty takes place in the absence of empathy. Humans do terrible things to each other. But acknowledging cultural beliefs doesn't excuse the crimes or make them any easier to comprehend. And this is maybe why our stories are so often gruesome, like the Grimm brothers' "Maiden without Hands" or the procedural crime dramas that dominate prime-time television. We read and watch and listen to these stories and ask, why are we so cruel, so flawed? In each telling we come closer to the answer.

I thought about how my former professor, Diane Goldstein, told me that in her scholarly practice she'd discovered a humane core at the center of the crimes she examined. She also conceded that sometimes divining that source is impossible; for some it will remain buried in the earth. I was upset, near tears, when we spoke, and she could hear this in my voice. She pointed out that as a mother I probably wouldn't be able to interpret witchcraft beliefs and practices that harmed children—in particular, children who shared a genetic condition with my daughter. She warned that I might be unable to tease apart my personal and academic selves. She was correct.

In all of the children I'd met over the past three weeks, regardless of age or gender, I'd seen my daughter. Every child's story represented my darkest, most exaggerated fears for her: the small children with sun lesions, the orphans, the maimed, and the murdered, how they were segregated, ostracized, taunted, and marginalized. How many of them were forced to live without a sense self-worth, without dignity, and in the absence of love.

And yet, as we drift away from Africa, I am not weighted with sadness. I'm surprised to feel uplifted, hopeful. It's the resilience that outshines the bleak tales. The buoyancy of a traumatized child; the strong, proud athletes of a soccer team that sporadically wins but always plays the game; the woman who saw injustice and, despite threats and challenges, walked right into the heart of fear and never looked back. These are the stories that come home with us. Stories about people whose lives, however briefly, touched ours and left a mark. Intersecting because of a quirk in the ladders of our collective DNA.

"We are breathing the particles of some of the earliest people on record," Andrew said on our last morning on safari. We were driving past the Great Rift Valley, where paleoanthropologists dated remains back 1.9 million years. The air was thick with dust. The grit seeped into our eyes, hair, and lungs. As humans we are linked through our makeup, which is complicated and complex, a million little parts, and in the end, there is just dust. We are connected by the air we breathe; the earth we walk on; the moon, fingernail or full, that hangs in our sky; and the sun, dangerous or fruitful, that lights our days.

LIFE SWIMS BACK INTO FOCUS. OUR SPRING GARDEN, WITH ITS ANKLE-high flat-leafed pea shoots. Sadie's trowel—blue-tipped with a wooden handle. Her red hoe. Andrew, smelling of freshly cut grass, one pant leg still rolled from riding his bike home from work. The dog, desperately earnest, unwalked and nosing my palm for attention. The padding of my feet walking from the fridge to the counter to the stove in a well-worn triangular path across the linoleum kitchen floor. The exasperating trail of crumpled pink socks that leads to Sadie's room, which is no longer a nursery but the place where a little girl lives.

It is there that in the dark hours, with the soft glow of her nightlight a permanent dusk, we rock. The chair, with its wobbly gait and loose slat, is where we reconnect night after night. Sadie curls into me, as she did when she was a baby, and we move rhythmically back and forth. Sometimes before bed, sometimes in early morning when she wakes and calls for me. Soon, maybe next week, maybe the week after, I need to discourage these nightly wakings. But for now, when she calls, I come.

THREE

BELONGING

CHAPTER 13

The Albino Farm

I'M SITTING AT A COURTYARD CAFÉ WITH BLACK WROUGHT-IRON BISTRO tables and chairs in Port Townsend, Washington. It's the first time I've left Vancouver Island since we returned from Africa two months ago. There is a slight breeze, and a late-day sun overhead. Wildflowers curl around the flagstones that spill out into a Wednesday-afternoon farmers' market, where I'd bought a bouquet of blue snapdragons and a half-quart of red-ripe strawberries.

I'm not far from home, just a ferry ride across the Salish Sea and a short drive along the base of the mountains that I see on my morning dog walks. I'll leave this sparkling sailboat town before night falls.

When we returned from our trip, we didn't immediately settle back into our life. Andrew had a job interview in Ontario, an intense fourteen-hour academic experience that included a professional lecture, continuous meetings, and a mock graduate-level class delivered to departmental professors. Then he left for a field season in the Great Bear Rainforest. I wrestled with Sadie's new behavioral problems, lingering effects of our temporary abandonment. Getting dressed was a monumental challenge that left us both sweating and emotionally drained. The answer to all of my questions was no. We worked through this while collecting rocks at the beach, eating the first tiny peas from our garden, and chasing the dog around the backyard, eventually finding our way back to normal.

What I couldn't quell was my nagging suspicion that we brought something troubling home with us from Tanzania. The bug bites on both of our ankles turned dark and seemed to multiply. I threw out our duvet. I washed and dried every pillow, blanket, and sheet in the house. Then, while Andrew was away, I called in an exterminator, whose indiscreet van pulled into my driveway for a few hours, then pulled out again and never returned.

"There is not a single trace of bed bugs in this house," the exterminator told me after an exhaustive search that included the folds in our backpacks and every corner of our bed and Sadie's crib.

The paranoia settled but the dreams persisted. As when I was in my twenties, I was once again feverishly traveling in my sleep. I was wading through airport corridors and train cars and unknown crowds. The sense of urgency and movement felt much the same, but the quest had changed shape. In the recent foreign dreamscapes, my role was as chaperone, sometimes with a child and sometimes searching for one I'd lost. My dreams had matured in tandem with my life. Now I am a mother in my waking and sleeping moments.

Today, however, I travel alone. From where I'm sitting in the café, I can see the back of the man who is singing and playing guitar. I can hear the melody but I'm too far away to make out the words. A young woman with auburn hair and a red backpack is his only audience. She is faithful or enthralled, and she was sitting there half an hour ago when I walked by. I noticed her because she turned to look at my dress as I passed. It's orange with a splash of green vines, and her gaze wandered up the pattern from hem to neck. We'd briefly locked eyes. *She has Down syndrome*, I thought. Then I wondered, *Is this every person's first thought when they see this young woman? What do they think about next, how do they react, and is it predictable? How does she feel, and what does she think about when encountering people in the world?*

My thoughts were prompted by a conversation I had with poet Erin Belieu that afternoon. We'd met at the Fort Worden State Park, a few miles from here, where she runs an annual writers' conference. We sat in the park restaurant, eating grilled cheese sandwiches with ketchup and talking about poetry and the perception of disability.

Erin has shoulder-length, sandy-blond hair and stylish boxy glasses that caught the window's glare. She wore a pink scarf wrapped around her neck. She had a straightforward manner and greeted me as if we'd been in the middle of a conversation, though we'd only just met. Her familiarity was comforting, and the conference attendees—writers at varying stages of their careers—periodically interrupted our meal with whispers of thanks, or to squeeze her shoulder, or to ask for more of her time.

I'd stumbled across one of Erin's earliest published poems, "Legend of the Albino Farm," while researching albinism references in folklore. Reading it for the first time, it had felt familiar.

Legend of the Albino Farm
Omaha, Nebraska

They do not sleep nights
but stand between

rows of glowing corn and
cabbages grown on acres past

the edge of the city.
Surrendered flags,

their nightgowns furl and
unfurl around their legs.

Only women could be this
white. Like mules,

they are sterile
and it appears that

their mouths are always
open. Because they are thin

as weeds, the albinos
look hungry. If you drive out

to the farm, tree branches will
point the way. No map will show

where, no phone is listed.
It will seem that the moon, plump

above their shoulders, is constant,
orange as harvest all year

long. We say, when a mother
gives birth to an albino girl,

she feigns sleep after
labor while an Asian

man steals in, spirits
the pale baby away.

A series of images formed in my mind as I read and reread the stanzas: a moonlit field; a woman with long white hair tills the dark earth; she wears a nightgown. After reading it twice, a phrase sifted to the top of my memory pile:

"Mostly they had her working in the fields at night during rainstorms."

In a flash, black-and-white and choppy like a silent-movie reel, I see her: the albino aunt. The witch forced to work the fields in darkness under rainfall. Blanket wearer by day, earth tiller by night. The arresting story doled out by an acquaintance at an afternoon party. The woman who lamented my genetic luck with a slow shake of her head. Then I remembered how another friend had intervened and challenged her facts.

"I've never heard that story," he said.

"She was a great-aunt," she retorted huffily.

She was my cousin's cousin; it happened to a kid at my high school; she lived in the town next to mine. Folklorists call these recollections FOAF tales because they are told as something that happened to a "friend of a friend." It establishes authority but removes the teller from the immediate event. Reactionary and hurt, I'd relayed the story countless times since, but in every retelling I missed this obvious clue. If this exchange had appeared in a literary narrative, I'd have recognized it immediately. Which is why it took the bold imagery of Erin's poem to show me that the woman's absurd social blunder was a retelling of a contemporary legend. Like most storytellers, she'd tweaked the geography and characters to suit her personal landscape and lend authority to the tale. And, like most people who share these tales, she probably believed the story or some aspect of it.

This woman was accustomed to being at the center of party chatter. When a white-haired infant was introduced at the event, the attention was focused, intense, and hard to penetrate. She bumped up against the narrative and then found a way in, a connecting thread, a way to reroute the audience back to her world, her life, her great-aunt. She was trying to belong, and this is something everybody wants.

After reading the poem, I emailed Bill Ellis, the contemporary legend scholar I'd spoken with about albino colonies, to ask for his opinion. He stressed that he needed to know the characters to make a "cogent interpretation" but agreed that the woman's comments were likely without malice.

"It seems to me that she was thinking, 'Some people would be utterly freaked out by a child who was albino and think that such a human would be utterly other. But I'm part of a family that had a member who shared this condition. Yes, she was handicapped by it, and this marginalized her, and other people's reaction ("she must be a witch!") further excluded her. But ... *she* was *my great-aunt* ... so albinism is not so deviant that it affects only one family in a million. It affected mine, after all.'"

The Albino Farm legend appears across the United States. It inspired a 2009 B-grade horror film, and crops up across the Internet on websites like Underground Ozarks and Weird NJ. The details change with locations, but usually the setting is an abandoned rural property and the albinos are the characters occupying the space. Sometimes they are dangerous and sometimes they are victims, like in my acquaintance's "great-aunt" tale where the protagonist was forced into labor at night and hidden under a blanket in daylight. They are often depicted as ghosts, people who haunt a landscape that wronged them. It isn't unlike the beliefs I learned about in Tanzania, where people with albinism are called zero-zero, meaning spirit, and seen as immortal souls.

I was curious to know what inspired the Albino Farm poem, so when I discovered that Erin ran a writers' conference just across the water from where I live, I contacted her and asked if she'd meet with me. Over lunch I told her how her work had helped me reframe an otherwise negative experience.

"It was while reading your poem that I realized this person was using the details of a contemporary legend—the aunt, the farm—to connect herself to my situation, that she had absorbed it and, like all contemporary legends, had made it her own," I said.

"She said it happened to her? Someone she knew?" Erin asked. "Interesting how she really wanted to take ownership of something legendry, which I guess is a very human need."

I agreed and told her about how Bill had interpreted it in a similar way. I asked how she came across the legend in the first place and why it had inspired her.

"My memory is that one of the reasons I wanted to write the poem was that the details of the legend were always really fuzzy and changed depending on who you were talking to, but none of the stories were consistent and none of them made sense. The shape of something was already there, but it was never complete, so I figured I could write the complete legend of it as a poem."

Erin wrote this poem about two decades ago and says it marked a turning point in her career; it was in this work that she became a poet. There was a deepness about it that felt intimate and personal. She related to the protagonists in the legend, she said, feeling an outcast in her small town for several reasons. She had a severe learning disability, and she also spent a year of her childhood in a wheelchair.

"So my awareness of difference might have been a little more attuned than some people's," she said. "And I'm also a poet—or I was a budding poet then—and I think that you look at a legend like that and you have to think about how it's predicated entirely on something absurd, which is just a pigment difference. So I was fascinated by the cruelty of it as well."

"It's interesting that you were conscious of albinism as a condition rather than a legend or something magical," I said. "It seems you were relating to the subject of these kinds of legends, which are often about groups of people with some kind of medical difference." I listed off a few of the other farm or colony legends I'd encountered about people with dwarfism or encephalitis or mental health issues.

"One of the things my poetry, throughout my life, has been interested in is the underdog, and power relations," Erin said. "My teacher when I was in graduate school was Robert Pinsky, and he talks about how poets have their animating obsessions, their monomanias, which are the questions they keep coming back to over time. Usually a poet has one or two things, a lifetime puzzle that they are trying to put together, and I think that for me has been kind of the central theme of how I write. So I guess it doesn't surprise me that would be the subject of my first really finished poem. Because if you look at all of my work over time—not that you should do this—it keeps coming back to this idea of difference and power relations and exclusions."

Near the end of our meal, I told Erin that, in addition to recognizing the legend, I also saw myself in her poem. "As the mother of a child with albinism I saw myself in a flash at the end," I said. "I have never seen myself in any literary form. I've seen some depictions of albinism, but I've never seen it from the parent's perspective. And then I thought, *Oh, that's me, I'm the person who gave birth to the pale baby girl.*"

Erin nods thoughtfully, then says, "I take that as a compliment. I'm glad the poem communicates in that way."

READING THE POEM HELPED ME TO THINK CRITICALLY ABOUT MY acquaintance's behavior, and by extension, my own. I'd exaggerated aspects of her personality and physique in retelling the story, when in reality she was fairly ordinary. Examining her actions through a scholarly lens allowed me a level of objectivity that hadn't previously been available. It made her comments interesting, rooted in meaning, and humanized her impulse to share and connect. It defused the situation, which was fleeting, but reoccurred vividly every time I shared or remembered the story.

Writers will often use a character's difference as a lens through which to see the truth in humanity. They explore how people negotiate life with an aesthetic difference or physical handicap, and how they are treated or perceived by others. Like Judah, the pale protagonist in Michael Crummey's *Galore*. Crummey said he used the character as a canvas on which the villagers could project their fears and desires. How people treated Judah reflected their greater nature. In this work, and in others, human differences are used as a cultural barometer. I can see how, in some ways, this degrades the person with the disability being portrayed: he or she becomes less a human character and more a plot device. But this doesn't have to be the case. It's the character's differences that make him or her relatable. The challenges are more pronounced than those of the general masses, but they act as a metaphor, an exaggeration of what it is we all feel when we're plowing through our days. Because to some extent everyone feels dissimilar from the rest of the population, alone, on the fringe, and we're all trying to find a way in, a way to belong.

What path to take is a constant puzzle. Like the poets with their animating obsessions, I'm searching for clues to my own mystery, querying why my daughter's life looks the way it does. The answers arrive in scraps of science and stories, in seeking new geographies and consulting the wise and experienced. This has illuminated patches, but I believe that the answers to who we are and why we exist lie within our family, a concept distilled early in childhood. ("It's a family swim," Sadie tells me one Saturday morning. "That means that you have to come to the pool with me and Daddy.") For a bigger picture, we query our antecedents, the people who came before (like the albino great-aunt), and reaching farther back, we question the historical, antique, sepia-toned people who live stoically in our frames, (un)smiling down from where they hang on the wall. The ancestors. Our stories, I would soon learn, begin with them.

CHAPTER 14

"*Before We Begin*"

In August 2013, Sadie and I visit my parents at their cottage on Lake Ontario. On our first morning, Sadie sits with my mom, collecting beach rocks into plastic cups. It's a familiar scene, one that might have been plucked from my own childhood. I'd also known the smooth turn of those stones in my palm, the sounds of the lake, and, like Sadie, my playmates were mostly adults. They were my much older half-siblings, my parents and grandparents, or my parents' unconventional visiting friends. Reaching school age, I discovered that my background was unusual. Back then, I sometimes found it taxing to explain the intricacies of my blended family, but I knew our story well, both our recent past and our ancestral history. I knew exactly where I came from.

Family tales can be a protective armor. Researchers working out of the Emory Center for Myth and Ritual in American Life found that children who were well versed in family history had higher self-esteem and better coping mechanisms than those with less knowledge of family lore. Specifically, the researchers asked questions pertaining to stories that the children couldn't know firsthand, ones about previous generations that had to have been passed on. These ancestral tales helped anchor the children in time, gave their life relevance and meaning on a temporal scale. The stories didn't need to be happy ones, or even true, but they needed to be told.

This is where Andrew would step in and point out the difference between causation and correlation. The knowledge of family stories didn't cause the children to be resilient; instead, it's the process involved in sharing the tales that yielded positive results. Storytelling occurs when there is an audience, as at a meal, a family event, or before bed. A family that gathers often has heightened communication, and this contributes to the psychological health of the people within its fold. The study inspired me to brush up on my family tales and learn more about Andrew's ancestry so that when Sadie begins questioning where she came from—and she might, more than other children, tussle with this question—I can pull from a polished repertoire.

So alongside our summer clothes and Sadie's sunhats and stuffed animals, I packed my digital recorder and a list of questions to ask my parents and in-laws over the holiday. I planned to learn more about Sadie's ancestors and how they lived. Details such as how my grandparents met, and the name of Andrew's grandfather who was shot in the arm during World War II. I also craved the deeper narratives within our DNA and felt these interviews might provide a few seeds from which I could grow a larger story. Knowing as much as we could about our family lineages might ameliorate some of the wonder about where my daughter's unique features came from.

I interview my parents on the second night of our visit. We are sitting at the long wooden farm table inside the screened-in porch. It's dusk, the lake is turning pink and gray. A few scattered dishes remain from the dinner we'd eaten that night—late harvest corn, green beans, and salmon. Sadie is upstairs sleeping in what had once been my bedroom. Andrew is at a conference in Minneapolis and won't arrive for another few days. It's just the three of us, as it had been for most of my childhood and teen years. Earlier that evening, I told my parents about my plan to record family stories. "I'd like to do it tonight," I said. Although they protested—"Can't we do it another time?"—I was firm. Our schedule is tight. We'll be gone by the end of the week.

When we are settled, our wineglasses refilled, candles lit against the falling dark, my father clears his throat and leans forward.

"Before we begin, we have something to tell you."

"What?" I ask.

"We think we know where the albinism gene came from," he says.

"This has never been corroborated," my mother adds. "But we do have evidence."

"We have pictures in an album—it's very old, from the early twentieth century and even earlier, the late nineteenth century—and there are pictures of my mom, your Grandma Urquhart, and she's just a baby, and in them are two women, maybe in their late teens, nice-looking girls, who definitely have albinism," my dad explains. "We looked for the pictures when your mother remembered something your grandma told her."

Here is what my mother thinks she remembers: her mother-in-law telling her about an extended family portrait taken in front of the Horseshoe Falls, early in the last century, and saying that there were "albinos in the photo." This conversation probably took place in the late 1970s when my parents were visiting my grandparents at their home in Niagara Falls. My grandmother, Maryon Morse Urquhart, was a soft-spoken woman whose small round hats matched her neatly tailored suits. She respected and revered the past, so determined to pass on family stories that for years after her death we discovered notes she had left us in the drawers of inherited furniture. In her neat cursive, she told us the details of the ancestor who made the item, and where it had sat in the family manor, the residence attached to the

Morse & Son Funeral Home in Niagara Falls. In her sophisticated, understated manner, she'd tell my mother some of the most gruesome tales associated with the family undertaking business. My mother, a writer, was an eager audience. She wrote some of these stories down, including them in her first novel, *The Whirlpool*, but she invented characters and fictionalized the details and locales. When the memory of the conversation with my grandmother surfaced, she worried that she might have invented that too.

She remembered this exchange in January 2011 when I'd sat in Sadie's nursery and cried over the phone. "They think there might be something wrong," I'd said, and somewhere, in the long hallway of my mother's memory, my grandmother opened a door.

My mother brought it up with my father, but he didn't know about the photo and didn't remember any relatives with albinism. He called his only sibling, David, but my uncle was unable to help. He was gripped by Parkinson's disease, which had induced early dementia. If the knowledge existed, it was locked in his frozen mind. His wife, Donna, who is also from Niagara Falls and had known the Morse family since her teen years, had never heard of the purported group portrait or the white-haired members posed within it.

Finally, my mother searched the weathered and careworn albums my father inherited after his parents died. She didn't find a family portrait taken by the falls. What she discovered were a series of snapshots from the early 1900s. The setting was the backyard at Morse & Son Funeral Home, the family business and residence. The first couple of photos depicted four adult women and a trio of children under the age of three. The youngest child is my paternal grandmother. The older two are her brothers. Two of the four adult women have snow-white hair and wear glasses. One of these two women appears in a third photograph, probably taken about a year before. Her hair is white. She wears glasses.

But is her hair white? In this black-and-white photograph, grainy, cracked, and worn with time, it was difficult to tell. When my mom showed the photograph to my dad, he was struck by a sudden memory of a great-aunt and her daughter, and how both women had white hair. It was a fleeting image, not anchored in time beyond the perimeters of his childhood.

When my parents weren't able to verify their memories or identify the women in the photos, they put the album away and stopped asking questions. It was a theory that ran on fumes and it had been exhausted. They decided not to tell me about the pictures. Maybe some time in the future, they reasoned, when things calmed down. Which, it seems, is tonight.

"Why don't you know who the people are?" I ask my dad.

"My grandpa died in 1937, when I was three, so I didn't know him. I have no idea whether his sister, my great-aunt Rosie, was a carrier, but I suspect that she was and that so was my grandfather. Because if it was from his side of the family, it would have to go through him, to my mother, to me," my dad says.

"To you, to Sadie," adds my mother.

"You see?" my dad asks.

I nod silently but my mind swims in circles. I understand the pattern of Mendelian inheritance and the intricacies of recessive genetic traits; what I can't grasp is why my parents kept the photos from me for so long.

"So you found the pictures two years ago?" I ask. "Why not tell me then?"

"I didn't feel it was a good thing to do if we didn't know for sure who these women were and if they had albinism or not," my mom says. "For a while we thought, well, unless we know, unless we have absolute iron-clad proof, why even bring it up?"

"But how come you know now?"

"We don't." She sighs. "But now you're doing this research, so I think it's time you know."

I go searching for scrap paper to draw out a family tree and find an invitation to one of my father's past art shows. The print on the cover is an ink, watercolor, and collage work from 1989. The title is "Five Trees." It is a craggy and bulbous four-tree arbor, with one little shrub growing in the middle. In the background, the hint of a stone wall, and beyond that, radiant beams of light. On the blank side, I draw six generations down, with Sadie being number seven, and I star the possible carriers the way I'd seen our genetic counselor do when sketching our family tree. The twinned trees, one in my father's hand, the other in mine, is a relic of this night. It will belong to Sadie one day. I return to it often in the coming months, marveling at how much information is there, but also at how much is missing.

Up at the house the next morning, my mother shows me the album. It is bound in black leather, wrinkled like a palm, and worn to a rusted red around its edges. The pages are tied together with black string and the word "Photographs" is embossed on the cover in gold script. The pages often come loose, so that you need to lie it on a flat surface and lift them one by one.

Sadie peers over the lip of the table as my mother and I go through the album.

"What are you looking at?" she asks us.

"We're looking for some pictures," I tell her.

"And they're hard to find," my mother says as she gingerly lifts the pages and scans the faded faces within them. They are mostly snapshots, with few formal poses.

"Okay, here's one," my mom says and hands over a page with four photographs fastened onto a black background.

The image in the top right-hand corner shows my grandmother, who is about two years old, sitting in the arms of a woman with white hair and glasses. My great-uncle Ronnie sits in the arms of another woman with white hair and glasses. The children's matronly Irish nanny and a neighbor named Rhea MacPherson, who is holding the oldest brother, Wesley, are also in the photograph. In a second shot of the same grouping, the adults are laughing. One white-haired woman's face is obscured by her elaborate floral hat, but the other hunches forward, giggling in the awkward and carefree manner of a young teenager. My grandmother was born on October 23, 1907, and judging by her age and the season, the photo was likely taken in the spring or fall of 1909.

The final photograph is an earlier shot, maybe taken in 1908, as my grandmother is still an infant and her brothers are toddlers. The Irish nanny is in the center, and to her right there is a young woman in a dark dress with white polka dots that gathers at the neck in a high lace collar. Her white hair is tied back with an enormous satin bow. She holds my great-uncle in her arms. She is seated in direct sunlight, and because her unpigmented hair is the same value as the sky, the camera cannot define where her head stops and the atmosphere begins. She wears glasses and her eyes are closed against the glare of the sun. With a magnifying glass, I can see her white eyelashes and eyebrows. She looks like the teenagers at the NOAH conference. She looks like my daughter.

Sadie leaves with my mom to rustle about the garden and pick flowers while I study each image more carefully. There are several pages of photographs, all taken on the same day. Although I'd never seen the pictures featuring the two white-haired women, I was intimately familiar with another image from this roll of film. In it the three tiny siblings stand in a row. The boys wear rounded hats that look like blackened halos. My grandmother is cherubic, dressed all in white. In her shy downward smile I see a hint of Sadie, her great-granddaughter, whom she would never know. I knew this picture because it hung on the wall beside my childhood bed.

For all the years that I slept there and woke staring at that photograph, until I left home at age seventeen, the two white-haired women—Were they sisters? Mother and daughter?—were always there. They were just a few paces outside the picture's square corners. Had they gazed on as the children were photographed? Did they call words of encouragement and try to make the small siblings smile for the camera? Now when I imagine the walls of my childhood room, I can almost see their shadowy images standing outside the wooden frame, hidden amid the pink floral pattern of the wallpaper.

FOR THE NEXT THREE DAYS OF OUR VACATION AT THE COTTAGE, SADIE and I are alone with my dad. He and I spend much of the time talking about the past while engaging in various forms of play with Sadie— kicking a ball across the lawn's soft grass, collecting rocks from the beach. One quiet hour, Sadie hovers inches from my dad's hands, watching him sketch. My dad is seventy-nine, older than Sadie's three other grandparents by fifteen years. I sometimes worried she wouldn't know him, know the paint-splattered lab coat he wore when working in his studio, the classical music blaring from the ancient record player in the corner. Worried because his world was also mine. I grew up in the corners of his studios, an area cleared for me to paint and draw, the deafening piano concertos filling the space between us.

Over these summer days, ghosts swim into my father's memory and whisper hints. We are sitting on a pair of lawn chairs while Sadie splashes in a wading pool in the shade, when he says, simply, "Spencer."

I look at him. "Spencer who?"

"No, the surname Spencer rings a bell."

Sadie hoists herself over the pool's edge, emptying half the water onto the grass. She's wearing a pink and orange full-body bathing suit that covers her from the cuff of her ankles down to her wrists and up to her neck. Her face is shaded by a waterproof wide-brimmed purple hat that she's worn all summer. I watch distractedly as she tears across the lawn.

"Whose last name is Spencer?" I ask my dad.

"Aunt Rosie's, maybe."

I tap these messages, straight from the mind's graveyard, into my smartphone, which frequently loses service by the lake. Eventually, a snippet of information drifts to the top of my search results:

012418-92 (Welland) Arthur A. SPENCER, 37, electrician, Stamford Twp, Niagara Falls Village, s/o Benjamin & Edna SPENCER, married Rosella MORSE, 22, Niagara Falls Village, same, d/o Marsena & Mary Ann MORSE, witn - Albert E. COOK of Niagara Falls & Emma DOUGLAS of Niagara Falls Village, 31 December 1891 at Niagara Falls Village.

What I find are details from a marriage license, housed on a genealogy website. It is a site designed to pique your interest, lure you with tips and hints of your ancestors until you are so beguiled by the past that you will pay a monthly fee just to access it over and over again. I pay the fee. I access it over and over again. I begin to check the site more often than Facebook, even though the people whose images and information I scan are all dead.

THAT NIGHT, I SIT ON THE FRONT PORCH WAITING FOR ANDREW TO arrive from the airport, reading the paper and periodically scanning the treed drive for his approaching headlights. It's near midnight when he pulls in, wired from travel, emptying crumpled boarding passes and receipts from his pockets onto the kitchen table. I guide him into the living room so we can sit down. He's describing his lunch—a Southern fried chicken sandwich from a Minneapolis food truck.

"It came with Parmesan truffle fries," he says, sinking into the couch cushions. "Doesn't that sound amazing?" He pulls out his iPhone to show me a photo and I have to interrupt.

"I have a photo to show *you*," I say and hand him the disintegrating album. While he looks at the photographs, I describe the night on the cottage porch with my parents and fill in the gaps with what I've learned since. I tell him that Rosella and Arthur Spencer were my dad's great-aunt and great-uncle, and that over the past two days I'd learned they had five daughters—Ora, Beulah, Edna, Alma, and Inez—all born between 1893 and 1901.

"So who are the women in these photos?" Andrew asks.

"Because of my grandma's age, we know the photos are taken around 1908. So she could be the oldest sister, Ora, or the next sister, Beulah," I say, pointing to the photograph of the woman seated in the grass. "They would have been teenagers at the time, and the other three sisters were still kids."

"Are the women in the other photos sisters?"

"I think they might be mother and daughter," I say, recounting my dad's memory of a parent and child with matching white hair. "I think it might be Rosella and her oldest daughter, Ora."

"How old is the mother?" he asks.

"She would have been thirty-eight in this picture," I say, holding the group shot under a magnifying glass. I turn to face Andrew. "Whatever their relation is to each other, or to me, I feel certain—as certain as your dad was when he saw Sadie's baby photos—that these women have albinism."

Andrew studies the images for a beat. I wait, anxious to hear his conclusion.

"I feel the same way," he says.

When I show the pictures to my older sister Robin the next night, she agrees that the women share Sadie's condition but is unsure of my mother–daughter theory.

"I think the woman you see as the mother looks younger than the daughter," she says, looking at the scanned images on my laptop screen.

Andrew, Sadie, and I are at Robin's house because she'd hosted a family party that night that included all of my siblings and my first cousins on my father's side, and their children.

My brother Aidan's children are close in age to Sadie and now she trailed after them with wild enthusiasm. She turned away from me when I occasionally approached to slow her down, or refit her hat, or insist she wear her life jacket in the pool. "No, Mommy, no," she'd say, pushing her hands out to stop my advances. She piled onto a hammock with her cousins, and Andrew pushed them so far they almost tipped forward onto the concrete. He did this a few times, catching the kids just before their heads connected with the cement patio. They loved it, of course. They were a thicket of intertwined limbs, an irrepressible hydra with its many heads shrieking. I stood on the deck, fifteen feet above them, with my sister-in-law Wendy, and we alternated between taking photos of the kids and calling warnings ("Too high!" Don't bonk heads!"). I thought of the black-and-white snapshots taken a hundred years ago: my grandmother, her brothers, and people who I think are her first cousins or possibly an aunt. Did they see each other often, or were those pictures taken on special occasions, like this one?

This family gathering was a rare arrangement outside of weddings and funerals, and was prompted in part by our visit to Ontario. At one point during the evening, my father suggested that I tell everyone about the photographs, but I declined. I hadn't seen my cousins in a decade, maybe since my older brother Marsh died eleven years ago. I couldn't tell them they might be carriers for a genetic condition. Albinism is simply a part of my life now, but there was a time when it had scared me. Besides, I had names but no way of linking them to the photographs. I wasn't much further than my parents had been, back in the weeks after Sadie's birth. Back when they felt the story wasn't worth telling because they didn't know the facts.

The next night, we are in Georgetown with Mary Lou and Don. Before we head to sleep, I tell them the story of the mysterious photographs and show them the scanned images on my computer. My in-laws are interested but unconvinced.

"It could be white, but it could also be blond hair," Mary Lou says. "It's hard to tell in these old black-and-white photos."

She hands the images to Don, and he looks at them for a long time. I am reminded of when he'd examined the first photographs of his granddaughter, how he'd shifted from grandparent to physician, unable to separate the two roles.

"It's conceivable," he says. Nothing more. I wonder if he's doubtful.

I am also uncertain, but for a different reason. I'm convinced that the two women in the photos have albinism, but I'm not sure I can successfully identify them. They lived a hundred years ago. The characters who populated their long-ago black-and-white world are now bones in the earth. To find them, I will need to dig.

CHAPTER 15

Family Folklore

"TELL ME A NIAGARA FALLS STORY, DAD."

"Which one? The one about the woman in the barrel, or the one about the tightrope walker?"

"The woman in the barrel with her cat, and then the tightrope walker."

This conversation was a nightly ritual in my childhood, the daredevils familiar like distant relatives. My dad told the stories as if he were standing on the bank of the river watching them unfold, as if he were holding his breath with the rest of the crowd when Blondin, the French acrobat, cooked and then ate an omelet while suspended on his tightrope wire 160 feet over the watery border between Canada and the United States. I'd almost believed that my father had been one of the men who helped Annie Taylor and her cat out of the barrel after they survived the 167-foot drop over the Horseshoe Falls. He'd described the trickle of blood that ran down her face as if he were the only one to notice.

A hint of gruesomeness, a struggle, an extraordinary feat, and an animal companion—the hallmarks of Western folktales existed in my father's hometown repertoire. His was a storied world, the peculiarities of which were further rooted in my imagination by family trips to visit my grandparents, until the late 1980s, when they died within a year of each other. There was the Niagara Falls Museum, where the dual-headed animals looked at me with glassy complacency from their display cases, the stitches ringing their necks visible through their worn and dusty coats. I remember drinking Shirley Temples in the revolving restaurant at the top of the Skylon Tower, my father's early career paintings—a series depicting historical Niagara events—lining the circular wall opposite the windows from which the diners hoped to glimpse the falls at least once over the course of their meal. The paintings were removed during a renovation in 2009, but the restaurant continues its slow turn today.

My dad grew up in the residence that adjoined the family business, a funeral home started in the early 1800s by my ancestral grandfather Austin Morse. Austin was a skilled cabinetmaker from upstate New York who immigrated to Canada in his early twenties. His talent in the art of casket-making extended naturally to burial services, and in 1826 he founded one of the country's first funeral homes, Morse & Son. My grandparents were the final Morse connection, selling the business in 1971 when they retired, ending a family enterprise that spanned 145 years.

Bodies arrived at my father's childhood home a few days a week. Most were Niagara Falls citizens who died ordinary deaths, but occasionally corpses of bloated daredevils and suicide victims were fished out of the water downstream from the falls and delivered to the back door. As a teen my uncle David saw the remains of a showman who tried—and failed—to shoot the falls without a barrel. His body was found a week later. "Not much left of him," my uncle told my dad. "Not much left at all."

My father's daredevil tales were part truth and part fiction. He had not stood on the riverbank watching Annie emerge from her barrel, and there's no record of her cat accompanying her over the falls. Nor did he witness the Frenchman's high-wire picnic. Both events happened around the turn of the nineteenth century. They were part of his mental anthology, a collection of family and published tales retold as his own, so vivid that all these years later I can still conjure Blondin's tightrope and how it swayed when one of the bracing wires was cut by a bookie who bet against him.

THE NOVELIST AND ESSAYIST THOMAS KING WRITES THAT "ONCE A story is told, it cannot be called back. Once told, it is loose in the world." I think what King is saying is that after you tell a story, you no longer own it or have any power over what form it might take. The story is a seed and it can germinate. As a folklorist, I know that tales are migratory and, like plants and human cells, they mutate across space and through time. They adapt. They persist, like weeds, through the cracks of generations. Once you tell your story, you relinquish all control.

Maybe this is why my parents kept the photo album locked away in the sideboard for two years and silenced their fleeting reconstructed memories. When I had asked them what took so long, they said they didn't want to share a story that wasn't rooted in fact. But this is unusual in my family. The story and its telling have always held precedent; truth is an afterthought.

The sole parenting guidebook on albinism warns against seeking a genetic culprit or pinning the blame on a particular side of the family because grandparents can experience guilt knowing that they passed on a mutated gene. The recently unearthed photos suggested culpability. They could prove, or at least strongly indicate, that my father was the carrier. ("Your father has strong genes," my mother says every time another great-grandchild is born with my father's nose on his or her face, or blinking out at the world through replicas of his pale blue eyes.)

I don't think it was guilt that kept my parents silent over the past two and a half years. Although in some ways it felt like a betrayal, I don't think their decision was rooted in deception. I believe it was a protective measure. Back in January 2011, my father-in-law had waited for Andrew to come to him before he shared his concerns about our daughter. He wanted his son to be ready. My parents were acting on the same principle.

I've made a career out of information recovery, in journalism and, more recently, in folklore. I spent the last six years of my life digging through archives and uncoiling aged microfilms; trampling the long grasses of historic graveyards; sitting in overheated kitchens across rural Newfoundland with my recorder running moments after knocking on the front door and introducing myself to the people who lived there. After my daughter was born, I turned to the stacks at the library and medical school and sought out the information housed in digital archives, and in academic and popular literature. It wasn't long before this inspired physical journeys—to St. Louis, to Tanzania. There was nowhere I wouldn't go to find the answers to my questions. My parents knew the photographs would light a fire I couldn't easily put out.

I think they were also afraid of what I might discover. I share this fear. If I dig, will I unearth lives of sorrow, destitution, or careers in the sideshow circuit? Although the group shots suggests otherwise, I worry that the white-haired women might have been ostracized by the family because of their difference—which might explain why my father didn't know anything about them. I knew two versions of the small city where these women lived. In one, there were staid gatherings at the Niagara Falls Club, polite company, white linen, cherry-wood furniture, and old-backed couches in the parlor. The second incarnation, the city's shadow, is peopled with exhibitionists and supernatural tales. The daredevils, characters of folly, a hint of desperation in their acts. The believe-it-or-not showcases of human feats and oddities. This shadow is where my dread germinates. Even a small, seemingly innocuous detail about the women, like spinsterhood, could be devastating because of what it might suggest. All of the information carries such weight, relating as it does, to my child.

ON LABOR DAY EVENING, THE SUMMER SLOWLY SLIDING INTO FALL, Sadie helps me spread a cotton cloth across the grass underneath one of the two apple trees in our backyard. When we've smoothed the creases of the picnic blanket, the dog lumbers over and collapses in the middle, and Sadie follows. They lie there intertwined, the dog, snout to sky, sniffing the aroma of the sausages Andrew is grilling on back-deck barbecue, and Sadie, her eyes closed against the sun, her arm snug around the dog's neck. She's wearing her favorite shirt, purple with a red-ruffled heart sewn across the front, the neck misshapen from endless washing, the long sleeves growing short at the cuffs.

I've come to love our 1950s' rental with its magical fenced-in yard. Moving away from Victoria now seems a distant and unlikely possibility, though Andrew's work contract is up in less than two years. Relocation looms on the horizon, but for now we're happy here.

After dinner I give Sadie her bath, filled with bubbles and a menagerie of plastic floating toys, and put her to bed. Then I retreat to the downstairs office, as I've done almost every night since we returned from Ontario, to study the family tree I pinned to the wall beside my desk. It is messy in its arrangement. There are late-stage additions and many corrections. It's amateurish, a genealogist's nightmare, but through it I can trace a genetic pathway that begins in the 1800s with the cabinetmaker-turned-undertaker Austin Morse, and his wife, Mira Cook, and ends with the birth of my child 210 years later. There are two important branches. The first is my own direct line, and the second is that of my great-great-aunt Rosella and great-great-uncle Arthur Spencer and their five daughters.

In an effort to find out more about them, I begin to send emails to strangers on the genealogy site whose uploaded trees include these ancestors. My messages have a whiff of desperation about them—too many exclamation marks, a bit earnest—and at first I hear nothing back.

Then a woman named Ruth Ruller in Brisbane, Australia, married to Arthur and Rosella's great-grandson, sends me an email that changes the focus of my search. "I heard that you were interested in the albinism factor in the Spencer family," she writes. "One of my sister-in-laws mentioned to me some time ago that there were four albino sisters."

She tells me that her mother-in-law, Marjorie Ruller, who lives in Niagara Falls, could tell me more. The women in the photographs are either Marjorie's aunts, or possibly her aunt and her grandmother. Marjorie is ninety years old, but Ruth assures me that her mother-in-law has an excellent memory, recalling facts from her childhood and married life with the precision of someone half her age. "She doesn't write because she has bad arthritis in her hands and arms," Ruth says. "But if you live near and want to visit her, I am sure you would find it worthwhile."

"FOUR KIDS WITH ALBINISM IN ONE FAMILY IS STATISTICALLY UNLIKELY," Andrew says when I tell him about the rumor I heard from Ruth.

"I know, but there must be some truth in it," I say. "Maybe the number got exaggerated over time."

Currently, two families tie for most siblings with albinism according to *Guinness World Records*: the Gaulin family in Quebec and the Sesler family in the United States. They each have four children with this condition. In the case of the Canadian siblings, their mother is a carrier and their father has albinism, meaning that there is a one-in-two chance with every pregnancy that the child will express this genetic disorder. For my great-great aunt and uncle (as it is for me and Andrew), there was a one-in-four chance that each baby would be born with albinism. If my relatives really did have four children with albinism, they are on par with today's world record-bearers. They would be an extraordinary example of genetic anomaly.

Marjorie is the one person who can prove or dispel the "four sisters" rumor, who can illuminate the lives of these long-gone ancestors. I want to meet her, not over the phone but in person. So when my PhD oral defense is set for late September in St. John's, I see an opportunity.

"I could go to Niagara Falls," I say to Andrew. "I could stop in Toronto on my way home and drive down for a night."

"You should go," he says.

"*We* should go," I say, though I know this isn't financially possible.

"Ask your dad to go with you," Andrew says.

I CALL DURING THE DAY WHEN I KNOW MY DAD WILL BE IN HIS STUDIO. When he picks up the phone, I can hear piano music playing in the background. I tell him about Marjorie, and how I want to visit her in late September. I ask if he'll come.

"Sure, Em," he says. "I'd love to."

I am my mother's only child and my father's fifth. The product of his second life. My closest sibling is almost a decade my senior, and so my childhood and teen years were mostly spent in a three-part unit with my parents. My dad was in his forties when I was born. He'd lived an entire life before I showed up. Then he lived another with me in it.

My dad was my first traveling companion. Together we saw London and Paris and too many French graveyards for me to remember. (He likes to draw the deteriorating tombs and finds inspiration in the dark caverns of open graves but claims this has nothing to do with being reared in a funeral home). It's been years since we've traveled together, probably since before I met Andrew.

Over the phone we hash out a few quick details before the conversation turns to daredevils. They'd been on my mind as I'd pored over the black-and-white images of Niagara Falls from the late nineteenth and early twentieth centuries—when most of his stories took place.

"Dad, do you remember the Niagara Falls stories you used to tell me before bed?"

"I remember your brother Aidan used to ask me to tell him Niagara Falls stories."

"But I did too," I protest.

"Oh?" my father asks, unconvinced.

"Yes, like the one about Blondin's picnic on the tightrope wire, and the one about Annie Taylor, the lady who went over the falls with her cat," I say, trying to prove my link to the remembered ritual.

"Oh yes, that's right," my dad says. Then he tells me a story I'd forgotten. It's a family tale. It was one of my favorites as a child because it centered on a little girl (my great-grandmother, Mayme Morse) in peril. There was an element of danger, and the possibility of death, which is exactly the kind of story that appeals to children.

When she was young, Mayme's parents sent her across the bridge that spanned the Canada–U.S. border to buy a loaf of bread. The bridge was being repaired and some of the slats were missing. There were gaps large enough for a small body to slip through and fall into the churning gorge more than 160 feet below. Riding her tricycle, she made it across easily and somehow without knowledge of the dangerous gaping holes. On her way back, a construction worker saw her coming and rushed to greet her. "You can't pass this way," he said, but Mayme was adamant. "I live on the other side, so I have to get back." The man picked her and the tricycle up in a kind of firefighter's carry and gave her one instruction: "Don't look down." But she couldn't help herself. As they stepped over a missing slat, she looked directly down to the black waters below, and at that moment released her grasp on the bread. The image of the loaf twirling down through space, getting smaller and smaller and then disappearing into the water with barely a ripple, stayed with my great-grandmother all her life. She told my father this story often because she could, because although the bread was lost forever, she'd made it across the bridge.

CHAPTER 16

Daycare

THERE WAS A FRIGHTENING ACADEMIC HAZING RITUAL TO PREPARE FOR, there was a return to my ancestral landscape to organize, there were plane tickets and hotel rooms to book, but none of these issues was more pressing than choosing the right daycare. It was getting hard to ignore the age difference between Sadie and her tiny peers at the childcare facility where she spent a few days a week. There had been a turnover of kids in the past year and now Sadie stands a head taller than the rest. She has been speaking in sentences for eight months while her little pals babbled and squawked back at her.

"Why does it matter if she's older?" my sister-in-law Tam asked when she was visiting in the fall. The truth is that I'm not sure it does, but the grandparents and the parenting experts believe she needs more stimulation, and so now I'm peddling my child to a series of local daycares and preschools.

Sadie's first sitter, Leslie, was a hardscrabble woman from beyond the overpass that divided the city of St. John's from the rest of Newfoundland. I needed eleven hours of childcare a week to cover my teaching schedule. Leslie worked for a friend in the Folklore Department, and when she stopped by, I described albinism and what adaptations might be made when caring for Sadie, who was eight months old at the time. When I finished my spiel—the first spiel I'd ever given—she said, "I know a youngster who has a feeding tube." I didn't feel she was trying to tell me that it could be worse. Instead, she was saying that life is complicated and filled with challenges, and so what?

I hired her on the spot. Next came Melissa, a pillar of organization during the whirling chaos of our house sale and in advance of our cross-country move. We discovered Serene about a month after we arrived in Victoria. True to her name, she can command a toddler-filled room without raising her voice above a whisper. She's run her five-child daycare from the ground floor of her house for two decades. We adore Serene and the calm atmosphere she carries with her. Looking elsewhere feels disloyal.

The first preschool I visit is run out of a low-lying church a few blocks from our house. The owner doesn't flinch when I describe some of Sadie's needs. "We like to say we'll take anyone," she says with a shrug and there is an echo of the hardscrabble Newfoundlander in this woman, which makes me hopeful. I visit a second daycare, also run out of a church, to compare. The owner shakes her head when I describe Sadie's vision. "I don't know," she says. "It's just that we have to be able to look after all the kids." She is also concerned about sunblock. "Maybe you put it on in the morning," she says. I explain that it needs to be reapplied every two hours.

"Mm-hmm," she says distractedly. "Maybe what you should do is ask for government funding so that I can employ a third caregiver."

We sit at a child-sized round table while we speak. The lights are dimmed and small children are in various stages of sleep, lying on mats spread out across the nursery floor. A three-year-old with a bowl cut sits on a miniature chair to my left, woefully awake, a stuffy nose keeping her from slumbering with the others. What separates this little girl from my daughter, I wonder. It is difficult for me to tease out their differences. Sadie is my first and my only child. I can't say if caring for her is limiting or burdensome compared with caring for other children her age. Sadie is adept and capable, often reminding me if I forget to apply her sunscreen or pointing out that she needs a hat. She shoulders some of the weight, but she does need careful attention: she should be positioned close to the storyteller reading the book, she will need help identifying a caregiver from a distance, her glasses need cleaning often, and she should always wear a hat when outside. This awareness flows naturally for me. For others, it needs to be learned.

I thank the daycare owner and tell her I will think it over. She hands me some literature about the center that we both know is destined for my recycling bin. I turn and wave at the stuffy-nosed little girl and she gives me a halfhearted salute. I push open the heavy front door and step outside, knowing that I will never go back.

I register Sadie for a part-time spot in the first daycare I visited. She'll start in the new year, when she is three years old. During my tour I'd seen a NO BULLYING sign on the door and had attempted a feeble joke about it with the owner.

"No, it happens," she said. "Three and four years old, that's when it starts."

I'm worried that Sadie, with her white hair and pink glasses, will be a target. When we're with her, we never focus on her albinism. She doesn't see herself as different from other children, and I don't want her to start feeling this way. I can't control what her playground peers might say to her or what she might overhear parents saying to each other while dropping off or picking up their kids.

It is getting harder to talk about albinism in front of Sadie, and that becomes increasingly clear during a low-vision clinic Andrew, Sadie, and I participate in over two days in late September. She sees a psychologist, a neurologist, an ophthalmologist, a speech therapist, and two occupational therapists. There are a battery of tests, two skipped naps, a few tears. Sadie, in her striped leggings and kitty-cat shirt, her hair cut in a cute bob because she refuses elastics and barrettes, barely meets the age requirements of these exams.

When the three of us meet with all the experts as a group, Andrew takes Sadie to the waiting room for a few minutes while I ask that they not emphasize Sadie's low vision. She knows that she sees an eye doctor and wears glasses, but she doesn't know words like "blind" or "low vision" or even "albinism" as far as we know. A few of these experts adhere to our request during the individual meetings but others blow right through using all the words we've been avoiding. For her part, Sadie doesn't seem to notice.

I vacillate between defending and rejecting the idea of disability. I don't want people to downplay my daughter's vision challenges, as if hovering near the legally blind mark with her glasses on isn't difficult, or suggesting to her that she might be able to see if she tried harder. She can't. What she can do is use technology like an iPad, magnifying devices, and a monocular to help her see distances, or to bring the world closer to her. She can hold a book inches from her face to make out the details of a picture or the subtle difference between the letter *p* and the letter *b*.

My dad is visiting during the time that we attend the low-vision clinic and after we describe the various tests to him, he mentions that quite a lot of sight is cognitive. He taught studio art for his entire career—spanning two universities and forty-five years. He pointed out that when it comes to sight, a lot of it needs to be learned. Students didn't arrive in his courses with the ability to reproduce perspective on the page. They needed to understand that objects in the distance appear smaller, and that on the canvas these objects need to decrease incrementally as they recede into the background in order for the viewer's brain to organize and make sense of what is depicted. The rules of perspective aren't necessary to create works of art, but you need to know them to subvert and manipulate them successfully.

I'd never considered that sight is partly learned. This is why people who are visually impaired can manipulate their world. They too need to understand perspective and distance to calculate the time it takes to cross a street or get from room to room within their house or shake someone's hand.

On the second day of the clinic, Sadie and Andrew head home early and I stay to discuss her results with the gathered experts. Eight professionals are in the room when I enter and take a seat. It feels bizarre having these people gathered here to discuss my two-year-old daughter. While I'd observed the various tests and felt she performed well, I was suddenly nervous. I hoped I wouldn't cry or become defensive. As each person steps forward to recount their experience with Sadie, it becomes clear that I didn't need to worry. In the tests administered by the psychologist, she scores in the very superior range for verbal ability, memory retention, and most surprisingly, visual-spatial recognition based on her age, meaning that this is where she falls among her regular-sighted peers. The results from our near painful hour with the über-patient speech pathologist are the same—Sadie's abilities rank in the ninetieth to one hundredth percentile. This trend continues with every expert's report.

"In summary, she's doing awesome," the psychologist says near the end of our meeting.

"Well, of course, we think so," I say, swallowing away the lump in my throat. "I just had no idea what to expect two and three-quarter years ago when she was born. It's too bad I couldn't have sat in on this meeting, seen into the future back then, but it's nice to be here now."

When the official reports from the clinic arrive in the mail, Andrew scans them and emails the document to both sets of grandparents. My parents hang it on their fridge and jokingly refer to it as "Sadie's first report card."

Sadie is developing at a speed I hadn't anticipated, and we have not kept pace. We need to talk freely about albinism in our house and in our daily life before it starts to look and smell like a secret. Parents tend to hold information back from their children for fear that what they say might alter or hurt them. It's a lifelong dance. I watched my in-laws struggle with the burden and subsequent release of know-ledge, and then witnessed my parents loosen their grasp on a secret they'd kept for over two years. Should my in-laws or my parents have acted earlier, or held onto their information any longer? I don't think so. Ultimately, those decisions were up to them. I am only in charge of one story, one life.

We decide to make a book to give to Sadie when she is three years old. In drawings, photographs, and words we will chronicle her life so far. It will include albinism but it won't be about it because that's not what defines her. I've looked into children's literature on disability and I understand these are educational devices, but sometimes I won-der why we can't have a story where the protagonist's difference is part of the background rather than the foreground. It is a part of who they are and shouldn't be ignored, but surely we don't need to focus on just one aspect of a child's multifaceted life.

With this in mind, Andrew and I gather on the couch after Sadie is in bed and draft a prototype. There are artistic differences. We are both stubborn about word choices, like the difference between describing Sadie's hair as white or white-blond. I prefer the Luddite method of drawing, whereas Andrew sketches on the iPad. At one point our argument gets so heated I think we will need to abandon the project. But slowly, we form a narrative. The dog plays a major role, as does the red tricycle. One page features the local pizzeria we bike to on weekends, where the server with the tattoos gives Sadie crayons and sometimes a gratis gelato. Somewhere in the middle we mention albinism, describing it in simple terms, but then, as in life, the story moves on.

CHAPTER 17

Legend

MARJORIE'S VOICE, UNWRINKLED BY TIME, CRACKLES LIKE A FIRE across the telephone line when we speak to arrange our visit. We sort out our interconnected pedigrees and she says that as a child she'd known about my father and his brother—her second cousins—but that "the families weren't all that close." She speaks with the casual precision of someone half her age and promises to dig up some family history before my father and I arrive. In the weeks that follow, I also unearth some family lore. It's hard to tell if what I find is fact or fantasy, and eventually I consult an expert to help tease it apart.

While researching my paternal family tree, I traced my lineage back to our earliest-known North American ancestors. I followed their paths through time and space, dipping slightly south into New York State and then heading slowly eastward, through Connecticut and Rhode Island until coming to rest in a place called Rehoboth, Massachusetts, which is where two sets of couples, my distant ancestors, settled after arriving from Britain in the mid-1600s.

The state of Massachusetts is 190 miles long and 50 miles wide. The first North American immigrants pitched up on its shores in the *Mayflower* in 1620, and my ancestors followed aboard a ship called the *Bevis* eighteen years later. When I looked at a map, I noticed that Rehoboth is less than twenty miles from Lakeville and Freetown, the communities where the purported albino colony members resided from the eighteenth to twentieth centuries.

I began to wonder if the people featured in those early news accounts I read, and who still appear in legend form today, might be connected to my ancestors. Could we all carry the same gene mutation? The surnames attached to reported colony members, Reynolds and Pittsley (which sometimes appeared as Pixley, Pigsley, or Hoggsley), didn't show up among my direct ancestors. However, tree branches meander and split. My family timeline and geographic location overlapped with theirs. Robert Pigsley, for example, was born in Dighton in 1690, and my ancestor Priscilla Carpenter was born in 1680 in Rehoboth, about five miles away.

The genetic link and shared landscape hint at the possibility that our two family lines crossed at some point, but I can't say for certain without tracking down descendants and drawing their blood. This is impractical at best and illegal at worst. What I know is that the family at the heart of the colony stories did exist. I'd cross-referenced their names and dates with census and cemetery records. Although I doubt their numbers soared anywhere near two hundred, as was reported, it is plausible that they had a high rate of albinism within their family, and this might have appeared for several generations.

Legends can sometimes reveal surprising truths. In a 2011 article published in the *New England Journal of Medicine*, researchers linked the mythological giants of Northern Ireland to a high rate of gigantism among people living in County Tyrone today and dating back to the sixth century. The best-known tale centers on a benevolent giant named Finn mac Cumhaill, who constructed a bridge of hexagonal stepping stones, known today as the Giant's Causeway, to reach Scotland and defeat an enemy giant, or, in a different variant of the legend, to reach a love interest on a nearby island. The scientific explanation is that the basalt columns are the result of volcanic activity, but along the Northern Irish coastline, at least since the third century, it is the giants whose stories prevail.

The study, led by endocrinologist Dr. Márta Korbonits, based out of Barts and the London School of Medicine and Dentistry, compared the DNA of people in County Tyrone currently living with gigantism and the 250-year-old skeleton of Charles Byrne, a self-exhibiting giant measuring nearly eight feet tall, who was born in the same region. Not only did Byrne and the five present-day families share the same gene mutation responsible for gigantism, they all descended from a common ancestor who had lived about fifteen hundred years ago. The genetic window could stretch back almost four thousand years, to a time long ago and far away, a time when perhaps giants roamed the rocky northern shoreline of the island.

"We think that this area has a higher percentage of positive samples than anywhere else in the world," Dr. Korbonits told me when we spoke on the telephone. "So we very much believe that the folklore surrounding this region was based on something which is now scientifically and medically proven to be true." She cites similar studies on gigantism that have been conducted in the north of Finland and on one of the Pacific Islands, and tells me that all three regions share a mythology peopled with giants.

Gigantism is caused by a tumor in the pituitary glands that causes an excess release of growth hormones. If identified in early childhood or puberty, the tumor can be surgically removed or the patient can be prescribed medication to stop the secretion. Both procedures can arrest the rapid height development and the child will become a regular-sized adult. Without medical intervention, people with gigantism typically die before middle age. For Charles Byrne, and for his ancient ancestors, these treatments weren't an option.

I asked Dr. Korbonits why she accepted mythology into her scientific practice. She's originally from Hungary and learned about the Northern Irish giant legends while treating her patients. She felt that connecting the stories to her research was a natural conclusion. "I come from a country where folklore is important," she said.

The Massachusetts albino colony has never been studied by scientists but not for lack of trying. Charles Davenport, an eminent biologist who founded the Eugenics Record Office at Cold Spring Harbor in 1910, heard rumors of the purported tribe and implored one of his sources, a sideshow performer with albinism named Rob Roy, to find out more.

"Did you speak to me of a colony of Albinos in Massachusetts?" he asked in an undated letter to Roy. "If you know anything about such a colony, I should be glad to learn where it is located."

Davenport published the first Mendelian study of albinism in *Science* in 1908, and he expanded on it in the *American Naturalist* in 1910, based in part on his work with the Roy family. There is no mention of the Massachusetts albino colony in these landmark papers or in his other published studies on albinism, so it's unknown if he was able to track them down. It was possible that Roy's knowledge of the tribe came from reading the same syndicated newspaper articles I'd come across a century later. He was literate, as his return letters to Davenport can attest. In these messages he is courteous and obliging, giving Davenport permission to use his name, and his wife's and son's names, alongside their images in scientific journal articles and medical texts.

Across Roy's letters, in slanted scrawl, Davenport wrote "albinoes" and filed them accordingly. The scientist may have enjoyed a pleasant business or even friendly relationship with Roy and his family, but it's difficult to see a proponent of eugenics in a gentle light. He advocated that people with genetic mutations, or vaguely defined undesirable traits like being feebleminded or alcoholic, should be sterilized to improve the human race.

Roy, a dislocationist, and his wife Annie, a sword swallower, were employed as performers with the Ringling Brothers in the late nineteenth century and later, along with their son, King, billed as a contortionist, with Barnum & Bailey. Like Roy, both mother and son had albinism. This type of employment wasn't unusual for people with genetic conditions in the late nineteenth and early twentieth centuries. In one news report, the Pittsley family was deemed haughty for their refusal to join the Barnum & Bailey sideshow. As if it were their destiny, their life preordained. The reporter wasn't certain if the story about the circus and the Pittsleys was truth or myth, and I'm unable to find any further information. Some of these details are lost in time, and some live on in local legends, small-town newspaper accounts, informal place names, and, I discover, on YouTube.

There is a section of road along Route 79 outside the town of Lakeville that is referred to by locals as Pink Eye Village. I can only infer that this name is referencing the persistent rumor that people with albinism have rose-colored eyes, and is a vestige of the albino colony legend from the previous century. It is a rural stretch less than a mile long, with a collection of small houses, most in need of repair, some with garbage-strewn lawns. I tour this road courtesy of a YouTube clip uploaded by a local realtor who makes disparaging comments as the dilapidated homes whiz by the car window.

"Ah, Pink Eye," he says. "There's a house up here that a goat ate the walls off of. That's barely habitable."

"I don't know how people can live in these things," a child's voice says from off-camera.

"I don't either, especially right here where it really falls off the edge" he says. "That's a hot mess."

In that moment, a legend passes from one generation to the next.

It's not a stretch to say that this child is being schooled in bigotry and classism at the same time. Legend and belief are closely intertwined. I'm not certain the realtor knows that he's connecting rural poverty with a genetic condition. Beliefs about albinism are so deeply ingrained that they are difficult for people to recognize. An informal place name, Pink Eye is synonymous with this desolate rural landscape, unemployment, desperation, and inbreeding. I watch the clip several times with a mix of dread and fascination and wonder about the people who live in those houses so carelessly written off by the narrator. Where do they think they live? What do they call it? Is there a connecting line between them and the Pittsleys or Reynolds? Could I be linked to this string of falling-down houses and their inhabitants?

It's conceivable that my lineage might overlap with that of the albino colony, but my knowledge of population genetics is limited. So I turn to the one expert I know won't immediately dismiss my theory, the first person to teach me anything about genetics at all: Dr. Lesley Turner, Sadie's pediatric geneticist who'd been tasked with delivering our DNA test results.

I'D YEARNED FOR NEWFOUNDLAND OVER THE PAST YEAR, BUT RETURNing isn't the homecoming I expected. At first I am distracted by the looming thesis defense, but once the theatrics are finished and my nervous sweat of a performance concludes, I feel disoriented. I navigate my five days there with an awkward ease—I am a visitor in a city so familiar, I know the cracks in its sidewalks. I feel lonely without Sadie and Andrew. A feeling that grows stronger when I visit the Provincial Medical Genetics Program offices at the Health Sciences Centre.

It hasn't changed since I was here last. The walls are pale, the tiles are institutional, and the small waiting room is empty. I remember how we filled this space while anticipating our early visits with Dr. Turner, piling our winter coats across the few chairs, moving the stack of magazines to balance Sadie's car seat on the coffee table. I can almost hear Andrew asking, "Is there enough time to get a coffee?" We could never get enough caffeine back then. By the time Sadie turned one, we had stopped bringing her here for appointments. Genetics gave us the blueprint, the rest of her care would be in the hands of other kinds of specialists.

Dr. Turner meets me at reception. It is an easy reunion, and I'm happy to see her. She's wearing a black dress with white polka dots and her hair is pulled back from her face. I follow her down the yellow hallway, past the examining room where we first met. When we're settled in her office, Dr. Turner asks about Sadie. I tell her about my daughter's recent "report card," her capacity for language, her mastery of the toilet, and how she still wakes up in the night and calls for me.

"I can't believe she's almost three," I say, sighing a little.

"Yes, on Boxing Day," Dr. Turner says, and I'm touched that she remembers Sadie's birthday. I think about the new cast of medical characters in our life. We are more case file than personal story to these physicians. It's not their fault. They never knew that extraordinary baby, so it's harder for them to care beyond the boundaries of our visits to their various offices. They will come and go, but Dr. Lesley Turner will always be a central character in the story of Sadie's life.

I tell Dr. Turner about what we've been doing since we last met, about the hundreds of white-haired delegates at the NOAH conference in St. Louis, the folk beliefs that brought us to East Africa, and most recently, the genealogical research into my father's family. I carefully pull the photographs from my bag and show them to her, starting with the image of the young girl seated in the grass.

"I felt there was no question, when I saw this photo, that this woman has albinism," I say.

"Definitely, for sure," she says, and I'm buoyed by her confident diagnosis.

"The next two are harder to tell," I say.

"Yes, it's harder," Dr. Turner says, examining the two group shots. "Because it could be graying hair."

While I spin the yarn of Rosella and Arthur and their progeny, Dr. Turner expertly sketches their genetic family tree on a piece of paper.

"Can you add that to my file?" I ask her. Our records are available to any future family members who request genetic testing. It will be easier to find the location of a possible mutated gene using our DNA as a map. If my theory holds, my father's combined nineteen grandchildren and great-grandchildren might want to access this information.

"There is something else too," I say, slightly embarrassed. I tell Dr. Turner the story of the albino colony in Freetown and Lakeville, Massachusetts, and how I traced my family line to a neighboring community. "Is it a wild assumption to think we could be connected?" I ask.

"Not at all. It's very likely. When we talk about genetic conditions that are frequent in certain populations, a lot of it can be attributed to the founder effect."

"So it has to do with migration?"

"Yes, it does," she says. "It just means that you have a small group of people who have come from a larger group—like twenty migrants coming from England to Massachusetts in the 1600s—and by chance, in that small group of settlers, several of the people are carriers, maybe because they are family. Then they all have children, and there is a higher incidence of carriers than there would be back home, in the larger population that they came from."

"Because people are intermarrying within the community?" I ask. Following Dr. Turner's lead, I do not use the term "inbreeding."

"Yes, the chance of them meeting someone in the community who is a carrier is going to be much higher than if they met someone from farther away, like New York," Dr. Turner says.

If two people are related, even distantly, the chance that they will carry some of the same genetic mutations is high. They might share some of the "seven really bad mutations" Dr. Brilliant mentioned, or recessive genes for a milder condition like albinism. If the community remains isolated because of its ethnicity—like the Roma of Eastern Europe or Ashkenazi Jews—or because of their geographic location, as with some of the smaller communities in Newfoundland or northern Sweden, the populations have higher rates of certain hereditary conditions.

When the supposed albino colony lived in the backwoods of Massachusetts, people didn't know the particulars of hereditary genetics. It was clear that albinism was correlated with reproducing among kin but not how, as evidenced by one reporter's observation: "It is believed that continual intermarriage has been largely instrumental in handing down the pink eyes and white hair. The Pittsleys were clannish. They wouldn't mingle with other families, much less take wives from them."

As our visit concludes and I carefully tuck the photographs back into my purse, I ask Dr. Turner if it's common for parents of children with genetic conditions to do this kind of research. "Do other people dig around in their past after a diagnosis?" I say.

"Some do," she says. "The fathers tend to be more concerned with the facts about the condition, whereas the mothers can be more interested in the family and where it came from. There are people who go on the genealogy sites and come back with books and have done a huge amount of work. It can lead—" She pauses for a moment. "Well, not just to the condition that they started with but to all sorts of things about the family."

I don't think Dr. Turner intended it this way, but by the end of the week I will look back on her parting statement and wonder if it contained a gentle warning.

CHAPTER 18

Niagara

It's been twenty years since I stood by the edge of the Horseshoe Falls. I never had a reason to return, but in the past month, coming here was all I could focus on. My dad ferried me to Niagara Falls from the Toronto airport this afternoon. It's dusk now and the light is turning blue. A faint rainbow shimmers in the water's rising mist. To get down to the falls we rode a funicular that lifts and plummets every few minutes, taking sightseers between the water's edge and the string of souvenir shops, chain restaurants, and hotels above. My dad pointed out invisible landmarks as we descended—the bridge where my great-grandmother dropped the bread, the hotel her parents had operated on Table Rock. I have to imagine how these structures might have looked because they've long ago disappeared.

The falls are a gaping insatiable mouth consuming the black waters of the Niagara River and devouring the landscape beneath, eroding the bedrock by a foot per year. It's not difficult to see why daredevils are also drawn into its pull. The falls have their own atmosphere, climate, and precipitation, but there is also a distinct culture. Tourists wearing white-bottomed sneakers, their gray hair tucked under baseball caps, shuffle along its banks taking in the view through the lenses of their digital cameras.

Next month, my father will return to the city to be inducted into Niagara Falls' Wall of Fame. He's a hometown boy with a venerable art career. I'd promised to send the award administrator a recent headshot, so I ask my dad to pose with the falls as a backdrop. He leans against the stone and wrought-iron fence—its spirals and leaves so familiar from my childhood, I could reproduce them from memory. He smiles. It's a genuine smile, not forced, and I can tell he's happy to be here. To be home.

It's been fifty-four years since my dad moved away from Niagara Falls, but the city's streets are etched in his memory. Within ten minutes of leaving our hotel the next morning, we're whizzing by the retirement residence where Marjorie lives. I'm anxious about the meeting and I consider opting out. We could just keep driving, but we don't. When we reach our destination, I take a few moments to get ready, shuffling photos, quietly fretting in the front seat. I'm worried that Marjorie might tell me woeful, tragic tales about the relatives who shared my daughter's genetic condition, and that my dad will be there to witness my disappointment. Or, worse, that she won't tell me anything at all.

The residence is a tan-colored three-story building on River Road, removed from the kitsch and phenomenon peddlers of the downtown core. We let ourselves in through a glass door and find an elevator at the end of a long hall. As we slowly rise, I reread my notes where I'd scribbled directions, though I've committed the address, including the room number, to memory. When we knock, we can hear a muffled call from behind the door before it swings open and Marjorie appears.

"Could you hear me say I was coming?" she asks. "Takes me forever when I hear a knock." She shakes her head and throws up her hands. "Well, I'm Marjorie," she says. "Come on in."

At about five foot nine, Marjorie is taller than I expected. She is wearing a pastel-green cashmere sweater with two pearl buttons at the neck and brown slacks. Her white hair is set in curls that frame her face, and she wears a pair of gold hoop earrings. She settles into an overstuffed purple armchair and invites me and my dad to sit across from her. Framed family portraits hang on every wall, and three more are propped on top of a bureau. I notice photographs of small children and babies on a coffee table that sits under the window. Her room faces southeast and I can see the rocky face and churning water of the Niagara River Gorge below us. The leaves on the trees are just starting to change color.

"Do you want me to tell you the whole story?" I ask once we're settled.

"Yes, I do," Marjorie says. "My daughter-in-law, Ruth, over in Australia, said you were coming to see me, and I thought, *Why? Who are they?* And then you told me a few things on the phone, but the whole story would be good."

"It started when my daughter, Sadie, was born in December 2010 with a head of white hair," I say, and I tell her about my father-in-law's diagnosis and the genetic testing that followed. I tell her about the folklore research I did and how it inspired our trip to East Africa, and how I mined my family history following our return. Then I tell her about the photographs and pull the copies I made from my purse. I kneel beside her so that we can look at the pictures together, and my dad stands and hovers above us.

Marjorie puts on her glasses and leans forward, scanning the images.

"These are really old," she says. Then she's silent for a while.

"This is the first photo I saw," I tell her, filling the quiet space with nervous chatter. I show her the picture of my grandmother as a toddler with her two small brothers, their Irish nanny, the neighbor

Rhea MacPherson, and the two white-haired women. "These are the people we are trying to identify. Do you know who they are?"

"Well, they're my aunts," Marjorie says with a small shrug.

"Here are the two women again." I show her the second group shot. "This girl here is laughing and she looks young, but she has white hair."

"That could be Ora. Ora was the oldest. Beulah died quite young, when I was just six, so I don't remember her face as well."

"So they could both be young women?" I ask. "Because I wondered if maybe their mother, your grandmother Rosella Morse, might have had albinism too? Maybe she is one of these women?"

"Oh no. No, she didn't have the white hair," Marjorie says, disproving my theory that the women are mother and daughter. My father's memory wasn't incorrect, but by the time he'd known his great-aunt Rosie, her hair had turned white with age. The two women were sisters, Ora, who would have been about seventeen, and Beulah, around sixteen.

Marjorie continues to study the photos. "It's kind of hard, but I can tell they're my aunts just by their faces. Because I do remember them. They both had that look about the eyes. I can see it in this photo."

"Here's the last picture." I show her the photograph of my grandmother as an infant sitting on her nanny's generous lap; my great-uncle Wesley, the fat baby perched in the tall grass to the left; and the sweet white-haired teenager holding my great-uncle Ronnie in her arms on the right.

"That to me looks like it could be Aunt Ora," Marjorie says. "She was a chiropractor."

I knew about Ora's profession because I'd cobbled together a gap-filled life history from census and archival records. She'd married a Scottish soldier named Blair Tainton when she was twenty-six. Blair was thirty-two, and he'd just returned from serving in World War I. He'd enlisted in August 1918 and they were married less than a year later. They had a daughter named Jean, born in 1920, but after appearing on a census in 1921, she doesn't appear again. Blair also disappeared, or at least his records aren't easily found online. Ora got remarried to a man named Alfred Biggar when she was about thirty. He operated a key shop out of their home in Niagara Falls, and the couple had two children together.

In her early twenties, Ora began nursing school but switched to chiropractic medicine during World War I. The Canadian Memorial Chiropractic College was founded in 1945, and she'd been practicing for at least twenty-five years by then. That means Ora trained in the United States, and on Marjorie's suggestion I contacted the Palmer College of Chiropractic, to see if she turned up in its matriculation records. Alana Callender, the senior director at the Palmer Foundation for Chiropractic History, couldn't find any mention of Ora, but she did give me some historical context. "About 25 percent of practicing chiropractors were women during this period," she wrote in an email, explaining that "a big push was put on for women students during and after World War I, including attendance incentives such as reduced tuitions for student wives."

Being visually impaired and a woman would have been major career handicaps at the time. Moreover, chiropractic medicine was then in its infancy, fighting to be accepted into the upper echelons of the medical world. Marjorie told us that Ora did a lot of pro bono work because she couldn't stand to leave a financially strapped patient in need.

"She did so much good," Marjorie says, shaking her head in wonder. "She was very well known."

WHEN WE SPOKE ON THE PHONE TO ARRANGE THIS VISIT, MARJORIE had told me that four of the five Spencer children had albinism, confirming the rumor passed between two of her daughter-in-laws. I ask her again today because I want to be certain. "So there were four sisters, Ora, Beulah, Edna, and Inez. Who had albinism? Had the white hair?"

"Yes, there were four sisters with the white hair," Marjorie answers. "My three aunts and my mother. Alma was the only one with dark hair."

"Did you know your mother and her aunts were albinos?" I ask, using the language of the time just to be clear.

"All we thought was that they had white hair, but I don't think we wondered why until we got older. None of my cousins or anybody had anything like it, and I mean anything, no white hair." Marjorie gestures to the family photographs lining the four walls of her small room. "I have six kids and nineteen grandchildren—the oldest is almost fifty—and twenty-two great-grandchildren," she says. "Over the years I have wondered if it might turn up."

"Now it has," I say.

I ask Marjorie if she knows anything about the sisters' eyesight. Both girls in the photo are wearing glasses and I wondered if this was unusual for the time.

"I don't know much about their glasses," she says. "I do know that with the white hair there's very poor eyesight. My mother could pass me on the street. Unless I spoke to her, she wouldn't know me. She had her glasses, which were thick, and she always had to use a magnifying glass to read. But she always read."

I am aware that it's difficult for Sadie to pick me out in a crowd, but I was surprised last spring when I approached her near the house and she didn't know me. She was in our driveway, playing with Andrew after he picked her up from daycare. I'd been grocery shopping, and heavy bags of vegetables and milk drooped from both shoulders. I approached without calling out to her, hoping to surprise her, but as I got closer, just ten feet away, it was clear she didn't recognize me. She'd surveyed me with mild curiosity rather than familiarity. *Is this a game?* I wondered. It was only when I spoke that she reacted.

"Hi, Mama," she said, smiling and running straight to me.

There is a range of low vision within albinism and we had hoped Sadie would fall into the higher end of the spectrum. She has surpassed all of our early expectations. Marjorie's description of her mother's eyesight would have upset me a few years ago. I might have been struck by the image of a mother who couldn't recognize her child. Today it's a different story. It's about how Edna used a combination of glasses and magnifiers to read, and that she read often.

Humans have been using tools since the Stone Age. I no longer believe the stylish ophthalmologist at SickKids who told us Sadie would never drive. I often see teens posting messages in albinism social media groups about their upcoming driving tests. They use a monocular to drive, and want to know which one works best, if others drive at night, and what the test might be like. On the final morning of the conference in St. Louis, we saw a white-haired driver at the helm of a minivan pulling out of the hotel parking lot. He was wearing a futuristic device attached to his head through which his world was magnified. It didn't look sad. It looked astonishing and progressive. Sadie will drive with the help of technology, if she wants to. Just as Edna used a magnifier and thick glasses because she wanted to read the daily news.

In advance of our meeting, Marjorie had collected some family biographies and made photocopies for me. These were newspaper accounts of weddings and funerals, with accompanying dates and pedigrees, that another relative had put together for her. My phone call had piqued her interest in family lore and she read the accounts with renewed interest. After going through them a few times, she noticed something peculiar that jogged her memory.

"I was talking to someone, I forget who it was, but they said that my grandparents were first cousins, and they always say that's a no-no," Marjorie tells us.

"Which side were they related on?" I ask. "I don't think it was the Morse side."

"Well, going through those papers on the Morses and the Spencers, I noticed an awful lot of Cooks in there."

"Austin Morse's wife was a Cook," I say, referring to our shared ancestral grandparents. "Maybe Arthur and Rosella weren't first but second or third cousins?"

"Maybe. Anyway, you'll find it very interesting reading the papers," Marjorie says. "They really go back quite a ways."

I am resistant to the idea of family intermarriage entering this story. I understand that it was not uncommon to marry your kin in the late nineteenth century. I can't help but think of Pink Eye Village, and the albino colony legends. Inbreeding is at the heart of so many derogatory beliefs and notions concerning albinism. Procreating with a relative, distant or close, can increase the chance of passing on this recessive genetic condition, but it doesn't spontaneously cause albinism. The parents need to be carriers. Although I'm uncomfortable with the concept, it's clear that Marjorie finds it interesting.

When I look at the papers she copied for me, I notice that she circled the instances where the last name Cook crops up throughout the texts. Later, while puzzling through these hints, I'll remember Dr. Turner's comment about how people often find more than what they initially were looking for when rummaging through the past.

Marjorie says that the Spencer sisters remained close as adults. Inez lived with her parents into their old age, and Alma, the sole dark-haired daughter, moved into a house just behind them so that the two families shared one large lawn. In winter, the sisters' husbands would flood the backyard to make an ice rink for their children to skate on. Before the Christmas holidays, the women held an annual meeting to decide who would be in charge of what dish and where the dinner would take place that year. Marjorie tells me about a picture of the family walking across the shared yard, everyone carrying chairs from one house to the other so there would be enough seats for the gathering. The grass was green. It was December 25, 1941. Marjorie had been married that year and she was pregnant with her first child. My seven-year-old father and his six-year-old little brother were eating Christmas dinner at the Morse & Son residence, a few blocks away.

After two hours have passed, I begin to worry that we will exhaust Marjorie with our questions. While I'd been prying into her family life, my father had been interjecting with memories of old neighbors, long-defunct businesses, and local lore. ("Who was your dentist? Did you see the Honeymoon Bridge fall in '38?") We are reaching the end of our visit, and there is something I need to know before we leave, just in case I don't see Marjorie again.

"I want to know if your aunts and your mother had good lives," I say. "Were they happy?"

Marjorie mulls over my question, then slowly nods her head. "I would say so. I would say they had good lives."

This is what I'd hoped for. Ordinary tales of women who lived like anyone else at the time. Women whose parents loved them, and who in turn found love themselves—in husbands, in children, and in Ora's case, also in vocation. The sisters befell routine tragedies, from which we are all at risk. There had been an early death, an absented husband,

and for Marjorie's mother, Edna, a family business that failed during the depression.

"I don't say my mother had a bad life," Marjorie says. "But she had a harder life than the others."

Marjorie describes her mother's married life as difficult. Her husband was twenty years her senior and had a few children from his first marriage. They ran a bakeshop. It was hard work, and the family suffered when it went under. At this point in the story, Marjorie stops and turns to face my dad.

"If it hadn't have been for your grandmother, well, she was very helpful when my dad lost the business," Marjorie says. "I remember her taking me and my sister to the dressmaker to have dresses made, and how she'd have us over for tea. We used to love to go to Aunt Mayme's house."

My dad is silent for a few moments. I worry that he's missed what Marjorie said, knowing how his hearing has decreased in recent years. Eventually, he nods.

"That was my granny," he says. "Yes, that sounds like her."

I think of my dad's grandmother, Mayme Morse, who once lost a loaf of bread into the Niagara River Gorge, taking Marjorie and her sister to the dressmakers, and it strikes me how connected our lives are. They overlap and interlace, running through the blood in our veins and threading together through ancestral lines that have faded over the last century. My great-grandmother's kindness had been returned to me today through Marjorie's graciousness, her willingness to sit through a two-hour session of questions about the past with a couple of strangers. Except that she probably doesn't see me, and certainly not my father, as strangers. Because we're not. We're family.

CHAPTER 19

Aunt Rosie

THE SPENCER HEADSTONE IS NOT DIFFICULT TO FIND. IT IS A FEW PACES from where my grandparents lie, across the gravel path that divides Drummond Hill Cemetery in two. It sits on the rise of a slow hill. My great-great-aunt and -uncle, Rosella and Arthur, are on one side of the family plot, and Beulah, the ill-fated second sister, is on the other. The other siblings, Ora, Edna, Alma, and Inez, are buried in cemeteries nearby with their spouses and children. My dad leads me to Austin Morse and Mira Cook's gravesite along the back fence. Beyond their shared granite headstone I can see the downtown hotels and the needle tip of the Skylon Tower. They lived so long ago. Austin was born in the last gasp of the eighteenth century, but my family home was crowded with his handiwork: joists and beveled edges, the intricate pattern of a shell on the headboard of my childhood bed. A trace of his skill lives on in my father's sculptures, three-dimensional organic landscapes encased in wooden boxes. Most of them have doors affixed by hinges that allow them to open and close, not unlike a casket or a sideboard.

On our way back to the parking lot, we pass by the MacPherson family site and my dad stops for a moment.

"Here's Rhea, the neighbor who is in the photographs," he says. I think of the woman who appears in the back row of the group shots and how I might recognize her today if she walked by me on the street.

In the shadows of high noon, the sharp light reflecting off the granite headstones, the cemetery has a dreamlike quality. So many of the characters who populated my recent thoughts are lying beneath my feet. Even those with bit parts, like Rhea.

From my archival research and the family papers that Marjorie gave me, I'm able to piece together a backstory, one that starts a few blocks from here on New Year's Eve 1891, when my great-great-aunt Rosella Morse married Arthur Spencer. She was twenty-two and he was thirty-seven. It was the first wedding to take place in the newly built Lundy's Lane Methodist Church. The rust-colored brick building, with its arched windows and tall spire, had replaced the red clapboard meeting house, the congregation having outgrown its one-room space. During construction, the turned ground unearthed soldiers' remains, bones of the men who had died in the 1814 Battle of Lundy's Lane. Their allegiances were identified by the buttons still clinging to their disintegrating uniforms.

In these cases, Rosella's father, Marsena Morse, who was a second-generation undertaker, was called to supply the coffin for the soldiers' reinterment. No shroud, no case or embalming needed for what was left of these beleaguered troops. The historical society footed the bill, which covered labor and materials, a quarter of the cost of a regular funeral at Morse & Son.

The temperature hovered around the freezing mark on the night of the wedding, and there was a scattering of snow on the ground from earlier in the week. Rosella wore a fawn-colored silk dress trimmed with swan down, her dark hair swept back from her face. She carried a bouquet of white roses. The pews were filled with guests; latecomers were forced to stand crowded along the back wall. Marsena walked his second-oldest daughter down the aisle toward her future husband as the organist played Mendelssohn's *Wedding March*.

After the wedding ceremony, Rosella's parents served the eighty invited guests a sit-down dinner in their home. Their residence had been spared from the fire that ravaged the adjoining structures a little over two months before. "The burning of my buildings took place on October 13, 1891," Marsena noted in a rare diary-like entry in his business ledger, which mostly chronicled the costs of the dead.

At 10 p.m., a carriage arrived and Arthur and Rosella, now Mr. and Mrs. Spencer, said goodbye to their gathered family and friends and climbed inside. They were headed for their new home at the corner of Clark and Ferry, about half a mile from Morse & Son.

Ferry Street would have been the most direct route. Tree-lined and mostly residential, the dirt road was inlaid with streetcar tracks, and the narrow wheels of horse-drawn carriages left criss-cross patterns in the snow and frozen mud. The houses were built close together, and there were no front lawns, so that the porch steps unfolded directly onto the sidewalk.

They probably passed lit windows on their way home, people gathered inside anticipating the new year. When Arthur and Rosella woke the next morning, it was 1892 and their life was just beginning.

When I try to imagine what came next, the birth of their first child on February 15, 1893, what I see hovers between the distant and more recent past. I try to envision their newborn daughter, but the baby I see is my own. They called her Ora, which I learned means "light" in Hebrew. I wonder if this was because of her hair color or if it was unrelated, similar to how we'd decided on the name Eira (Welsh for snow), but it rained the night our daughter was born, so we used our second choice and called her Sadie instead.

Ora's parents may have known immediately that their child had a genetic condition, or they might have learned over time, when their infant failed to make eye contact or track a moving object. Maybe they didn't suspect anything until the following year, when their second child, Beulah, was born with the same features. By the time their third child, Edna, arrived in 1897, Rosella and Arthur would have expected her to have albinism. It was Alma, their fourth daughter, who came as a shock when she was born, in 1899, with dark eyelashes, brows, and hair like her mother. The final baby was born a year into the new century. They named her Inez. She was pale, with a crown of white hair, like three of her four older sisters.

I try to imagine how my great-aunt felt when her children were born. Rosella was a God-fearing woman who devoted her life to the Lundy's Lane church. Today there is a room named in her honor where her portrait hangs on the wall. If she hoped with each pregnancy that the child would be born with pigment, she would have been equally resigned to see their differences as part of God's plan. I'm not religious but I understand the sentiment. It's a little like our first babysitter's implied "So what?" It's a little like my own beliefs, which sometimes straddle the line between the natural and supernatural world, and often stray into the territory of fate. It's a little like learning the wonder and intricacies of genetic science, accepting that you don't know why this happened but you do know how, and then moving on.

What I can say for certain is that Rosella and Arthur worried about their daughters. I didn't learn this from Marjorie, though she did tell me that her grandparents treated their children fairly, with acceptance, and that they encouraged them to have normal lives, and loved them. I know this because I am a mother. Sadie is my constant fret. She is at the forefront of every small or large concern in my life. She takes up so much of my brain, I'm sometimes shocked there is room for anything or anyone else. One day, Andrew turned to me with astonishment, a thought having crossed his mind for the first time: "All the parents we see love their children as much as we love Sadie," he said. "I'm surprised that we aren't crashing our cars and walking into walls. It's amazing there's still order in the world."

MORE THAN A CENTURY AFTER ROSELLA AND ARTHUR'S CARRIAGE pulled up to their marital home, I'm standing at the corner of Clark and Ferry. It's impossible to imagine the Spencer residence here, despite Marjorie's generous description. It's been obliterated like the rest of the homes that once lined these streets. The trees were stolen too. Even the topography has changed. The roll of a hill visible in old photographs has been smoothed and leveled. It was death by tourism. A spate of chain restaurants and low-slung motels rose in the wake of the demolished houses, which were too close to the main attraction to be spared the wrecking ball. "Only steps to the falls!" the motel billboards scream.

"Do you remember your grandparents' house?" I asked Marjorie earlier that morning.

"Yes, I can still see it in my mind. It was a big brick house and it had a veranda. You can go up and down Ferry Street and Clark Avenue and there are no homes now," she said. "Everything is gone."

Today, a three-story motel called Admiral Inn sits on the corner lot where the Spencers once lived. We park beside it, and my dad and I walk across the concrete that had at one time been the adjoining lawn between the two family homes—where they carried the chairs between houses on Christmas Day. We stand at the corner for a few minutes as I snap photos in all directions, despite the lack of any historical context. When I finish, we walk into the inn's reception, which sits under a pair of faux Grecian columns. The man behind the counter is curious. It's on the cusp of off-season. In the height of summer he charges $200 or $300 a room, but in winter the rate hovers somewhere around $50. They probably don't get many walk-ins.

"We are looking for number 633 Ferry Street," I say to him, using a street address I'd found on an old census.

"That wouldn't be around here," he says.

"Well, it was here," I protest. "It was the number of a house on this corner in about 1910."

"That would be a hundred years ago," he says, smiling kindly but clearly baffled. "It wouldn't exist anymore."

I will never stand on the veranda that wrapped around the Spencer home. I won't let myself in their back door and peer into the room off the kitchen where Arthur died, the last place Marjorie had seen him when she was a small child. I won't know the parlor or the green lawn that joined the two family homes in later years. I will not know the squeak of their floors or the rise in their stairs, and I will not look at the world through their windows. Everything, as Marjorie told me, and the innkeeper confirmed, is gone.

Even the church where Arthur and Rosella were married, and which presided over most of their social life, has been reincarnated into a modernist work of concrete architecture. There is only one place that does still exist, and it marks our final stop before my dad delivers me back to the airport. This is the funeral home, which continues to operate, in name only, as Morse & Son.

My siblings, one of whom is almost two decades my senior, remember the funeral home well, as my grandparents operated the business until the early 1970s. I arrived six years after it was sold. When I knew them, my grandparents lived in a modest bungalow that seemed to sigh under the weight of Austin's furniture.

Morse & Son loomed large in my imagination but, the occasional funeral aside, it was never a tangible part of my childhood. I knew it from black-and-white photographs. It was a piece of the distant past to which I was tangentially connected, until today.

I follow my dad as he paces across the funeral home parking lot, which had once been his grassy playground. He shuffles from side to side, trying to plot where the group photograph was taken.

"This is where the shed was," he says, lifting his arm and tracing an invisible structure. "And the playhouse was over here."

Then he scans the facade of the building across the street and tries to line it up with an image stored in his mind. There is a mature tree growing out of the parking lot's cement. In the photograph there is a sapling. I don't know if it's the same tree. I can't tell if the branches split in exactly the same way. Although I try to help by comparing the existing landscape with the old images, I acquiesce to my father's memory.

"I think, probably, they were just about here," he says. I join him where he stands and try to imagine how it might have looked when the shot was taken. The view is somewhat unchanged—I'm looking at the green grass of a defunct schoolyard and beyond that the Drummond Hill Cemetery, where we'd just come from.

My father holds the camera, as his grandfather had one hundred years before, and he takes my photograph. When I smile, I imagine Sadie looking at this picture when she's older. By then she will know why I was here. She'll know it's all about her.

When Marjorie handed me the biographical papers and pointed out the scattering of Cooks across the Spencer and Morse families, I knew her theory on Rosella and Arthur being related was correct. I couldn't immediately pinpoint how, but if I followed the clues in the biographies, they would lead me to an answer. Intermarriage wasn't unusual before the turn of the nineteenth century. It wasn't cast in the cruel, disdaining light it is today. Initially, I ignored the evidence because I'd grown protective of the Spencer family. I didn't want to hear any snickers. It reminded me of the shame I felt when Sadie's first ophthalmologist asked if I was related to my husband. It made me think of the realtor showing off Pink Eye Village. I didn't want any part of these narratives of backwardness linked, even tenuously, to my daughter's family history.

Unlike me, Marjorie shrugged it off. "Marrying your cousin is a no-no," she said. "We know that now." Maybe you need to be a nonagenarian to accept the past and reconcile it with the present. Inspired by Marjorie's attitude, I decided not to judge historical actions by a contemporary value and knowledge system.

I used a combination of census information, birth certificates, gravestones, and the family papers from Marjorie to find where the Spencer and Morse pedigrees overlapped. My fourth great-grandmother, Mira Cook, the cabinetmaker's wife, provided the clue. Her parents—Haggai Cook and Sarah Durham, born in the late 1700s—appeared in both the Morse and Spencer trees. Rosella and her husband, Arthur, shared great-grandparents and this made them third cousins.

Marsena Morse, Rosella's father, and Edna (Cook) Spencer, Arthur's mother, were first cousins born only three years apart. A little more than three thousand people lived in Niagara Falls the year Arthur and Rosella married. Edna and Marsena would have grown up together; their children must have known each other as kin. What they likely didn't know was that their marriage might have genetic repercussions when their children were born.

Scientists at the time were working toward understanding the correlation between procreation among relatives and albinism, but the link was more theoretical than solid. Karl Pearson's definitive *Monograph on Albinism in Man* was published in 1911, ten years after the Spencers' last child was born. He prefaces the genetic tome by saying there is still much to be untangled; in particular, he wonders "if there is evidence to show that albinism occurs relatively more frequently in secluded districts, mountain valleys or islands, where we may suppose the population sedentary and much endogamy to prevail? To what extent does inbreeding in man, cousin, or even closer marriage seem to lead to albinism in the offspring? To these problems the reader may find some contributory suggestions, if far from complete answers, in the following pages."

What I learned about my ancestral grandmother Mira Cook changed the shape of my history, and not just because her pedigree unraveled how the Spencers were cousins. It strongly suggests that the albinism gene traveled down from her side of the family, and this meant that I couldn't lay claim to the Massachusetts albino colony. Unlike the giants of Tyrone, I did not have a mythology to ascribe to the twist in my genetic lineage. Mira's maternal and paternal lines meandered eastward like her husband's family had. They too showed up in the Eastern Seaboard, and in some cases, the state of Massachusetts. But her side of the family lived north of Boston, fifty miles from where the Morses overlapped with the Pittsleys. The distance makes it seem far less plausible. The nineteenth-century New England albino colony has been shelved as a family legend, which can be fact or fiction depending on how you tell the story.

CHAPTER 20

A Late Guest

I'M IN THE KITCHEN MAKING SALAD DRESSING WHEN MY SMARTPHONE alerts me to an incoming message. It's a surprising photo from my sister Robin. I'm distracted, using the phone to read a vinaigrette recipe while at the same time trying to keep Sadie's drifting fingers from the knife's blade as I chop walnuts, so at first I don't open the message. We'll be leaving for a potluck dinner shortly. The day had slipped by. The night before, Andrew and I joined friends at a live music show, a rare after-dark venture for us that involved draft beer and an ill-advised text to the babysitter imploring her to stay later when we decided on a nightcap. Sadie woke us up this morning, predictably, at dawn.

Sadie picks up a walnut, lays it in her palm, and then pops it in her mouth. She does this a few more times and I know I should stop her from touching the food I plan to serve to our friends later, but I'm too tired to care. I reach for my phone. It's late October, and Robin is with my dad in Niagara Falls, there to see him inducted into the Wall of Fame. I expect the image to show some aspect of the ceremony, but when it materializes I see that it's not from today. It's a family portrait and it was taken more than one hundred years ago.

I don't need to read the accompanying text to know that the people in the photo are Arthur and Rosella Spencer and their five daughters. I'm so intimate with their records that I know their first and middle names, the surnames the girls would take when they married, how long each family member would live, and the slanted physician's scrawl across some of their death certificates. Knowing their birthdates, I can guess that the image was taken in about 1905, when the youngest sister was four and the oldest was twelve.

My great-great-aunt Rosella's face is soft and kind, set in a mild expression of concern, as might be expected when herding a cacophony of young girls into still poses. It's the first photo I've seen of her. Her dark hair, mirrored in only one of her daughters, is pulled from her face and wrapped into a bun. She wears a dress with puffed sleeves made of dark fabric that gathers at the collar in a panel of lace. Her husband, Arthur, is bald, and there's a hint of a smile visible under his bushy mustache. He's leaning back, his legs casually crossed. It seems like he's enjoying the process of the portrait, proud to be showing off his brood.

The girls and their parents are sweetly entwined, small hands placed on Rosella's lap and Arthur's shoulder, as well as linked with one another's. The two youngest wear matching white dresses; the two oldest wear glasses and are elaborately adorned in dark cloth like their mother; and the middle child, Edna, who is Marjorie's mother, anchors the center in silk tartan.

Minutes pass while I pore over the image. I see my daughter in every one of the girls—in their eyes, faces, eyelashes, glasses, hair, and lovely little hands. In Rosella I see myself. It's not unlike the sensation I had at the conference in St. Louis when I caught sight of a familiar woman, before realizing it was my reflection.

My chest swells. I'm honored to share a branch of my family tree with this demure group. I will frame their portrait and hang it on the wall amid our collection of family pictures: black-and-white snapshots of our grandparents; our moms as children; a group shot from our wedding day on the rocky outcrop in Bonavista Bay. I'll hang it so that Sadie will grow up seeing it every day, and know that she's connected to her past, seeing aspects of herself in the images of her long-ago relatives, and that all the people featured in these photos are part of her tribe. She belongs to them.

It was my dad's first cousin, Susie Morse Berger, who had brought the portrait of the Spencer family to the ceremony. My dad telephoned her a few weeks ago to invite her to the event, and during that conversation he mentioned our visit with Marjorie and told her about Sadie. Susie thought immediately of the portrait, which belonged to a distant Morse relative she'd got to know in recent years. She borrowed the original and had a copy made for me.

I am surprised that Susie knew about the Spencers. Her link to Rosella was as tenuous as my father's had been. The difference is that my dad left Niagara Falls half a century ago and Susie remained. "It's not common to live in the same place as your ancestors these days," Susie says when I call to thank her for the photograph. "But we do, and so you don't forget. You drive by places that remind you of people and stories every day."

AFTER SEEING THE PORTRAIT, I WONDER IF I'VE OVERLOOKED ANYONE else with a connection to the Spencers. I call Marjorie and ask her, for the second time, which of her first cousins are still living. During our visit she'd mentioned two women, one who was gravely ill, and a second who lived in Trenton, Ontario. I'm surprised to learn that there is a third cousin, Inez Mae Twocock, who is eighty-eight years old and lives in Niagara Falls. She is Ora's daughter.

It was the photograph of Ora, her closed eyes under wire frames, her white eyelashes, that convinced me to begin this search. At first she was a portent from the past, a distant light in the fog. When snatches of her life fell into view and she slowly materialized, I saw her story as a possibility. Her life symbolized my daughter's potential. Knowing that the Spencer sisters married, had children, and led the kind of lives that were regular for the time was important to me. Learning about Ora's career as a chiropractor, a woman with albinism practicing alternative medicine in the early twentieth century, my relative, had been thrilling.

If my late grandmother had been alive when Sadie was born, she would have used Ora's life as an example of what my daughter could achieve. It's been more than twenty years since my grandmother died, but she was stubborn, persistent in her quiet elegance. She'd found a way to tell me about Ora, the same way she detailed the lives of the ancestor who'd carved our furniture, by leaving handwritten notes in the drawers for us to find after her death. She was determined that the past would persist in her progeny's lives. She'd left my father the album that held the photographs of the Spencer girls. She'd told my mother about this family, a wisp of conversation that was seemingly unimportant at the time, but remembered three decades later. She'd orchestrated this discovery but could only take me so far. My grandmother couldn't tell me the small details of Ora's life, so I call the one person who can.

Inez Mae picks up on the third ring and I introduce myself, laughing a little nervously, concerned she might not understand why I'm calling. I needn't have worried. Our visit to Marjorie hadn't gone unnoticed by the Morse descendants who live in the Niagara Falls region. There'd been chatter.

"You're the girl with the albino daughter," Inez Mae says. "I'm very interested in hearing about your child."

"I'm very interested in hearing about your mother," I tell her, and we spend the next hour and a half talking.

One of the first things Inez Mae tells me is that her mother drove a car.

"She did? It's pretty unusual for someone with albinism to drive," I say and then tell her how the handsome pediatric ophthalmologist at SickKids said Sadie would never get behind the wheel of a motor vehicle in her lifetime.

"You know, Emily, back then there were very few cars on the road," Inez Mae says, laughing. "Some of the women used to tell me, teasingly, that they would phone people and say, 'Ora's driving!' So, in other words, everybody look out! I mean, that was a joke, but they did look out for her."

Inez Mae, who was named for her Aunt Inez, Ora's youngest sister, tells me that her mother saw patients in her home office but also made house calls (hence the driving). She wore a uniform with a small pocket over her left breast, where she kept her magnifying glass. She also wore thick, pink-tinted glasses. Like her sister Edna, she read the newspaper every day. She was left-handed. She detested housework and hired a live-in caretaker for this duty. She was strict about her children's health, seeing it as a personal affront when any of them fell ill. She played euchre with friends on weekend evenings, holding the cards up close to her face to differentiate the hearts from the spades. Mostly, however, she worked.

The Biggar family lived near Niagara Falls's Little Italy, a neighborhood named for the influx of Italian immigrants who'd settled there. Ora had several patients from this community, and some believed she had special powers based on her appearance. This supernatural thinking could just as easily have extended to Ora's profession—partly because chiropractic medicine was in its infancy when Ora started practicing in Canada and people were unsure of how alternative therapies worked, but also because she provided remedies to people with seemingly incurable problems.

She helped a young polio survivor relearn to walk, jettisoning the leg braces the girl had been condemned to use following her illness. She worked on children with mental and physical disabilities, helping them to relax and to move freely.

"I saw men come in on their hands and knees because they'd injured their backs at work, and they would walk out of that house," Inez Mae says. "To me as a child, these were miracles."

Later, when Inez Mae's only son was born with an intellectual disability, Inez Mae remembered the children her mother had worked with, how Ora had handled them with respect and afforded them a level of dignity they might not have received in the more traditional medical practices of the time. Inez Mae says she found solace in this.

I think back to the photograph of Ora sitting in the grass. She's holding my great-uncle Ronnie, who was also born with some form of disability, something which then had no name and remains a mystery. "He had a downward look" is how it was described to my dad, which means his chin was often pinned to his chest. He didn't speak, though there is a family myth that he could communicate with animals. He was twenty-four when he died.

A FEW DAYS AFTER WE SPEAK, INEZ MAE CALLS ME BACK. SHE'D BEEN thinking a lot about Sadie and there was something she needed to know.

"I hope you don't mind my inquiring, but is your daughter okay?" she asks. "Is she functioning as a regular three-year-old?"

She'd heard that people with albinism could also have intellectual disabilities, a relic from earlier medical texts that I'd also encountered in my research.

"Yes," I say, explaining that eyesight is the main hurdle for people with albinism and that there is no connection with any other form of

disability. I begin to tell Inez Mae about the low-vision clinic assess-
ment but trail off. Those two days of aptitude tests don't illustrate
Sadie's life. Instead, I tell her about Halloween. "She went trick-or-
treating for the first time this fall. She dressed as a paper doll."

I describe the costume to Inez Mae and tell her that it was based
on a picture book Sadie and I both love. One afternoon, Sadie lay on a
piece of blue bristol board and I traced a dress around her body. We'd
made a paper bow for her hair and a mini-Sadie doll to fit in her front
pocket. She walked stiffly but with pride through our neighborhood,
garnering compliments along the way—mostly about her costume, a
few about her hair. Then I told Inez Mae about how we had traveled to
Alberta earlier in the fall for a wedding and how Sadie had sprinted the
length of Banff Avenue at dusk, weaving through tourists' legs, heading
straight into the shadow of Cascade Mountain. I describe how she com-
mandeered the dance floor at the Calgary Polo Club until midnight,
when eventually we climbed aboard the hotel-bound school bus and
she fell immediately asleep in a lump of snoring taffeta and silk ribbons
across my lap. I describe our home life: pulling carrots from the garden,
red-tricycle afternoons, walks along the beach with her dog, a soggy,
wet-snouted conspirator. It's been a good fall. No—it's been a good life.

"Well, there you go," Inez Mae says. "That's wonderful."

A week later, a package arrives from Inez Mae. It's like opening a
time capsule. There are photographs of her mother and aunts from
various stages of their lives. In one, the women are in their twenties,
on a picnic with their husbands, shaded under a canopy of tall trees.
There are several Model T Fords parked in the background, and
the hint of a river in the dappled light beyond the forest. It feels
intimate, as if I were watching them, unseen, from a few feet away.
There are photos of the sisters' children, a few wedding shots, and
an updated version of the Spencer family portrait, with all the girls
grown. Along with the photos, Inez Mae included a series of letters

from the minister of health, the mayor of Niagara Falls, the local MPP, and several official chiropractic associations congratulating Ora, in 1965, on fifty years of service.

In the message accompanying the package, Inez Mae wrote that as the mother of a disabled child, she suffered some insensitive attacks from "supposedly mature adults." She said she wasn't making a comparison between her son and Sadie, but between us, as two moms. If I ever found myself upset by hurtful comments or behavior in regard to my child's difference and I wanted to talk, she said she'd "go there with me." Her offer felt sincere and it reminded me of the letters I'd received from friends and family after Sadie's diagnosis, messages of love, understanding, and kindness, now bundled with twine and carefully tucked away in a shoebox on a shelf in my office.

She'd also enclosed an overview of Sadie's astrological sign, Capricorn. She told me how she had taken comfort in astrology after her only son was born—she felt it might offer some insight into who he might have been had he not been born disabled. This made me think of my great-grandmother Mayme Morse, and my great-uncle Ronnie, her intellectually disabled first-born child. I'd recently learned that she'd taken him to faith healers, attempting to cure him. I was surprised because she was described as stern, sophisticated, and unflappable. Interactions with the supernatural seemed out of character. I can only imagine that she was desperate. The faith healers weren't able to help. No one could understand why Ronnie seemed trapped within himself.

Inez Mae and Mayme didn't find the answers to why their children were born the way they were, but, like me, they discovered a certain kind of salve in the search. I think this is why Inez Mae was so quick to send me all the family photographs and information about her mother. She knew my journey, or at least a version of it, and she understood how much each scrap of knowledge meant.

When I first sifted through the package, I was most interested in the photographs of the Spencer sisters and the information about Ora. Looking at the images a second time, I was struck by a series of photographs from a Morse family gathering to celebrate my great-grandmother Mayme's eightieth birthday. They'd rented the recreation room at the Culp Street YMCA to accommodate all the guests. One image shows my grandmother, Maryon Morse Urquhart, sitting at a table with Inez Spencer Dobson, the youngest of the five Spencer daughters. The second photograph is taken in the same room from a different angle. It shows my dad as a round-faced young man, before he'd grown a beard. His soon-to-be first wife, Madeline, sits to his left, her dark hair fashioned into a pixie cut, her eyes sparkling. My Aunt Donna, elegant, wearing white knee socks, and my Uncle David, goofily licking an ice cream cone, sit across from them. In the third picture from the party, Mayme, wearing pearls and a satin dress, a corsage pinned to her left breast, is cutting into a rectangular cake topped with sugar rosettes.

It's strange to imagine my young father in the same room as the women I'd worked so hard to identify. By then, Mayme's nieces, the Spencer girls, were in their late fifties and early sixties. Their white hair wouldn't have stood out as unusual. My father couldn't have known their fair complexions were a result of a genetic condition, one that he carried in his cells and that would turn up fifty years later in his youngest grandchild.

Looking closer at the photo that shows my dad, I see a date stamped near the white border: June 1958. This was a significant year for him. He'd just finished art school. A month after the picture was shot, he married his first wife. That fall they sailed to La Havre, France, on a Hamburg Atlantic ocean liner and spent eight months in Europe, living off the proceeds from my father's first major art show the year before. They first lived in Paris, then traveled slowly south to shelter the winter in Spain's Costa del Sol. The experience had a profound influence on my dad's work, and he has returned to Europe every year since. His career was taking off around this time and would reach new heights in the next decade. He couldn't have known all of this at that late spring family gathering, nor could he have predicted that his marriage wouldn't last. That after four children together there would be a sad disintegration, and how he'd move away from London, Ontario, where they lived, leaving behind his former wife and two of their children. He'd take a new job at the University of Waterloo while single-parenting his two unruly teenage daughters and seeing his two young sons on weekends. A few years later, my mother, a young widow, would return to the University of Guelph to finish her degree as a hopeful distraction from her grief. Neither of them could know that through the luck of geography or fate, they'd meet, fall in love, and marry. Back then, he couldn't have predicted that at forty-two, seventeen years after his first child was born, my dad would have me, his last. How I would return to this party, a late guest, and understand all of what was to come. The events, happy and sad, that would unfold over the next half-century are the fated movements that linger in my genes.

CHAPTER 21

Origins

After Sadie's birth, we observed a nightly ritual on the maternity ward. Babies were placed in their plastic bassinets, then trolleyed down to a room at the end of the hall where they were bathed and weighed. On our first night, we arrived at the room on the heels of another couple. They looked impossibly young to me, a decade our junior. The father wore a flat-brimmed baseball cap pulled low over his eyes. The mother's face was wide-open, freckled, her expression a blend of hope and fear. As we waited in line I peered in at their baby, a regular, dark-haired, scrawny newborn, and cooed over him, congratulating his parents.

We watched the nurses, efficient and starched, swirl around the room in choreographed harmony. Strong-armed and adept, they lifted and unfurled the bundled babies in one fluid motion, dipping their naked squealing bodies into small tubs of warm water, washing their hair, if they had any, in a circular motion toward the crown, then toweling their papery skin dry.

When it was our turn, we sidled up to a weigh station beside the young couple we'd met in line. The nurses continued their well-worn routine, whirling along, until, one by one, they spotted our child and came to an abrupt stop. "That hair is some white," they'd sing, straying off script. None of them mentioned the second infant in the room. In that moment, I felt sorry for the other parents. Surely they noticed how our baby was upstaging theirs.

Already I'd convinced myself that the attention and focus on my baby was part of a grand narrative, one that included the birth of an astonishing child, and was symbolic of a magical, wonder-filled life to come. I knew my daughter was extraordinary. What I didn't know then was that all parents feel this way about their children. The young couple in the bathing room probably didn't notice or even hear the comments about Sadie. They were focused on their own miraculous offspring. They felt the same way about their baby as we did about ours.

Skip ahead three years to a night in early winter: Andrew, with a wet tea towel thrown over his shoulder, is washing the dishes from dinner. Sadie, bathed, tucked-in, feeling the hard-won exhaustion of a preschool day, is asleep in her room. Under the kitchen table the sleeping dog yawns, shifts, stretches, then slumbers on. In the living room, I bend and stand in a circular motion, collecting the day's gathered detritus. When I finish I fall onto the overstuffed couch.

Andrew joins me. I'm holding my notebook and a pen. I want to record something he'd said to me earlier in the week. We were talking about how different our life looks from how we envisioned it might, back in the foggy early months spent visiting the genetics department of the hospital, a time I remember as being in perpetual dusk.

"You said that life then and life now is like walking in the woods before and after studying biology, right?" I ask.

"Yes, before you know about plants, you can walk into a forest and it all looks green," Andrew says. "It can still be moving and beautiful, or at least enjoyable, but a million stories go untold. Maybe you notice different shades, or that some plants are tall and others are small, but you don't differentiate species. In a sense, learning the plants—their names, their habitats, their needs, and their dependents—is like learning how to read. And once you learn the plants, you can't return to seeing them as nameless greenery."

In the beginning, it had been impossible to see the outline of our daughter's future because it in no way resembled our pasts. We wanted to be the best parents for her but, startled, and with no map, we didn't know how. In his book *Far from the Tree*, Andrew Solomon uses the term "horizontal identity" when referring to children who are different from their parents. In these instances, mothers and fathers are forced to rewire their default versions of the world. When our daughter was born, Andrew and I needed to relearn how to see. Like my dad's art students, we needed to understand perspective in order to make sense of the view.

Initially, this seemed a singular task. A long road with few traveling companions. But as we moved forward I heard stories from every corner of my universe, all pertaining to children with some form of difference. Some cases were mild and some were tragic. I related to these tales, but what surprised me were the parallels I discovered between our story and the narratives of seemingly ordinary children. There was a common thread, in all instances, that tied our stories together. A string that binds us all. Our children's lives and challenges varied, but in our concerns, our hope, and our love for them, we were all alike.

I filed these tales alongside my collection of albinism lore: old newspaper articles about a legendary backwoods tribe in New England; Noah and his hair the color of white wool; accounts from early anthropologists and their misguided searches for a fair-haired race in Panama; and the story of four white-haired sisters born one hundred years ago, which, in the end, turned out to be true.

The traces of our ancestors manifest in surprising ways. I understand inheritance now in its scientific distillation, but I also know its richer, deeper, more mysterious forms. It's something I've been think-ing about since my daughter turned three. Sadie received an easel for her birthday. Standing upright allowed her to come closer to the page and see what she was working on. This freed her movements from the cramped, hunched position she had previously assumed while drawing. My parents were visiting, and after setting up the easel, Sadie and her grandfather sequestered themselves in the corner of the living room to draw. This happened for about an hour every afternoon for the rest of my parents' visit. Sadie, standing with a marker in her hand, would draw while my dad sat at her side and encouraged her, suggesting ways to approach a white space and fill it with life and color.

After my parents returned home, I noticed that Sadie's drawing style had changed. The blended colors spreading across the page held a faint echo of my father's paintings. I wondered if, when she was draw-ing, she was thinking about her grandfather, the memory of his gentle directions informing her work. It surprised me that she absorbed his lessons so acutely. Then I had a different thought. Maybe her ability isn't learned. Maybe it's passed on; something alive in her cells. Maybe her artistic talent is genetic.

Watching Sadie grow creatively, but also physically and emotion-ally, I am keenly aware of how fortunate we are. She will face chal-lenges in her life but, unlike her peers in East Africa, she does not live in fear.

Under the Same Sun continues to tally the attacks on people with albinism in African countries, both the death toll and the survivors. The two most recent attacks in Tanzania have been on children—a teenage girl and a four-year-old boy. Both victims survived. The girl fled and is now safely at school through the UTSS scholarship pro-gram. The boy's mother brought her son to the police station, implor-ing the officers to help. This incident marked the fourth attempt on his life. "We are the keepers of such immense tragedy," Don Sawatzky said to me during a conversation we had in winter 2014. "Globally, this is as bad as it gets."

I'd called Don to ask about some of the people we met in Tanzania last spring, specifically the boys we visited at the school outside Dar es Salaam. We talked about Adam, and how he was struggling a bit academically but otherwise faring well. He'd been back to Vancouver for follow-up surgery, and the physicians who operated on him were planning a trip to East Africa to help other children and adults who'd lost limbs to poachers. I asked about Mwigulu, the sad and broken boy we met who'd been silenced by his trauma, whose body had hummed with terror.

Don tells me that a few months after we visited, Mwigulu attended a week-long summer camp for children with albinism organized by UTSS. Based near Mwanza, the program was designed to promote each child's sense of self-worth. "We wanted these kids to leave feeling that they were valuable human beings," Don explained.

The theme drummed through their activities and songs, and motivational phrases were stitched into the camper's baseball caps and emblazoned across their shirts. After the camp ended, Mwigulu returned to his school dorm with renewed energy. His expression, once set in a dull stare, was now animated and lively. His eyes lifted and met the faces of the people around him. He started talking again, engaging in soft-spoken conversations with his teachers and the other children at his school. "Something shifted for him," Don said. "He's started to enjoy people and life again."

Afterward, Don emails me a photograph of Mwigulu, taken at the July summer camp. He's wearing a shirt made from black and orange block-print fabric. The stump of his left arm is exposed and you can see the deep red scars from where it was severed above the elbow. He's looking down into the camera, a contemplative expression on his face, his mouth twisted, ever so slightly, into the hint of a smile.

When we first spoke in February 2012, Peter Ash warned that he wouldn't see an end to the witchcraft killings in his lifetime. But along with the Under the Same Sun staff—people like Vicky, Omary, Don, and others—he's made a tremendous impact in the five years since founding the nonprofit organization. In June 2013, shortly after we returned from Tanzania, the United Nations passed a historic resolution on the rights of persons with albinism. This marks the first time in history that the attacks and discrimination against people with this genetic condition have been recognized and addressed in an official and international capacity. The resolution was prompted, in no insignificant part, by Under the Same Sun.

Sadie occasionally asks if she can come to Tanzania with us "next time." The nurse at the travel clinic had been right about a lot of things, including my desire to return to Africa. When we came home, I was grateful to slip back into our simple pace, but gradually a small part of me longed for Dar's chaos, the frenzy of kids on the beach in Stone Town, the life we witnessed along the country's roadsides.

I promise Sadie that we'll take her to Tanzania when she's older. We will watch Albino United practice in the dusty field off Ocean Road and visit Mitindo Primary School in the west (and this time we'll bring a ball for the children to play with). We'll go on safari so Sadie can see the orange sun setting over the plains and the animals grazing in the bowl of the Ngorongoro Crater, however she might view it— through a monocular, or even better technology yet to be developed. I will introduce her to Adam and to Mwigulu and, meeting them for the first time, she'll understand and know these boys in ways I never will. Until then, that future, pale light hovering on the horizon, we'll continue to take our well-worn paths.

IN THE EARLY DUSK OF A WINTER AFTERNOON, I'M WALKING FROM THE grocery store to the library, tugging Sadie, who is telling me she wants to be carried. She's flagging, done with errands and with walking, and she wants to go home. At three, she's healthy and robust, not a wispy child I can place on my shoulders or sidle onto my hip.

"I'm going to show you a secret path," I tell her. This works. Her pace livens. It's a narrow walkway that snakes around a community center and empties into the lot where I parked the car.

"Why is it here? Why is it a secret? Does Daddy know about it?" she asks.

"It's a shortcut for tired little people, and if the big people knew, they'd all take it," I tell her.

"Why?" she asks.

We move in a slow doddle, caught up in the question-and-answer banter that occupies so many of our waking hours. I'm startled when a figure appears close on our heels. In the dim light I see she's an older woman but lithe in her yoga wear, her hair pulled back into a youthful ponytail.

"Excuse me, does this path go all the way through?" she asks.

"Yes," I tell her.

She nods and smiles, then places her hand on Sadie's head and lets it rest a moment.

"Reminds me of my youngest," she says, sighing. "Someone in your family have that hair color?"

"Yes," I say, surprising myself. "It runs in the family."

It took a long time to distill our story into those five words: *It runs in the family*. We always knew this, of course, but now we have a group of ancestors whose lives can both anchor and mirror our own. In life's harried moments, the simple explanation will do fine. Some will want to hear the full story, the one that started three years ago and continues today, as we walk together, hand in hand, heading forward, buoyed by the past and what we know, all those secrets in our cells, the journeys we've taken, but also by what's to come around the corner, what lies ahead.

"What was the lady asking about?" Sadie wants to know when the woman disappears down the passageway.

"Your hair," I tell her.

"Why?"

"She wants to know more about you, about us and our family," I say, turning to face my small daughter and bending so that our eyes meet. "She wants to know who we are and where we came from."

Afterword

OUR SON WAS BORN IN THE FIRST WEEK OF 2015.

He had a one-in-four chance of having albinism, but the numbers never meant anything to me. I put as much faith in the scientific roll of the dice as I might in a palm reader's clairvoyance—both are predictions, not destiny. We decided to have a second child, embracing the genetic probability, and have prenatal testing done as a means of preparing for either outcome.

When I envisioned Sadie's sibling I saw a white-haired child with rosy cheeks who held books close to his bespectacled nose. A pigmented child never strayed into these fantasies, and eventually I realized that this was fine.

Then, on a sunny day in August, this imagined child disappeared when our genetic counselor called with the results of my amniocentesis test.

"The baby inherited one mutated gene and one regular gene," she said. "So he will be a carrier but will not have albinism."

"Whose gene?" I asked.

"Yours," she said.

I hung up the phone and thought of my father. I heard my mother's voice reminding me about his "strong genes." The Spencer family portrait came briefly into focus. Then, for a long time, I cried. I called Andrew and, with difficulty, told him what I'd learned.

"Of course I'm not disappointed," I'd said. "But I don't feel relieved either. I'd expected a different scenario, and I feel like I'm letting go of something forever. Like I'm saying goodbye."

"Look how far we've come," Andrew said.

When a baby is born differently than expected, parents can experience grief for the child they'd imagined. I was surprised to find this to be true when the results of our son's test showed that he would not have albinism. The child I'd conjured, not just over the months since I'd been pregnant but for three years before conception, vanished in an instant. Mourning him was an unexpected sorrow.

But just as my feelings morphed and relaxed concerning Sadie's genetic difference, I also accepted that my second child would differ from my first. That's all we really know about him for now—he's a boy, and he doesn't have albinism. Like all children he is a slow mystery who will unravel over time as we—the parents—watch, cheer, guide, hope, and above all, love.

Acknowledgments

I spoke with a constellation of people while writing this work and their names appear in the context of those discussions throughout the book. Each of these people helped illuminate, clarify, and shape the text, and I'm thankful for the time and ideas they shared with me.

There are also individuals with whom I had important conversations that informed this work but whose names do not appear in the pages. They include Dr. Bruce Beckwith, Dr. Debbie Felton, Dr. Patricia Lund, Dr. Barbara Rieti, Ryan Trant, and Dr. Rick Thompson. I am grateful for their contributions and for the time and expertise they shared with me.

Some conversations lasted longer than others. Over the course of a year and a half, Don Sawatzky of Under the Same Sun provided counsel and advice. I am grateful to him, and to Peter Ash and the Under the Same Sun employees in Canada and Tanzania for their invaluable guidance. Under the Same Sun is a registered charity. To find out more about the organization, please visit its website at underthesamesun.com.

Mike McGowan, director of NOAH (National Organization for Albinism and Hypopigmentation) was a great casting director, putting me in contact with a wide variety of people within the albinism community. I was lucky to have his help.

In Tanzania, I'd like to specifically thank Jacob Mwinula and the Albino United soccer team, Vicky Ntetema and Omary Mfaume of Under the Same Sun, Alfred Kapole of the Mwanza Region Tanzania Albinism Society, and the staff and students at Mitindo Primary School and at Mount Everest School. Thanks also to NoZone Clothing Company, of Victoria, British Columbia, for donating all those little red UV-proof hats.

In Niagara Falls, I'd like to thank Ernie Morgan of Morse & Son Funeral Home, who provided me with information and scanned pages from my great-great-great-grandfather's undertaking ledger. City Historian Sherman Zavitz answered my questions on nineteenth-century life in the area, and the staff at the Welland Public Library archives helped confirm dates and names by providing archival news sources.

Thanks to Ben Hyman, executive director of BC Libraries Cooperative (and information extractor), who dredged up historical Niagara Falls weather patterns for me.

I'm grateful to Max Bailey, who helped to connect me with my Niagara Falls relatives. I'd like to thank my newfound extended family, including Ruth Ruller, Marjorie Ruller, Inez Mae Twocock, and Susie Morse Berger.

Thank you to Sandra Martin for guidance in the early stages, and to John MacFarlane for giving this story its first home in the pages of *Walrus* magazine. Also, thank you to Stuart McLean for vouching for me along the way.

When the idea of this book took shape, my agent, Samantha Haywood, acted as a guide, confidante, consultant, and dogged enthusiast, and I feel lucky to have her in my life. I'm grateful to her and everyone at the Transatlantic Agency. Iris Tupholme was a generous, insightful editor with a keen eye and a huge well of empathy.

I am wildly fortunate to have worked with her on my first book. I am grateful to Iris, Noelle Zitzer, Judy Phillips, Allyson Latta, and to everyone at HarperCollins Canada.

I'm honored to have been a part of the Folklore Department at Memorial University of Newfoundland for six years; its professors and collegial atmosphere provided me with resources, direction, and breadth from which to draw while writing this book.

Early readers of this work provided me with sound feedback and direction. They include Rasha Mourtada, Anna Foat, Dr. Luise Hermanutz, Dave Innes, Stephanie Sinclair, Dr. Carissa Brown, and Dr. Diane Tye.

My parents and in-laws offered unique expertise beyond their roles as grandparents. I'm grateful to them for their unwavering support and their continued interest in this project, for caring for my daughter during some of the research phases, and for graciously understanding why I wanted to write about our family. I am lucky to have such wonderful parenting role models in my mom and dad, and in my mother- and father-in-law.

The events in this book took place in many geographic locations, but the composition and writing happened on the shores of the Salish Sea, within the homeland of the Songhees First Nation. I am grateful for my home, and for the inspiration from this landscape.

Andrew Trant, who believed in me so fiercely, is my greatest cheerleader and ally, and I could not have written a word without his support. Andrew, I'm so happy that you wandered into the Ship Pub that spring night so many years ago.

To Sadie, who told me, "I'm going to be a writer too, Mama, so you better get another chair at your table," thank you for inspiring this journey.

Bibliography

Abraham, Carolyn. "Unnatural Selection: Is Evolving Reproductive Technology Ushering in a New Age of Eugenics?" *Globe and Mail*, January 7, 2012.

Adams, Rachel. *Sideshow U.S.A.: Freaks and the American Cultural Imagination*. Chicago: University of Chicago Press, 2001.

Ann Arbor Argus. "Cape Cod Albinos: A Colony of Pink Eyed and White Haired People." October 25, 1895.

Baker, Charlotte, Patricia Lund, Richard Nyathi, and Julie Taylor. "The Myths Surrounding People with Albinism in South Africa and Zimbabwe." *Journal of African Cultural Studies* 22, 2 (2010): 169–81.

Baruch, Susannah, David Kaufman, and Kathy L. Hudson, "Genetic Testing of Embryos: Practices and Perspectives of US in Vitro Fertilization Clinics." *Fertility and Sterility* 89, 5 (2008): 1053–58.

Beckwith, Bruce. "Congenital Malformations: From Superstition to Understanding." *Virchows Arch* 461 (2012): 609–19.

Berton, Pierre. *Niagara: A History of the Falls*. Toronto: Anchor Canada, 2002.

Besner, Linda. "Distinct Society: Discovering Montreal's Deaf Community." *Walrus*, May 2013.

Bloomfield, Steve. *Africa United: How Football Explains Africa*. Edinburgh: Canongate, 2010.

Braathen, Stine Hellum, and Benedicte Ingstad. "Albinism in Malawi: Knowledge and Beliefs from an African Setting." *Disability and Society* 21, 6 (2006): 599–611.

Brockton (MA) Gazette. "The Pink Eyed Pittsleys." May 25, 1887.

Browne, J. Orde. "Witchcraft and British Colonial Law." *Africa* 8, 4 (1935) 481–87.

Cartier, L., Lynn Murphy-Kaulbeck, and the Genetics Committee. Society of Gynaecologists and Obstetricians of Canada Committee Opinion. "Counselling Considerations for Prenatal Genetic Screening." *Journal of Obstetrics and Gynaecology Canada* 34, 5 (2012): 489–93.

Chahal, Harvinder S., et al. "AIP Mutation in Pituitary Adenomas in the 18th Century and Today." *New England Journal of Medicine* 364, 1 (2011): 43–50.

Clarren, Sterling. "A Thirty-Year Journey from Tragedy to Hope." Foreword to *Damaged Angels: An Adoptive Mother Discovers the Tragic Toll of Alcohol in Pregnancy*, by Bonnie Buxton, xi–xiv. New York: Carroll and Graf, 2005.

Crummey, Michael. *Galore*. Toronto: Anchor Canada, 2009.

Cusk, Rachel. *A Life's Work: On Becoming a Mother*. New York: Picador, 2001.

Davenport, Charles B. "Degeneration, Albinism and Inbreeding." *Science* 28, 718 (1908): 454–55.

———. "Heredity of Albinism." *Journal of Heredity* 7, 5 (1916): 221–23.

Davenport, Charles B., and Gertrude C. Davenport. "Heredity of Skin Pigmentation in Man." *American Naturalist* 44, 527 (1910): 641–72.

Diamond, Jared, and Jerome I. Rotter. "Observing the Founder Effect in Human Evolution." *Nature* 329 (1987): 105–06.

Duke, M.P., A. Lazarus, and R. Fivush. "Knowledge of Family History as a Clinically Useful Index of Psychological Well-Being Prognosis: A Brief Report." *Psychotherapy Theory, Research, Practice Training* 45, 2 (2008): 268–72.

Dundes, Alan. "The Psychoanalytic Study of the Grimms' Tales with Particular Reference to 'The Maiden without Hands' (AT 706)." *Germanic Review: Literature, Culture, Theatre* 62 (1987): 50–65.

Eberly, Susan Schoon. "Fairies and the Folklore of Disability: Changelings, Hybrids and the Solitary Fairy." *Folklore* 99 (1988): 58–77.

Ellis, Bill. *Aliens, Ghosts and Cults: The Legends We Live*. Jackson: University Press of Mississippi, 2001.

———. "Contemporary Legends in Emergence." *Western Folklore* 49 (1990): 1–7.

Feiler, Bruce. *The Secrets of Happy Families: Improve Your Mornings, Rethink Family Dinner, Fight Smarter, Go Out and Play, and Much More*. New York: William Morrow, 2013.

———. "The Stories That Bind Us." *New York Times*, March 15, 2013.

Fivush Robin, Jennifer G. Bohanek, and Widaad Zaman. "Personal and Intergenerational Narratives in Relation to Adolescents' Well-Being." *New Directions for Child and Adolescent Development* 131 (2011): 45–57.

Fraser, J.A., and Rita Crane. "Obituary: Arnold Sorsby, Editor, Journal of Medical Genetics, 1962–1969." *Journal of Medical Genetics* 17 (1980): 410.

Froggart, P. "The Legend of the White Native Race: A Contribution to the History of Albinism." *Medical History* 4, 3 (1960): 228–35.

Garrod, Archibald, and H. Harris. *Inborn Errors of Metabolism*. London: Oxford University Press, 1963.

Golden, Janet. *Message in a Bottle: The Making of Fetal Alcohol Syndrome*. Cambridge, MA: Harvard University Press, 2005.

Goldstein, Diane E. *Once Upon a Virus: AIDS Legends and Vernacular Risk Perception*. Logan: Utah State University Press, 2004.

Greaves, Mel. "Was Skin Cancer a Selective Force for Black Pigmentation in Early Hominin Evolution?" Proceedings of the Royal Society Biological Sciences 218 (2014): 1–10.

Harris, Reginald G. "The San Blas Indians." *American Journal of Physical Anthropology* 9, 1 (1926): 17–63.

Hathaway, Feighanne, Esther Burns, and Harry Ostrer. "Consumers' Desire towards Current and Prospective Reproductive Genetic Testing." *Journal of Genetic Counselling* 18 (2009): 137–46.

Huet, Marie-Hélène. *Monstrous Imagination*. Cambridge, MA: Harvard University Press, 1993.

———. "Monstrous Imagination: Progeny as Art in French Classicism." *Critical Inquiry* 17, 4 (1991): 718–37.

Hume, Mark. "Faced with Corruption in Africa, This Vancouver Resident Refused to Back Down." *Globe and Mail*, December 28, 2012.

Jones, Kenneth L., and David W. Smith. "Recognition of the Fetal Alcohol Syndrome in Early Infancy." *Lancet* 2 (1973): 999–1001.

Jones, Kenneth L., David W. Smith, Christy N. Ulleland, and Ann Pytkowicz Streissguth. "Pattern of Malformation in Offspring of Chronic Alcoholic Mothers." *Lancet* 1 (1973): 1267–71.

Kane, Tara. "Tall Tales a Problem for 'Midgetville': Vandals Make Trouble Looking for Pint-Size People of Myth." *Bergen County (NJ) Record*, April 27, 2002.

Keeler, Clyde. "The Incidence of Cuna Moon-Child Albinos." *Journal of Heredity* 55, 3 (1964): 115–20.

Kennedy, Dan. *Little People: Learning to See the World through My Daughter's Eyes.* New York: Rodale, 2003.

Kilgannon, Corey. "Are There Midgets in Midgetville? Don't Ask the Residents." *New York Times,* June 2, 2002.

King, Thomas. *The Truth about Stories: A Native Narrative.* Toronto: Anansi, 2010.

Kolatafeb, Gina. "Ethics Questions Arise as Genetic Testing of Embryos Increases." *New York Times,* February 3, 2014.

Lambert, Bruce. "Dr. Josef Warkany, 90, Pioneer in Study of Prenatal Health, Dies." *New York Times,* June 25, 1992.

Landsman, Gail H. "Reconstructing Motherhood in the Age of Perfect Babies: Mothers of Infants and Toddlers with Disabilities." *Signs* 24, 1 (1998): 69–99.

Lemoine P., H. Harouseau, J.T. Borteryu, and J.C. Menuet. "Les Enfants des Parents Alcooliques: Anomalies Observees Apropos de 127 Cas." *Ouest Medical* 21 (1968): 476–82.

Luande, J., C.I. Henschke, and N. Mohammed. "The Tanzanian Human Albino Skin: Natural History." *Cancer* 55 (1985): 1823–28.

Martin, Charles D. *The White African American Body: A Cultural and Literary Exploration.* London: Rutgers University Press, 2002.

Mayr, Ernst. *Systematics and the Origin of Species, from the Viewpoint of a Zoologist.* Cambridge, MA: Harvard University Press, 1942.

McGreevy, Ronan. "Study Suggests Tall Tales of Irish Giants Had a Grain of Truth." *Irish Times,* January 7, 2011.

Mesaki, Simeon. "Witchcraft and Witch Killings in Tanzania." PhD diss., University of Minnesota, 1993.

Morden, James. *Historic Niagara Falls.* Niagara Falls, Ontario: Lundy's Lane Historical Society, 1932.

Mundy, Liza. "A World of Their Own: In The Eyes of His Parents, If Gauvin Hughes Mccullough Turns Out to Be Deaf, That Will Be Just Perfect." *Washington Post,* March 31, 2002.

Munro, Joyce Underwood. "The Invisible Made Visible: The Fairy Changeling as a Folk Articulation of Failure to Thrive in Infants and Children." In *The Good People: New Fairylore Essays,* edited by Peter Narváez, 251–83. New York: Garland, 1991.

National Organization for Albinism and Hypopigmentation (NOAH). *Raising a Child with Albinism: A Guide to the Early Years.* East Hampton, NH: NOAH, 2008.

New York Sunday Telegraph. "Cape Cod's Albino Family." March 18, 1900.

Newman, Lucille F. "Folklore of Pregnancy: Wives' Tales in Contra Costa County, California." *Western Folklore* 28, 2 (1969): 112–35.

Northcroft-Grant, June. "Papakura, Makereti." In *Te Ara—The Encyclopedia of New Zealand*, updated December 17, 2013. http://www.TeAra.govt.nz/en/biographies/3p5/papakura-makereti.

Ntetema, Vicky. "In Hiding for Exposing Tanzanian Witch Doctors." *BBC News*, July 24, 2008.

———. "Living in Fear: Tanzania's Albinos." *BBC News*, July 21, 2008.

Onojafe, Ighovie F., et al. "Nitisinone Improves Eye and Skin Pigmentation Defects in a Mouse Model of Oculocutaneous Albinism." *Journal of Clinical Investigation* 121, 10 (2011): 3914–23.

Parker, Michael. "The Best Possible Child." *Journal of Medical Ethics* 33, 5 (2007): 279–83.

Pearson, Karl, E. Nettleship, and C.H. Usher. *Monograph on Albinism in Man*. London: Dulau, 1911.

Perry, Deborah F., DiPietro Janet, and Kathleen Costigan. "Are Women Carrying 'Basketballs' Really Having Boys? Testing Pregnancy Folklore." *Birth* 26, 3 (1999): 172–77.

Pew Research. "The World's Muslims: Unity and Diversity." *Pew Research:*

Religion and Public Life Project, August 9, 2012.

Provine, William. "Ernst Mayr: Genetics and Speciation." *Genetics* 167 (2004): 1041–46.

Rieti, Barbara. *Strange Terrain: The Fairy World in Newfoundland*. St. John's: ISER, 1991.

Sacramento Daily Union. "Pink-Eyed Albinos." September 14, 1895.

Savulescu, Julian. "Deaf Lesbians, 'Designer Disability,' and the Future of Medicine." *British Medical Journal* 325, 5 (2002): 771–73.

Scuerman, Mark, and Mark Moran. *Weird NJ: Your Travel Guide to New Jersey's Local Legends and Best Kept Secrets*. New York: Sterling, 2005.

Shaw, W.C. "Folklore Surrounding Facial Deformity and the Origins of Facial Prejudice." *British Journal of Plastic Surgery* 34, 3 (1981): 237–46.

Shelley, Edwin Taylor. "Superstition in Teratology." *Journal of the American Medical Association* 48 (1907): 308–11.

Smolenyak, Megan. *Trace Your Roots with DNA: Using Genetic Tests to Explore Your Family Tree*. New York: Rodale, 2004.

Solomon, Andrew. *Far from the Tree: Parents, Children and the Search for Identity*. New York: Scribner, 2012.

Sorsby, Arnold. "Noah: An Albino." *British Medical Journal* 5112 (1958): 1587–89.

Stout, D.B. "Further Notes on Albinism among the San Blas Cuna, Panama." *American Journal of Physical Anthropology* 4, 4 (1946): 483–90.

Tanner, Ralph. "Ideology and the Killing of Albinos in Tanzania: A Study in Cultural Relatives." *Anthropologist* 12, 4 (2010): 229–36.

Tatar, Maria. *The Hard Facts of the Grimms' Fairy Tales*. Princeton, NJ: Princeton University Press, 1987.

Tikao, Kelly, Nancy Higgins, Hazel Phillips, and Christine Cowan. "Kāpo (blind) Māori in the Ancient World. *MAI Review* 2 (2009). http://www.review.mai.ac.nz/index.php/MR/article/view/237/271.

Ulleland, Christy. "The Offspring of Alcoholic Mothers." *Pediatric Research* 4 (1970): 474–74.

Vandervelde, Marjorie. "Moon Children of San Blas Islands." *Expeditions: The Magazine of the University of Pennsylvania*, July 1973.

Warkany, Joseph. "The Importance of Prenatal Diet." *Milbank Memorial Fund Quarterly* 23, 1 (1945): 66–77.

Warkany, Joseph, and Rose C. Nelson. "Appearance of Skeletal Abnormalities in the Offspring of Rats Reared on a Deficient Diet." *Science* 92, 2391 (1940): 383–84.

Weiss, Meira. "Conditions of Mothering: The Bio-Politics of Falling in Love with Your Child." *Social Science Journal* 35, 1 (1998): 87–105.

Wikaira, Martin. "Patupaiarehe— Encounters with Patupaiarehe." In *Te Ara—The Encyclopedia of New Zealand*, updated July 8, 2013. http://www.TeAra.govt.nz/en/photograph/11075/urukehu.